"A lush memoir and richly detailed exploration of a pivotal era in Spain."

—*Kirkus Reviews*

"Desire drives both art and life, and Isidra Mencos's memoir pulses and glows with it. Her prismatic exploration of desire reveals everything desire can be, from natural, alive, and free to shamed, broken, and destructive to tenderly and determinedly reclaimed. Mencos excavates her most intimate experiences of becoming whole with the unflinching scrutiny of a scientist, the boundless curiosity of a child, and the astute devotion of an artist."

—Jeannine Ouellette, award-winning author of
The Part That Burns

"*Promenade of Desire* offers a brave and unblinkingly honest portrait of a young woman's sensual and sexual awakening in the face of censure and repression, and her refusal to be held back by the constraints of her family, culture, and religion. The same joyful spirit that expresses itself in Mencos' love of dancing shines through in her story of her own personal dance into a brave new world beyond the one her mother prescribed for her. Her story is shameless, in the very best sense of the word."

—Joyce Maynard, *New York Times* best-selling author of
Labor Day, To Die For, and *Count The Ways*

"*Promenade of Desire* is many things at once: a page-turning coming-of-age tale, a gutsy examination of family, a vivid portrait of a vanished time and a place, and a profound meditation on the nature of desire. Mencos is a sure-handed, open-hearted storyteller whose yearnings reflect our own."

—Aaron Shulman, author of *The Age of Disenchantments:*
The Epic Story of Spain's Most Notorious Literary Family
and the Long Shadow of the Spanish Civil War.

"*Promenade of Desire* sets the author's sexual coming-of-age story against Spain's sexual and political awakening in a unique and intriguing pairing."

—Julia Scheeres, NY Times bestselling author of *Jesus Land*

"Mencos takes readers on her compelling, personal journey of rebellion against the backdrop of her country's evolution to democracy. Fighting against family, tradition, and society's expectations of women, she ultimately triumphs."

—Andrea Jarrell, author of *I'm the One Who Got Away*

Promenade of Desire

Promenade
of
Desire

A Barcelona Memoir

Isidra Mencos

SHE WRITES PRESS

Copyright © 2022 Isidra Mencos

All rights reserved. No part of this publication may be reproduced, distributed, or transmitted in any form or by any means, including photocopying, recording, digital scanning, or other electronic or mechanical methods, without the prior written permission of the publisher, except in the case of brief quotations embodied in critical reviews and certain other noncommercial uses permitted by copyright law. For permission requests, please address She Writes Press.

Published 2022
Printed in the United States of America
Print ISBN: 978-1-64742-251-6
E-ISBN: 978-1-64742-252-3
Library of Congress Control Number: 2022907467

For information, address:
She Writes Press
1569 Solano Ave #546
Berkeley, CA 94707

She Writes Press is a division of SparkPoint Studio, LLC.

All company and/or product names may be trade names, logos, trademarks, and/or registered trademarks and are the property of their respective owners.

Names and identifying characteristics have been changed to protect the privacy of certain individuals.

To my husband, Luis E. Medina.
Thank you for believing in me more than
I believe in myself.

To my mother.
How I wish I had given you the tight, warm
hug I so longed to receive from you.

"In my fantasies, healing comes up like a plane to pull me out of the water. Real healing is the opposite of that. It is an opening. It is dropping down into the lost parts of yourself to reclaim them."

—Melissa Febos

"I, myself, am made entirely of flaws, stitched together with good intentions."

—Augusten Burroughs

AUTHOR'S NOTE

A FRIEND ONCE TOLD ME that after her mother passed and she and her siblings reminisced, she concluded, "We all had a different mother." I found this accurate. We all put our own imprint in our reality, shaping it through our emotional experience and our fickle memory.

In this memoir I've told my story as truthfully as I could. I double-checked facts when I could through research, re-read journals, and showed pages to people who appear in the book. During this process I discovered differences between what happened and how I recalled it. For example, a scene during a political demonstration developed as I tell it, but in talking to a friend I realized I had misremembered who was with me that day, so I corrected the error. I chose not to show the manuscript to my siblings—although I did ask some of them about specific details—because I wanted to reflect as honestly as I could the emotional impact of my upbringing without their own imprints interfering with my perspective. Coming from a very private and laconic family, I was also afraid my memoir would feel to them like a betrayal and their reaction might dissuade me from publishing it; I didn't want to run that risk. I see this book, however, as a gift to them: the gift of being open about the past while accepting that no family is perfect and that we can still be connected, flaws and all.

To protect the privacy of individuals in the story, I have changed some names, locations, and identifying details. I have also compressed some events and times to maintain narrative fluidity.

There's More Than Meets the Eye

THE DAY AFTER SCHOOL ENDED, my siblings and I, Mama, and Papa got into the blue station wagon. Mama sat shotgun, the baby in her arms and our dog, Ney, at her feet, and five of us sat in the back seat pressed like sardines. Our maid, Quica, and my three older brothers had traveled earlier in the morning.

It was an hour-and-a-half trip from Barcelona to San Julián de Vilatorta, a small country town where we always spent our summers. Papa loved *rancheras*, and we made the ride bearable by singing "Allá en el rancho grande" at the top of our lungs or mourning a lost love with the tragic "La cama de piedra." When we got tired of *gritos* and drama we attacked children's songs, tongue twisters, and games.

Once we were close, we craned our necks toward the car's windows, trying to find the two towers of Santa Margarita, my grandfather's house. The first one who spotted them gave a triumphant yell. That meant we had almost arrived, so we celebrated with our usual singsong: "San Julián de Vilatoooooorta, San Julián de Vilatoooooorta." Every time we said *"torta"* we tried to slap each other's cheeks, because *torta* means cake but it also means slap. Our cheeks got redder and redder until Papa told us to stop.

By then we were already in front of our summer home. Mama got out, holding the baby while she opened the gate. Ney jumped right after her, his tail wagging with the thrill of three long months of fields and sun.

1

As soon as Papa parked, I rushed through the garden, to the secret path behind the bamboo row, to the boxwood shrub so big one could hide inside, and to the carob tree that was my summer throne. Papa opened the garage door. I dragged out my tricycle and took a few spins around the garden.

Mama set out two foldable chairs and a table close to the tree. She sat down with the newspaper, sipping coffee from the small white cup that Quica had brought on a tray. I knew what would come next. She would go straight to the last page of the newspaper to fill in the crossword. Sometimes I tried to help her, but it was hard. I didn't understand the clues. Mama, on the other hand, guessed one word after the other as if she had invented the puzzle and was just checking that it all fit together correctly.

"Can I have a coffee drop, Mama?"

"Okay, but only one."

She took a sugar cube, dipped it into her coffee, and handed it to me. I grabbed it by the bit that was still hard and climbed up to a low branch of the tree, savoring the hint of bitterness hidden behind the grainy sweetness. I sat astride the thick branch imagining myself on top of a horse. As I moved forward and backward with its trot, a tingling rose from the branch to my belly. It felt good. I forgot about the horse and moved some more to see if the nice tickle would come again. It did. It felt like a big wet lick on a melting ice cream sandwich.

Mama heard me panting a little.

"What are you doing?"

"I'm riding a horse. Look how fast it goes!" I said, rubbing myself against the branch.

"Come down right now. You're going to fall."

"I won't fall." I rubbed myself faster to make the tickle come again.

"I said now!"

Her voice barked like Ney's when he saw the neighbor's cat. I climbed down from the tree and went to her. She put her arms around me and said, "We don't do that."

"Climb the tree?" Silly Mama. Of course she wouldn't climb the tree, but that didn't mean I couldn't do it, did it now?

"No. We don't move like that. Don't do it again."

Ah! She was worried I would fall out of the tree if I kept riding the horse.

"Okay, I won't do it again."

Mama smiled.

"Go look for Papa and tell him his coffee is getting cold."

That evening, after dinner, my younger brother, the baby, and I were put to bed. I complained that since I was almost six years old I should be allowed to stay up longer, but it was no use.

I lay down, rough cotton sheets pulled tight around my body, the house creaking and grunting, a door banging downstairs, a motorcycle revving up outside. Although I had inspected the bedroom for centipedes and spiders, I shuddered with the thought of one inching up the quilted cover.

My hand went down between my legs. Placing it flat over my panties, I moved it up and down, mimicking my movement on the "horse." A little rumble began building up, like thunder from a storm starting far away. It became stronger when I left my finger over a little button and moved it side to side. Soon the tickle came, and I fell asleep.

In the morning, the luscious aroma of baking cookies wafted upstairs. Quica made them with the cream of boiled raw milk that had been dropped off at dawn in shiny aluminum containers. They were my favorite treat. Although we never ate them for breakfast, I knew she would sneak one to me if I got to the kitchen before the rest.

I went downstairs in my nightgown and hugged Quica from the back while she opened the oven door. She turned around, startled, and when she saw my eager face she laughed. Her small blue eyes crinkled at the corners behind her black-rimmed glasses.

"I know why you're here, you little rascal."

"Can I have one, Quica? Just one!"

"Okaaay. Somebody might as well enjoy them when they're freshly baked." She gave me chocolate milk and two cookies she grabbed right from the tray in the oven.

As I finished the last morsel, Mama walked in with an armful of swimsuits. "There you are! Here's yours," she said, handing me the one-piece with a navy blue frilled mini skirt. I loved that swimsuit. I rushed upstairs to put it on, threw a pair of shorts and a short-sleeved T-shirt on top, and skipped to the garden to play with Ney.

The fresh summer day stretched its lazy arms around me, and I swayed with the chirps of the last scattered crickets.

Among the forty-seven grandchildren *Abuelo* Ignacio had, I was the only one born at Santa Margarita, like him and Mama. Abuelo was so thrilled about it that on the wall outside the bedroom, he inscribed in ink: "My granddaughter, María Isidra, was born in this room on September 23, 1958, at 1:10 a.m." Every summer I went upstairs to look at the inscription.

Santa Margarita was a castle-like mansion. It was built with limestone taken from a quarry on the property's land that would later be covered with soil and become vegetable and flower gardens. The stones, in soft hues of gray and tan, polished, and bonded with a pale ribbon of mortar, formed an intricate lace that made the walls sing. Its two towers, one square and one round, peeked over the trees from miles away. An enormous clock on the round tower played the melody of the hours drifting away in the long summer days.

In the mornings, there would always be thirty or forty of us, children and adults, lounging at the pool. The water was freezing because it was surrounded by pine trees that didn't let one ray of sunshine pierce through. We all begged Abuelo to cut down at least one tree to let a little bit of sun in, but he refused because he had planted them with his father when he was a child. Rumors abounded about the times my uncles had to break a layer of ice to jump in the pool, but I never saw it.

At lunchtime, we went back to our home in San Julián, a mile away, but we returned to Santa at five to meet the rest of the gang. *Abuela*, Mama, and my aunts sat drinking coffee and chatting in the *marquesina*, a covered porch in front of the house, while we kids disappeared for hours on end.

The first afternoon that summer, as usual, I visited Abuelo in his studio when we arrived in Santa.

"*Hola*, Abuelo." I looked around from the threshold. Abuelo was sitting behind his enormous mahogany desk. A few pinecones and stones that he had picked up during his walks and painted silver or gold were scattered among his papers. The wall in front of the door had floor-to-ceiling wood shelves with lots of books and some portraits. One of them showed a man in military uniform who had a thin mustache like Abuelo's. It was General Francisco Franco, who had won the civil war twenty-five years earlier and become Su Excelencia el Jefe del Estado. I knew about him because whenever we went to the movies, we had to watch a state-produced newsreel called "*No-Do*," and Franco was all over it, opening a reservoir, visiting a car factory, or talking to kings and presidents of other countries.

"¡Hola, *paisana!*"

It made me feel special that Abuelo called me *paisana*, as if being his countrywoman had forged a unique connection. I didn't know yet that relationships are like plants. They need to be tended to grow up strong. My relationship with Abuelo was affectionate but distant. It wasn't just me. There was a clear boundary between children and adults. We crossed paths at certain points and times of day but, for the most part, led independent lives.

"*¿Quieres un anís?*" Abuelo always offered us an anise candy when we visited. That might have been the reason I went to see him daily.

"*Sí.*"

He picked up a box from the shelf by the door. It was round, about the size of a coffee can, made with thick dark wood, almost black. He took the cover off and held it in one hand, offering the box with the other. Inside were many balls the size of garbanzo beans, immaculately white against the dark wood.

"*¡Gracias,* Abuelo!" I bolted outside with the anise in my mouth, ready for adventure.

I loved going to Santa, running free with my cousins in the forest, visiting with the cows and the rabbits, playing hide-and-seek in the granary, riding in the cart with the donkey when Luis, the farmer, took us for a short stroll.

At six o'clock we showed up in the kitchen, where Quica had joined Abuelo's maids, and they gave us a snack: slices of sour peasant bread drizzled with olive oil and sugar or toasted and seasoned with a rubbed garlic clove, olive oil, and salt, or a stack of cookies with two pieces of chocolate. And off we went again, searching for four-leaf clovers in the fields, climbing the loquat tree, picking up wild berries by the pool, running all the way down to the big cross—engraved with an homage to the war's fallen—that marked the border of the property.

When we got tired of sun and flies, we ducked into the bowels of the house, marveling in front of the Virgin Mary who presided in the chapel, jumping among mountains of potatoes in the dark room in the basement, gawking at the collection of stuffed animals in *el Quijote* (the room where our mothers played cards), turning in one of the two swiveling chairs in the barber room, now out of use, and sliding in the long hallways with their checkered black-and-white-tiled floors. Then up we went to the attic where Abuelo had hidden a priest during the war, tiptoeing in the dark room full of spider webs, and down again to the big hall where an old billiard table rested and eight *tresillos*—matched sets of one couch and two armchairs, each different from the other—lined the eight walls.

I suspected the house would never reveal all its secrets. I knew this was true when one of my cousins showed me a passage, hidden behind a bed's headboard, that I had never seen after years of exploring Santa from top to bottom.

It was a bit like my family and like Spain itself. Problems lurked in the dark, waiting for the day we wouldn't be able to keep them hidden any longer.

The Rumors of Franco's Death
Are Not Exaggerated

THERE WAS SOMETHING ELEMENTAL suspended in the air, some new slant to the way the light struck the buildings lining Las Ramblas, a restless energy in the rising and the falling of conversations among students, workers, and even families gathered around tables set for typical Sunday lunches.

Spain was bracing for change after four decades of dictatorship. The voices repressed for so long couldn't be contained any longer. They emerged in protest songs and in slogans yelled in street demonstrations. They surged in sermons by progressive priests such as Bilbao's bishop, who demanded recognition of the Basque language and culture and was condemned to house arrest. They shook our cities through terrorist attacks.

I was a freshman in college, studying Spanish and French literature. The humanities classes were in prefabs on Calle Diagonal, a wide avenue that cut Barcelona from east to west and, according to some, divided the city between the haves in the north and the haveless in the south. I would soon cross this border for good to start a new life on the vibrant lower side of the city.

Freshman courses were sown with older students who flunked on purpose so they could stay behind and encourage activism in the new crop. I was ripe for the picking.

For the last few years, our lunches at home had buzzed with

politics. Mama and Papa had evolved from conservative upbringings to center-left, guided by their Christian faith. The Second Vatican Council and the Latin American Theology of Liberation's emphasis on social justice resonated deeply with them. They had even moved our Sunday Mass from the old-fashioned church close to home to the Caputxins de Sarriá. These friars had become famous when they used the church to shelter a group of youths as they formed an illegal student union, while the police laid siege outside for three days.

Discussions in the news and around our family table focused on the tug of war between those who wanted *apertura* (opening) and those on the ultra-right—which everybody called *el bunker*—who wanted to preserve the status quo. We had watched with horror the coup d'état in Chile, lamenting Allende's death, and we had rejoiced when the Carnation Revolution in Portugal ended that country's four decades of dictatorship. Surely our revolution couldn't be far behind.

Franco had been in bad health for over a year. In September, he vanished from view. By the end of October there were rumors he'd been dead for weeks and the government was hiding his passing for fear of a rebellion.

Everyone watched the news and read the papers obsessively, interpreting medical reports down to the last detail, trying to decipher if he was close to dying or already dead and preserved in some icy chamber in his namesake hospital. In many homes, bottles of champagne were secretly chilling for weeks. Not in ours. Although Mama and Papa yearned for a democratic government, they wouldn't have dreamed of celebrating anyone's passing with a glass of bubbly.

Still, when Franco's death was announced, on November 20, my brother Guille bragged that he had indeed uncorked a bottle of *cava* with his friends and toasted the end of the dictator without an ounce of guilt.

I couldn't help but wonder, would freedom pour forth with the same ease as the bubbles that were erupting everywhere?

Two days after Franco's passing, I spent the weekend with a group of friends. Prince Juan Carlos, Franco's handpicked successor, was scheduled to accept the crown in a televised speech. We all bunched up on the sofa and on the floor in front of the TV, wondering if he would do anything to bring about change.

Dressed in a military uniform, the newly minted king talked in the monotonous voice that would become his trademark. His first sentences confirmed our fears. His praise of traditions and Franco fell on us like a stomping herd.

Then, there was a strange shift in his speech.

"Today begins a new era in the history of Spain," announced Juan Carlos. He talked about Spaniards' right to exercise their liberties, about recognizing cultural and regional diversity, and about the necessity of integrating Spain into Europe.

The words fell from his lips in his dull intonation, like bombshells disguised as plainly wrapped gift packages.

After the speech ended, we tried to interpret it.

"He said we should be more like the rest of Europe. I think there's hope," I said.

"Nah! He's just tossing a scrap to appease the masses," said a friend.

"Did you see how everybody applauded when he mentioned Franco? That garnered the loudest applause of the whole speech!" said another, discouraged.

After going back and forth, we ended up siding with a cautious pessimism. What we didn't know was that Juan Carlos had been secretly meeting for years with the leaders of the illegal political parties in France and in Madrid. Some had snuck inside his residence in the trunk of a car. They had been plotting a transition to democracy that, although full of hurdles and bumps, would be achieved a few years later.

Every day at university members of the illegal political parties ran clandestine meetings, rousing the troops. We were all caught up in the effervescence of the moment, ready to make our voices heard. I attended the meetings and marched with my friends in protests, exhilarated by the vigor of revolt after my tame upbringing and by the sense of belonging to a united group.

I once had the brilliant idea to attend a demonstration wearing clogs, which were fashionable at the time. A bunch of students took the green metro line from Zona Universitaria in Diagonal to Liceo, in the middle of Las Ramblas. This wide pedestrian promenade was the heart of Barcelona. It ran from Plaza Cataluña to the harbor, where the statue of Cristóbal Colón rose, his finger pointing alluringly to the New World across the seas.

There were dozens of people milling around, ready to march up to Plaza Cataluña, when we came out of the metro. At noon, we all linked arms and walked, a throng of several hundred, mostly students, fifteen bodies wide.

"¡*Amnistía, libertad*! ¡*Amnistía, libertad*!" we bellowed, demanding freedom for the thousands of political prisoners still in jail.

When that slogan got old, we chanted, "¡*Somos gente pacífica, y no nos gusta gritar*!" ("We are peaceful people, and we don't like to shout!") We sang it louder and louder until we were yelling, a thunderous uproar that made us giddy.

All of a sudden, police jeeps rushed to a stop on both sides of Las Ramblas. Dozens of policemen in their hated gray uniforms stormed the street, batons or rifles in hand, Plexiglas masks attached to their helmets obscuring their features.

"*¡Los grises! ¡Los grises!*"

We sprinted in all directions amid terrified screams and the crack of batons crashing onto backs and heads.

I tried to run, but my feet kept slipping off the clogs. I had foolishly stopped to put one back on when I heard heavy steps nearing. I looked back and saw a policeman rushing toward me, his baton raised and ready to strike. Only then did it dawn on me that this was real life, not a theoretical exercise of youthful rebellion. Suddenly, someone grabbed my arms and propelled me forward like a rocket. Two friends had come to my rescue. With their arms firmly hooked under my armpits, I ran faster than I'd ever run, followed by the smell of tear gas.

The protests continued for years, swelling to crowds of over a hundred thousand. *Los grises,* dressed in their threatening gear, sometimes observed the masses without intervening directly. Other times they used force to disperse them. I kept attending demonstrations but, just in case, I stayed close to the perimeter, ready to escape if the situation got out of hand.

Tickled and Locked Out

MAMA RAN THE HOUSE like a sergeant runs his army. Everything was always on time and done with precision. Lunch was at two o'clock sharp and dinner at nine, and nobody dared come late. Beds were made after the rooms had been aired, and the sheets were stretched until there wasn't even a hint of a wrinkle.

"A room can be clean, but if the bed is unmade, it will look like a mess," she always said.

She taught my older sister and me how to make beds the right way, with the corners tucked in tight. In the summer, since we didn't have to rush out to school, it was our chore to make all the kids' beds. Our brothers didn't have to do anything. I thought it was unfair, but there was no use complaining. That was the order of things: girls did chores and boys did whatever they pleased.

Although Mama's house rules were strict, she let us run around freely by ourselves in San Julián or at Santa Margarita.

"Aren't you worried they'll get hurt?" some friend would invariably ask.

"They all came with a guardian angel over their shoulders," she'd answer with a confident smile.

It may have been true, because most of the time we kept out of trouble, except when Guille cut his knee with a hatchet that was lying around in the yard. Luckily, he didn't split his leg in two, but the scar was impressive.

Coming from such a big family, I heard many times the same assumption: "With so many brothers and sisters, you must not need friends; you have your own best friends at home. How fun!" But that wasn't my experience. I had a friend at school who was one of fourteen children. Her family, like ours, received an award from the government every year for being prolific. It wasn't much money—more like a badge of honor for helping rebuild the country, which had lost hundreds of thousands of people in the war and postwar executions and exiles. My friend often described what she had done with her sisters over the weekend and how much fun they had in the evenings, laughing and talking with their lights off in the bedroom she shared with three others.

I wished I could say the same, but this intimacy was foreign to me. My older sister and I shared a bedroom, but she came upstairs later than I did, and when we were both awake in bed, we kept quiet, each of us reading our own book. My younger brother and sister and the girl who came later were too little to be my friends. My five older brothers lived in their own world.

Mama and Papa were nice, but they didn't speak much. I admired Papa from afar. I found him dashing. He had blond hair like mine combed straight back, a wide forehead, and light brown eyes. In San Julián, with his city suits and lawyer's office left behind, he came alive. When he jumped over hills on his motorcycle or came home with partridges hanging from his belt and a hare's ears peeking from his satchel, his dogs close behind him, he looked like a hero.

I sometimes longed to be a puppy, to be trained and walked and petted and taken on splendid adventures with him. I longed for that tender look Papa gave his dogs when he was relaxing in the yard after lunch and he dropped his hand from the armchair to caress their heads. But Papa wasn't the demonstrative kind. He didn't kiss Mama on the lips or hug her and twirl her around like in the movies. As for us kids, a kiss on the cheek, his neck stretched to bring his face closer to our lips, and a gentle but distracted smile were all we could expect.

Mama, like Papa, kept her feelings to herself. She never said, "I love you." Full bellies, mended socks, and punctual rides to school were how she showed she cared.

As a teenager, I went on expeditions around the house, snooping in every drawer, hunting for images that proved Mama had indeed loved me.

In one of my favorites, she's seated, short black hair, capri pants, pointy flats—a Spanish Audrey Hepburn. I'm standing up by her, holding another photo, and she's looking at it, leaning her head warmly against mine, smiling. I'm wearing a short white dress, hair pulled back with a white ribbon, short white socks, and white shoes. I must have been three years old. I'm pointing at something in the photograph, and I look happy, relaxed.

When I came upon this image, I hid it with the rest of my stash. There it lay on top of another that showed Mama crouching beside me and two of my siblings. I'm standing next to her, my arm wrapped around her shoulders, her arms around my waist. Her jet-black bee-hive bun contrasts with my blond pageboy. She has a gentle Mona Lisa smile, her dark brown eyes as soft as her lips. With her by my side, everything seems right with the world.

What age did she think was the limit to touch and be touched? Six, seven? It must have been earlier, or I would have remembered it.

"We are playing a game. Do you want to play?" asked my brother Diego.

"Yes." Although he was only three years older, Diego didn't play much with me. This was a welcome change.

"Let's go to my bedroom," he said.

There were several boys inside: another brother and a couple of cousins. "We are going to play doctors," said Diego.

One by one, we lay on a bed with our pants and underpants down by our ankles and our legs bent so our thighs spread open. Each kid took a turn looking without touching. Since I was the only girl, when it was my turn to lie down, a good long time passed while all the boys filed by me, wide-eyed and hushed.

I felt lucky. They had only one girl to look at, while I had four boys. It was also more fun for me because I could ask them to shrink and extend their *pito*, but I had no tricks up my sleeve.

After two or three rounds the game got boring, so I left.

Quica was washing clothes outdoors in one of the two stone sinks facing each other, right by the kitchen.

"I want to wash too, Quica!"

"What a little helper," said Quica, smiling. She dried her hands on a dishrag and went indoors. I followed her to the pantry. She got a wood box that had zucchinis and potatoes in it and put the vegetables on a shelf. Then she went outside and placed the box in front of the other sink, upside down, so I could stand on it. She gave me three white handkerchiefs and a bar of soap the same color as the *café con leche* that Mama and Papa drank in the mornings. It was still covered in cellophane. There was a green lizard drawn on it and some letters.

"L–A–G–A–R . . ." I started spelling, and then it dawned on me what it said. "¡*Lagarto*!" I shouted. Now the lizard made sense.

"How smart you are!"

"What does it say below that, Quica?" I didn't realize that she read with as much difficulty as I did. She looked at the soap for a long time, and then said: "*Jabón natural.* That means it's good."

Quica took one of the handkerchiefs and spread it over the sink's surface, which slanted down and had ridges. She opened the faucet, splashed some water over the hankie, and scrubbed it with the bar of soap. It smelled clean already. She left the soap on top of the sink, folded a corner of the hankie and scrubbed the rest with it over the sloping surface.

"Now you," she said.

The sink came up to my chest, even as I perched on the box. I took the bar of soap from Quica. It was so thick I could barely close my hand over it. When you passed it over the hankie, it left lines of a beige paste over each sink ridge. I put the soap aside and touched the paste. It was soft and squishy. I started scrubbing the hankie, marveling at the foam that formed on it.

I scrubbed and rinsed for a while, feeling proud of how white the hankies looked after I finished. Quica held me up so I could hang them myself on the line hidden behind the row of bamboo. My fingertips were as wrinkled as the sink's surface.

Mama came out the dining room door. "Leave this alone, María Isidra, we're going to Santa Margarita." Her voice sounded snappish. She always seemed bothered when I spent time with Quica, but I couldn't keep away from her. Quica's easy laugh delighted me, and her lilting Andalusian accent, so different from ours, made everything she said more fun to hear. When she smiled, her lips parted to reveal perfect white teeth, which may have been dentures.

Quica had come to live with us when I was a baby, and she would stay until I turned thirteen. She worked primarily as a cook but helped as well with childcare, laundry, and cleaning. A short, stout woman, she seemed to have permanently settled at around sixty years of age. She always wore navy blue or black housedresses with small white prints, buttoned from top to bottom. Maybe the dark colors were a sign of mourning, for Quica had lost not only her husband but also ten of her fourteen children when they were infants. She came from a peasant background, poverty-stricken in the postwar years, and in that world infant death may have been a fairly common occurrence.

When she told me about her past, I was awed that she could march through life so cheerfully, her warmth as enticing as the mouth-watering scents that rose from her pots and pans. It may have been a combination of the fatalism that helped people from the south bear their bleak circumstances and an innate positive spirit that allowed her to revel in the riches of the present. Her four surviving kids were doing fine, she was alive and healthy, and she had a roof over her head, abundant food, and a secure job that allowed her to save.

I relished spending time with Quica in the kitchen. She hustled and bustled, frying minced onion, garlic, and tomato for the *sofrito* that is the foundation of Spanish cooking or laying on the cold white marble whole armies of croquettes, a thick béchamel mixed up with grilled and ground chicken and minced fried onion, or enveloping boiled egg quarters that miraculously kept their shape. "The secret is to get a firm consistency in the sauce. See how it separates from the pan when I move it with the wooden spoon? Let it cool and harden before you mold the croquettes, then dip them in beaten egg and add the breadcrumbs," she explained.

When we were in Barcelona, I often went downstairs to spend time with her while she relaxed before dinner. We sat in the iron-ing room at a round table with long skirts that hid a brazier with piping hot coals. Quica made lime blossom tea and served us a cup, and we listened to *la señora Francis*, a *Dear Abby*–style program, on the radio. A romantic jingle opened the show, followed by women's letters detailing their problems. La señora Francis recommended patience with their husbands, self-sacrifice with their kids, and dedi-cation to their homes. Quica and I discussed her advice as we felt the warmth of the brazier at our feet and savored the honey-colored tea, all of it cozy like the golden light that hung right above the table and encircled us with its soft hue.

Sometimes I begged Quica to let me comb her hair. She kept it neatly tucked into a bun. I took out the pins and unrolled her long but thin salt-and-pepper mane. I brushed it gently while she read yesterday's paper, following each letter with her finger.

In later years, after she retired, she bought a modest apartment on the outskirts of Barcelona, which she shared with her sister until the end of her life. For a while, she did a monthly trek—a train, a bus, and a cable car—to spend one day with us and cook our favorite dishes. By the time she grew too old to subject herself to the long journey, I was too caught up in my messy life to visit her often. The selfishness of youth, however, did not tarnish the deep love I felt for her. I bawled at her death as I had not done for my lost grandparents.

After lunch, I snuggled in the family room with a comic book. Mama came to pick up her bag of yarn. She was always knitting a sweater for one or the other of us.

"What are you doing inside on this beautiful day?"

"I'm reading." I couldn't read well yet, but I loved comics, especially the adventures of Asterix and Obelix.

As Mama was about to leave the room, she stopped in her tracks. I was holding the comic with my left hand. With my right hand, I was searching for the nice tickle between my legs. Mama came to me and yanked my hand away from my body.

"I told you not to do this." There was no longer any doubt what she meant.

"Why?"

"It's dirty."

"But why is it dirty?"

"It just is. Promise me you won't do it again."

I didn't understand why it bothered her. Was playing doctors with my brothers also dirty, then? It was all so confusing. Still, I loved Mama more than anything else in the world, except perhaps black licorice, and I didn't want to make her mad. I promised.

I tried to keep my word and stop rubbing myself down there, but I couldn't do it. The tickle felt good, and I wasn't hurting anybody. When sleep didn't come right away, it was better than counting sheep—I only knew how to count up to ten anyway. It never got boring because there were many ways to make it happen. Sitting on my tricycle and pushing my body front and back with my feet on the ground worked pretty well. But every time Mama found me, she scolded me, so I decided to do it only at nighttime, under the covers.

One evening, I was at it when she came to say goodnight. As she approached the bed, I stilled my finger. I didn't realize that even motionless, my hand made a little mound right between my legs.

Mama was about to kiss me when she squinted. She pulled the sheet and bedspread off me in one big swoop, uncovering my body from neck to toes. The sheet rose and fell to the side with a thick flapping noise, like a sail swollen by a violent gust of wind. My hand stayed between my legs, frozen.

Mama's face puckered up, nose wrinkled, lips pursed. "How disgusting!" she spat out. Revulsion shot from her eyes like daggers pinning me to the bed. I shut mine. The heavy clatter of her steps on the stone floor hit me like cracks from a whip. I heard the door banging shut. I opened my eyes. She had left without switching the light off.

It was the first time Mama hadn't tucked me in and prayed with me. I grabbed the sheet and the bedspread and covered myself. I felt cold.

I tossed and turned, willing sleep to come to the rescue, but the same film played behind my eyelids over and over. Mama had never looked at me that way before. I wanted to cry. I hoped tears would lighten the weight oppressing my chest, but they wouldn't come out.

That night, my world split in two. Before, I knew Mama loved me. After, I was not sure. How could love share space with loathing?

A few minutes later, my sister came up. I faced the wall while she put her pajamas on and got into bed. Soon she was breathing steadily.

My hand crept back between my legs, but no matter how much I rubbed down there, I couldn't relax. My legs became iron rods, stiffened right off the sheet, my forehead scrunched up almost as tight as my shoulders, and the frantic speed in my finger made my arm tense. I gave up and fell asleep out of sheer exhaustion—the first of many nights when I was locked out of my own body.

Iron Woman

IT WAS MID-SEPTEMBER, time to return to Barcelona. We left San Julián after dinner and arrived after dark. When Papa parked the car, I rubbed the sleepiness off my eyes and followed him up the steps. As he opened the front door, the smell of the house hit me. San Julián smelled of thyme and manure. The house on Avenida del Tibidabo, perched on the highest hill in the city, had an austere scent of wood polish and mothballs mixed with a tantalizing hint of *sofrito*.

I ran to the second floor and opened the costume trunk. We never took our disguises with us in the summer. I didn't miss them because each house had its own treasures. Having not seen my fairy veil for three months, it thrilled me to pick it up and put it on, just as saving the *turrón* for Christmas—even though you could buy the sweet almond nougat year-round—made it more delectable.

We would be going back to school in a few days. I was eager to see my girlfriends, especially my cousin Sylvia, who was only twenty-four days older than I was and as close as a twin sister. I enjoyed school as well: knowing what to do and how to do it, singing songs in French, writing rows of carefully rounded "oes" with the top line sitting on their head like the bills of sideways caps, sniffing the tangy sheets of paper, so white they almost shone half blue.

El Sagrado Corazón de Sarriá—The Sacred Heart from the Sarriá neighborhood, in the upper side of the city—was a Catholic all-girls school. Most of the teachers were nuns. The huge salmon-colored buildings rested on grounds that had belonged to my ancestors, who had donated them to the nuns as a dowry when my great-grand-aunt took vows. One of them had been their summerhouse before Barcelona demolished the Roman walls that constricted the old city, swallowed the towns of Gracia and Sarriá, and converted them into neighborhoods. Other buildings were partly funded by Abuelo's great grandmother, *Doña* Dorotea de Chopitea.

Dorotea, a devout grand dame of Barcelona's high bourgeoisie, had donated her fortune—a product of her father's and late husband's businesses—to charitable works that financed the construction of schools, churches, shelters, and hospitals, many devoted to caring for destitute children and managed by Jesuits. She died penniless, supported in her last years by her daughters, who had inherited the other half of their father's wealth. This streak of fervent Catholicism and philanthropy ran deep in our family. It would one day determine my parents' future.

I had seen Dorotea's portrait in Santa Margarita—a serious old lady with a black dress that went all the way up to her chin—but I didn't know anything about her or her ties to my school. All I knew is that I loved walking under the double row of mulberry trees during recess, jumping over the hopscotch squares to reach *cielo* in the play-ground, and going up and down the majestic marble stairs in the entrance. The banisters were so polished that I yearned to slide down them. On the other hand, I was relieved it was forbidden. I was afraid I'd fall midway.

A precise routine organized our school days. Mornings began with prayer. In the dining room, there were rows and rows of long tables. Your seat was assigned. You had to wait for the nuns to come around and fill your plate, and you couldn't eat until grace was said. Our sober uniform, which I would come to hate, was a navy blue dress with three vertical pleats on the front, a loose belt in the same color and material, long sleeves, and a little white collar. We wore long socks, so only our knees showed. During mass, black veils covered our hair.

Although every hour of every day was regimented, unlike the spontaneity and freedom of San Julián, I enjoyed school. Most of the nuns were nice, even maternal, although a few crabby outliers applied strict discipline. Punishments included kneeling in a corner by the blackboard looking at the wall and, worst of all, taking the walk of shame through the classrooms with a donkey hat: a paper crown with two pointy ears that you had to put on if you did something terrible. I only saw it happen once. The practice must have been discontinued when I was six or seven years old. A subtler way to keep you in line was the list of *Marcadas* and *Distinguidas* on the blackboard. Seeing your name under "Marked" all day was slow torture, while accumulating "Distinguished" mentions for good behavior could get you a coveted pink sash to wear during school functions.

I was a good student who didn't cause any problems, unlike my cousin Sylvia, who was always getting into trouble. Once I was playing in the sandbox during recess when *Madre* Caridad—who couldn't have had a less appropriate name, as she was not particularly charitable—came walking resolutely toward me. Her big mass of black with the white halo of her wimple on top threw shade on my sandcastle. I looked up, apprehensive. She grabbed me by the ear and pulled me to my feet.

"Ayyyyy!"

Madre Caridad paid no attention to my cries. She dragged me toward the classroom.

"You are in trouble, missy. You can't have recess."

"Why? What did I do?" I whined.

I can't remember the offense, but I hadn't done it.

"What do you mean you haven't done it? So-and-so said it had been Sylvia Mencos!"

"But I'm not Sylvia; I'm María Isidra Mencos!"

Madre Caridad let go of my ear.

"Why didn't you say so before?" Her voice raised angrily, like it was my fault. "Where is your cousin?"

"I don't know!" I rubbed my ear, which burned like a hot coal.

"Go play," she snapped.

Sylvia and I shared a few laughs through the years every time I reminded her that I had saved her from a good ear yank.

I wonder what Madre Caridad would have done if she had found me as I was sometimes, with my hand in my pocket hidden by the desk, rubbing furiously between my legs to conjure the elusive tickle.

Push back, pull to the front. The tooth was held in place by a tiny fleshy thread. When I wiggled it forward, I fit the tip of my tongue under it and felt a hole surrounded by sharp edges. No matter how much I tried to distract myself, I couldn't stop thinking about my tooth. What if I bit something hard, broke the thread, and swallowed the tooth with the food? I was also scared that my brothers would make good on their promise to knock it off with a punch.

Mama told me that if I left it under my pillow, el ratoncito Pérez would come in the night, grab it, and leave me a coin. I imagined the little mouse used all the teeth he collected to build a castle. Where would he place mine? Perhaps it would go on the rail of a balcony with an elaborate embroidery fit for a queen.

I twisted the tooth on its thread. All of a sudden, a pang of pain told me I had succeeded.

"Mamaaaaa!" Mama and Papa were reading the newspaper and drinking coffee, as they did every day after lunch.

"What is it?" said Mama.

I opened my fist and showed her the tooth, the first one I had lost. She glanced at it and said, "It's yellow!"

I examined my tooth. It was true that it didn't look as white as a fluffy cloud on a clear day. It had a pale yellow hue, like a raw kernel in an ear of white corn.

I ran upstairs to the bathroom, smothered my toothbrush with Signal, and brushed my tooth for a long time. Every few minutes I applied more toothpaste and scrubbed with all my might each teeny surface, including the dark hole on the underside, until my arms ached and the tooth shone. I rushed back to show it to Mama.

"It's white now, Mama. See?"

"Who cares about this tooth? What's important is the ones in your mouth, and those are still yellow."

I took a step back, as if she had punched me. I ran to the bathroom again to look at my teeth. I brushed them every morning before breakfast, side to side, as Mama had taught me. Why weren't they whiter? The image of the *ratoncito* Pérez's palace dissolved, leaving only the anguish that I was dirty.

I don't remember finding the coin under my pillow the next morning, but I'm sure it was there. Mama made a point of preserving the magic rituals of childhood. That helped balance her insensitive outbursts.

Perhaps her harshness had to do with growing up during the war. She talked often about those three years. In spite of the constant hunger that made a fried egg the best-ever birthday present, she remembered them as happy times because she spent them with her siblings and cousins in a house deep in the countryside, playing all day. But that's also when she learned she had to be tough.

The war broke out in July of 1936. It being summer, the family was, as usual, in Santa Margarita. San Julián was in the hands of *los rojos*, the leftist Republican (anti-monarchy) groups that battled the right-wing coup d'état by General Franco. The town's Republican committee paid Abuelo a visit and told him that as long as they were in power, he and his family didn't need to fear for their lives or their property. Abuelo had donated considerable funds for many projects in San Julián, from the construction of the enormous School for Orphan Children and the church bell to traditional festivities. His generosity helped him evade the fate of other wealthy landowners. Dead bodies, including priests and family friends, appeared close to Santa Margarita. They were the fallen honored by the cross at the boundary of the property.

When Republican officials from Barcelona took over San Julián's City Hall, Abuelo had to flee and hide in an undisclosed location. Abuela stayed behind until the Republican government demanded the use of Santa Margarita for their troops. They gave her forty-eight hours to vacate the property and permission to take with her anything she wanted. She packed up everything in the house—furniture, art, valuables—and had it transported to the orphans' school, where it stayed hidden until the end of the war. The priests who ran the school had changed into lay clothes as the war began, and since they performed a social service by educating orphaned and low-income children, they were not bothered.

Abuela, her nine children, a maid, and Mademoiselle, the French tutor, moved to Abuelo's cousin's house deeper in the countryside, where they stayed until the end of the war.

Mama was only nine years old and the third of nine siblings when the war broke out, but before Abuelo went into hiding, he took her aside and said, "You are the strongest of them all. Promise me, if anything happens to me, you will take care of your mother and your siblings."

She never forgot it. She told us this story more than once.

Could that be why Mama didn't allow any fissures in the armored bunker of her façade? Her strength anchored my childhood in a feeling of safety, but it would also become a burden, for her and for others. Just as she wouldn't let anyone help her with household chores when she was in her 80s, no matter how bone-tired she felt, she didn't approve of anyone needing help.

Mama was convinced that you could conquer any challenge through sheer willpower. If you didn't, you were a weakling or simply lazy. Years later, she would berate Papa for not eating his lunch while he was writhing in agony from a kidney stone, the rest of us looking at our plates in silence; seeing my father's yellowed skin and the weak attempts he made to bring a spoonful of soup to his mouth, I had enough. "He is in pain and he cannot eat! Don't you see it?" I snapped. "Go to bed then, if you are not going to eat!" she snarled at Papa. "You will never get better if you don't make an effort!" Papa got up from the table, shakily, and shuffled to his room while we finished our meal. Did Mama's anger mask a feeling of powerlessness from seeing her husband so sick? I don't know.

Similarly, she blamed her sister for not trying to calm herself down or lift herself up even though she had mental health issues. My aunt would visit us and walk nonstop in San Julián's backyard, wringing her hands, words running over each other, flowing turbulently from her lips, while Mama commanded her to sit down, to stop making herself more nervous than she already was—denial overtaking compassion.

At fourteen, one day I had cramps so painful I felt dizzy. When I complained, Mama said, "You are such a drama queen. It can't be so bad!" A few minutes later I threw up and she sent me to bed with a hot water bottle and an aspirin. She checked on me a couple of times through the morning, and for lunch she brought me her special rice and garlic soup that would heal you even if you had one foot in the grave. In a crisis she might not give you a hug, but you could count on her to soldier on and rescue you.

Family challenges—from mental illness to money troubles—were kept under wraps. Perhaps Mama was trying to protect us by hiding or downplaying problems, but instead I concluded that it was preferable to not speak of difficult issues than to tackle them.

Guarding the Fort

JUST AS THE COUNTRY WAS TRYING to navigate life without Franco, I was trying to navigate my own private limbo. I was not a good girl in Catholic school anymore, and I had no idea where I was headed or who I wanted to be. I had chosen to major in literature because I loved reading and writing. Mama encouraged me. She had once dreamed of becoming a nurse—if she hadn't gotten married and given birth to ten children. "Study what you like," she said. "With time you'll figure out what job to pursue."

The first year of college the lectures were boring, but being out of the school I had attended for over a decade, surrounded by boys, and enmeshed in the political ardor of the time made up for the required classes' drudgery.

In January, my friends and I attended a concert by singer–song-writer Lluís Llach at the Sports Palace on Montjuic, the broad hill overlooking the harbor. I wasn't a big fan of his forlorn, monotone style—I liked the Beatles' upbeat music better—but that evening exhilaration seized me and my friends. Llach had been considered persona non grata by the Franco regime. His performances had been forbidden, so he exiled himself to Paris and returned to Spain only after Franco's passing. This concert, one of a series of three attended by more than 30,000 people, became another battle cry.

At the arena, we raised our lighters up and our voices even higher to accompany Llach on "L'estaca," a song about a rotten stick that's about to fall. It expressed how we felt to perfection: we were still tied up by the remnants of the dictatorship, but if we pulled hard—one from here, the other from there—we would surely be set free. Once the concert ended, we walked down Montjuic with a multitude of people, feeling invincible.

As much as liberation excited me from a political standpoint, it was harder to unlock the shackles of my upbringing, which had imprinted in my brain that sex was only for marriage and, even then, for procreation.

I had started dating Ramón, a senior agronomy student born and raised in Berga, a town in the northeast of Barcelona province. Ramón had never lived in Barcelona before his studies, hated big cities, spoke Spanish with a marked Catalan accent, and longed to get back to Berga and his family farm as quickly as possible.

He was three years older than me, tall and well built, with long-ish black hair and sexy green eyes. I liked him, but his forwardness scared me. I had a taste of it when I visited him at home. He lived with roommates in a flat typical of the Ensanche neighborhood, long and narrow, with a *galería cubierta* in the back—a sunroom that ran the width of the house, with windows from ceiling to mid-wall overlooking the *patio interior*.

In Ramón's home, filled with sloppy bachelors, a musty smell of dirty socks, and hardly any furniture, the *galería cubierta* was the most welcoming niche. It had a long wooden table where we camped out with our books and where I spent more time fending off his advances than studying. He first pushed a lock of hair back from my face and smoothed it down my shoulders. Then came the hand on the thigh and the kiss on the neck.

"Let me read, Ramón, please, I have an exam on Friday."

"Just a kiss, come on."

The kiss became two kisses, and soon he was on second base, while I pushed his hands away.

"You have nice breasts," he said, his eyes bright.

"What's so nice about them?" I asked, puzzled. To me, they were regular breasts, but then everything about me felt regular. I didn't have a sense of my own appeal: the smooth skin, the hazel eyes, the small nose and cherry lips, the long blond hair, the perfectly proportioned body. I was pretty, but I couldn't see it, like the boys who had surrounded me since childhood in San Julián never seemed to see it. Aside from a childhood crush when I was seven years old, I had never had any suitors among my summer friends. Once I developed, men whistled when I walked by construction sites, but I credited it to their lust, not to my beauty.

"They are round, they are perky but also soft, they are the perfect size . . ."

After that, I declined when he suggested going to his house, alleging that I studied better at home. This wasn't the first time a guy had touched my breasts, and my previous experience hadn't ended well.

The year before, when I was in college prep, was the first time I had attended classes with boys because coed schools had been banned during most of Francoism. My high-school girlfriends had either moved from Sagrado Corazón to a public school for this last year or left school altogether, but I stayed and formed a new group of friends.

Reading a journal from that time, I find an earnest girl who pushed for having serious talks about the meaning of life, God, politics, and other such grave subjects instead of just goofing around. If I was the philosopher in my group, Nico was the comedian, always cracking jokes and making us laugh. His sunny character helped me forgive his misogynist comments. According to him, women were not as intelligent as men, and they shouldn't work in the same jobs because they couldn't perform as well.

I had grown up with men's and women's roles clearly etched in my mind, but I didn't think women were less capable. I remembered watching a TV program on which couples were interviewed separately. The host asked the man and then the woman who was more intelligent. Mama instantly said, "I would answer that your father and I are equally intelligent, each in our own realm." At first, her comment surprised me, because men always appeared more important than women. On second thought, though, it made sense. Papa worked and supported us all, but Mama kept the house running like clockwork and was raising ten kids, which took considerable smarts and effort. Nico's point of view, however, was quite common. It was 1974. It would be another year before women were allowed to work or even open a bank account without their husband's written permission.

My group of friends also included Vicens and Remei, a committed couple, Joan, a lanky guy, outgoing and likeable, and a few other youths. Sometimes we went camping. It surprised me that Mama let me spend the weekend with boys since she was so set against sex before marriage, but she seemed to trust that I would be safe far from her watchful eye, as she did when she gave us free rein in San Julián. After all, I had never strayed from the rules (at least, not out in the open). She wasn't misguided. When we camped, Vicens and Remei slept in their own tent, but the rest of us lay chastely side by side, packed in a row of sleeping bags like sausages.

For a few months I admired Joan from afar, languishing when he played the guitar and led us through the Beatles and Bob Dylan catalogs. I hung on his every word and fantasized that he was singing his songs for me, but he treated me with the same detached affability as he did everybody else. This coolness changed when we spent a weekend at his summerhouse instead of camping.

Vicens and Remei took the master bedroom. Two boys plopped their backpacks in a bedroom with twin beds. There was only one bedroom left. Joan and I left our stuff on the beds and joined the others for a walk.

The whole day I had butterflies in my stomach. I forced myself to act naturally, but I was a wreck. Would Joan kiss me if we slept alone in the same room? I could only hope. It didn't cross my mind that he might go further.

That night, after dinner and a long chat around the fireplace, everybody said good night and we went to bed.

I changed into my pajamas in the bathroom. When I got to the bedroom, Joan was already in bed, his aquiline nose rising from the pillow, barely visible in the streetlight's glow that seeped through a crack in the shutters. He folded open the sheets and patted the mattress, inviting me to get in bed with him. I hesitated, but this was the first time he had shown an interest, so I slipped in beside him, trembling. After a little banter, he kissed me on the lips. My first French kiss! I tried to follow his lead, but I worried I was doing it all wrong.

A few minutes later, Joan slipped a hand under my pajamas and grabbed my breast. I almost jumped, but I caught myself in time. Wasn't this a sin? Maybe I should get up and leave. But then he would never want to be with me again. I pushed his hand away, but I kept kissing him. Suddenly, he kicked his pajama pants off, grabbed my hand, and wrapped it around his cock. I had grown up surrounded by brothers, but I had never seen a man naked, let alone erect. That thick throbbing animal startled me, but I tried to hide my discomfort. I didn't want Joan to think I was a prig. Still, I withdrew my hand.

Joan grabbed it again and brought it back to his cock. This time he kept his hand over mine and started moving both up and down. I was thirsty for caresses, for whispered sweet words, but he was careening down a one-way street. All pretense of togetherness fell away. He lay on his back, his attention focused on the mechanical pumping of our hands.

I yanked mine away without saying a word. I turned my back to him and curled up in a fetal position while he finished the job.

The rest of the weekend is a blur. I itched to go back home and bury myself in my bedroom until the piercing cry of "¡A cenaaaar!" would force me to go sit at the table for dinner. I didn't have anyone to share this experience with, and in any case, I felt too ashamed to talk about it. I'd been in bed with a boy, which was forbidden, but the worst part was that he hadn't loved me. At least I had kept him at bay, but I still felt sullied.

Almost a year to the day after the incident with Joan, Ramón drove me home one evening to Avenida del Tibidabo after dinner with friends. He parked across the street, on a dirt path that led to a park, so we could make out. It was past midnight. The mansions on either side of the elegant avenue were dark and the street was deserted. Ramón unbuttoned my blouse, got my right breast out of my bra and fumbled with it. Some of my girlfriends were already having sex, so I thought I should make concessions, even though I didn't want to. After a moment, Ramón unzipped his pants. I was petrified. The thought of his body over mine awakened more fear than excitement.

Right then we heard a brusque tapping on the window. A couple of *tricornios*—so called due to their three-pointed hard hats—stood outside. These guards regulated traffic, but they also acted as the arm of the still-repressive post-Franco regime.

Ramón moved away from me and cranked down the window. I buttoned and smoothed my blouse, my cheeks burning.

"Papers," barked one guard, tilting his head to eye me better. Ramón reached over me to the glove compartment. He offered his driving license. I noticed his hands shook a little. A shudder ran down my spine.

"I'm just taking my girlfriend home. She lives right there." He pointed to my house.

"And why did you park here if she lives across the street?" asked the second guard, smirking. They were clearly enjoying our flushed faces and lowered eyes.

"We were talking."

"Hmmmpff," snorted the first guard, as he examined Ramón's papers, front and back. "I could take you to jail for indecent behavior, you know?"

We didn't say anything. We knew this was true. Public displays of sexual behavior were censored and could be punished.

My mind raced. What would my parents say if they got a call from the police station to come get me? Thinking about Mama's disappointment froze my insides.

The two guards whispered to each other. After a few seconds, the first one handed back the papers.

"We'll let you go this time, but you have to take her home right now."

"Of course, right away, thank you," said Ramón, his voice docile.

He backed into the street, did a U-turn, and parked in front of my door. I got out without saying goodbye, opened the gate, and rushed up the stairs.

From inside the front door, I saw Ramón's car going down the avenue while the guards drove up the street. Trembling from head to toe, I went to my bedroom. My heart's thumps were so deafening I expected they would wake my sister.

After the adrenaline rush subsided, anxiety swelled. Would I have to marry Ramón, given how he had groped me? I wasn't ready to marry, but I had let him touch my breasts instead of withdrawing, as I had done with Joan. For all I knew, such intimacy, if you were a sincere Catholic, meant you had to rush straight to the altar. Luckily, Ramón's hand had never made it to my crotch. Perhaps I was in the clear.

I fretted we might get closer to forbidden territory when he invited some friends and me to his house in Berga in mid-June to attend La Patum, a festival that had been celebrated since the fifteenth century. It was my first time witnessing it, and the pandemonium that took over the streets astounded me.

A mass of people jumped in concert with the drumrolls, ran to escape the fire-spitting dragons, rejoiced with the parade of demons, mules, Moors, and Christians, and, at the culmination of the party, danced in counterclockwise circles around enormous papier-mâché figures carried by prancing men hidden under the giants' tunics. The fervor of the crowd had a life of its own, with the ecstatic revelers chanting and moving in unison and booing the musicians every time they stopped until they blasted off another round of music.

The relentless explosions of firecrackers, the boisterous crowd, the penetrating sound of multiple wind instruments, the grave foundational thump of *el Tabal*, the main drum, was exhilarating and almost dizzying. Ramón asked if we wanted to join in. I was tempted to say yes, but my friends were reluctant to participate, and I had some fear about being run over. We stayed off to the side, taking in the chaos.

I wondered why the long arms of Franco's regime hadn't strangled this exuberant party. Perhaps they didn't bother because it was in a small town and it happened during Corpus Christi. Anything that could be remotely tied to a religious festivity got a pass.

As the evening approached, I grew more nervous. Would I be able to keep Ramón off me as we had kept out of the dance? The wildness I saw in the streets had put me on guard.

That night, Ramón and I shared a bed, but I insisted on sleeping with my clothes on. When he tried to escalate his advances, I feigned crying. He had to accept defeat.

Once the school term ended, Ramón graduated and moved back to Berga. We said goodbye without drama or regret. Well, with a tinge of regret on my side because he took with him a black-and-white photo of my First Communion, where at six years old I looked angelic in my gauzy white veil and white flower crown, my limpid eyes and open smile all goodness and light. I've always wished I hadn't gifted this photo to Ramón, who probably ended up trashing it at some point, while for me it would have been a precious relic of the innocent girl I once had been, a moment in time that was rapidly receding from view.

1964, Barcelona
Red Balloon

I WAS IN THE FAMILY ROOM alone with my dolls. The door opened
and in came my brother Guille. He sat by my side and asked if I
wanted to play a game. I was in awe of him. At thirteen, he was boisterous, strong, the leader of the gang. I said yes.

He asked me to lie on the sofa, belly up, and I did so. He lay on
top of me, belly down, and grabbed my wrists with his hands. He
was heavy. He ground his body against mine. He pushed hard down
there, between my legs, where Mama had told me I shouldn't touch
myself. Even though we had clothes on, I felt naked. I told him to
stop, but he didn't. I tried shoving his chest away with my elbows,
but I couldn't move him an inch. I turned my face to the side. I saw
the brown bristles of the sofa and felt them pinching my cheek. I
wiggled my body, but his legs pinned me down in place. Grind, grind,
wide eyes, his lips curling. I had trouble breathing. "Stop, stooop,"
I pleaded.

All of a sudden, he stopped, jumped up from the sofa, and told
me the game was over. He walked out the door and left me there.

I didn't understand what he had done, but I knew it must be
wrong. I remembered Mama's revulsion when she bent down to give
me a good-night kiss and caught me with my hand between my legs.
Now Guille had ground his body against mine down there. Would
Mama be mad if she knew? Just in case, I didn't say anything.

Life went back to normal. Guille still didn't talk to me or play with me unless we were playing all together or having lunch, when everybody spoke over each other. A few times—one, three, five? I don't remember—when he found me alone in the family room, he made me play "the grinding game," even though I didn't want to. (Decades later, the weight of a man's body on my own would still constrict my throat, my mind going into flight, my flesh into freeze.)

One afternoon we had cousins visiting. We were all running after each other, playing Mamas and Papas. One of my cousins said that I had been a bad girl and Papa had to spank my bottom. Guille was Papa but he didn't want to spank me. My cousin insisted. I went along because I was a kid and kids do what Papa says. I bent down on my brother's legs. My cousin asked him to pull down my panties to spank me better. Guille said that wasn't necessary. He hit me twice, weakly, on top of my skirt, and let me go as if I were burning. He seemed embarrassed. Perhaps he realized he was too grown up for silly games. Or maybe he didn't want to cause me any more harm. He never sought me out alone again. (In my mind, the two things were related: my brother not wanting to spank me and avoiding lifting my skirt and the fact that we never played the grinding game again. But they may have been unrelated. I don't know, because I never asked. We didn't talk about anything personal.)

I kept touching myself. I had gotten into the habit over the summer and now it became an obsession. I did it every night and sometimes during the day, making sure nobody noticed, but it didn't feel good. Like a bright red balloon just out of reach, the tickle dazzled me. I tried to trap it, straining my body to reach up higher. Sometimes I clutched its string between my fingers, fleetingly, but it escaped. The small red balloon floated away while my body hurt from the effort to grab it, my legs rigid.

Preparing for my First Communion later that year, I agonized over the confession. I wondered if I should tell the priest about my nightly communion with my body, but I was too scared to mention it. What if they didn't allow me to participate in the ceremony?

The black-and-white photos of that day show a lovely six-year-old girl with straight hair and big pure eyes. Dressed in a long, white dress like a miniature bride, she's earnestly pronouncing her vows with her hand on a Bible or smiling with the rare joy of garnering, if for only a day, everybody's attention. Those eyes reveal the innocence and happiness that colored my childhood, no matter the moments of anguish that marred its shine.

The following summer, I spent a month with my cousin Sylvia and her family in the mountain town where they had a house.

One afternoon I taught Sylvia that there was a button down there that, if she rubbed it, would tickle her insides. Alone in the dollhouse that sat in the yard, or in our bedroom during the mandatory naptime, we fabricated little stories that fleshed out the exploration of our bodies.

In one of our tales, which I remember vaguely, a master ordered her slave to climb up the ladder to the top bunk bed with her panties off. As the slave stopped midway, the master "tortured" her by touching the slave's button from below. It was my favorite fantasy—"forced" pleasure couldn't induce guilt. And it thrilled me to know that I wasn't the only bad girl.

These games ended a year or two later, when Sylvia flunked a course and we saw less of each other, but my compulsion to chase the slippery tickle endured. It would one day spur one of the biggest regrets of my life.

A friend invited me over for her tenth birthday party. The house was full of kids when I arrived, but I didn't know anyone except this girl, whom I had recently met. After a while, I ambled through the long hallway as if looking for the bathroom to escape the rowdy strangers in the living room. A toddler was playing in a room in the far end. I sat with him, pushing his choo-choo train and helping him build a tower with his blocks. It was peaceful here, the shrieks of the girls reaching us faintly through the door I'd left ajar. I lay on the carpet and started rubbing between my legs. It wasn't because the boy was there; it was because that's what I did, anywhere, anytime.

I rubbed vigorously, with my finger over my panties, but nothing happened. The little boy approached me. I took him in my arms and, without even thinking, put his wiggly little body over mine, his diaper against my crotch, and moved him up and down. He looked at me, intrigued, and tried to reach my face with his chunky hands, but I was focused on what was happening down there, which was still nothing.

He didn't like being held without peekaboo or any other game. He whined. I put him on the floor, and he ran back to his toys.

A wave of shame and fear engulfed me. What had I done? And what if his mother had seen me? I got up, smoothed my clothes, and I never did it again, not to him or anybody else.

For months I yearned to confess, to ask for forgiveness, but I couldn't bring myself to do it. I was too embarrassed, too scared. I mulled over how I could tell the story so the priest would understand, but it seemed impossible. I couldn't understand it myself.

Decades later, shame still smothered me. How could I have used this child to feed my own twisted mania? It didn't matter that it was just a few seconds, that he didn't even notice, that my clothes were on, that his clothes were on, that I was only eleven. The fact remained that I had done to him the same thing my brother had done to me.

As much as I like to think that I'm a good-hearted person who always tries to help, the truth is that I've wronged others. Good girl, bad girl. The coin always has two sides.

Pablita's hair felt soft, like cream just whipped. I fastened the clasps on the back of her pink dress and turned her around. Tying the satin bow at the collar so both sides looked perky and the ribbons hung at the same length took three attempts. Her thighs played peekaboo through the lace hem, like mine.

I was with Pablita in the family room when the door opened and in bolted two of my cousins, followed by two of my brothers. They yanked Pablita from my hands. "Give her back!" I yelled, but they ran away.

I dashed out to the hall. They were climbing up the staircase, two steps at a time, and had almost reached the second floor. What were they up to?

"Give her to me!" I cried again.

"Just a minute; we're doing an experiment!" yelled a cousin.

They propped Pablita on the banister.

"Here it goes, ladies and gentlemen, the flying dooooooll!" shouted one of the boys. He pushed her over the banister. It only took two seconds for Pablita to land on the polished white tiles of the hall with a soft thud.

"Aaaayyyyy!" I ran towards her and examined her. She seemed fine.

The boys rushed downstairs and grabbed Pablita again, yelling triumphantly.

"Let her go!" I held on to her legs.

"Don't worry, don't you see that nothing happened to her?" said one.

"Last time, I promise!" said another. Face flushed with excitement. Voice urgent.

"But I don't want you to!"

They pulled Pablita out of my hands and rushed up the stairs.

Complaining to Mama and Papa crossed my mind, but the thought of the boys singing that nasty tattletale song—*"Acuseta, marraneta, calzoncillos de bayeta"*—stopped me. Besides, Mama and Papa's policy was that the less they intervened, the better. Our home was big. Most of the time we were out of their sight, left to our own devices to resolve our disputes. A common resolution was a slap on the face from the older to the younger, or the threat of it: *"Te voy a romper la cara."* ("I will break your face.") Knitted brow. Menacing eyes that drilled you in place. You had to shut up and take it.

This hands-off parental style had its advantages. No constant scolding or orders to lower your voice. No imposed rules about whose turn it was to do something. Just a bunch of kids, masters of the garden, the family room, the stairs, the bedrooms, the terraces, the basement . . . My cousins loved coming over, especially those from my father's side, who had a stricter upbringing. They went a little wild in our home, jumping on sofas, yelling and running nonstop like overwound mechanical bunnies.

Our rigorous pecking order sometimes got out of hand. Once, Guille, Diego and some cousins forced my brother Jorge, who was a little younger, to drink pee. They told him it was lemonade. Although he didn't believe it, he couldn't escape the circle of excited faces around him. I felt bad for him, but I shut up and retreated to my bedroom, fearing I would be next. Another time Guille forced Diego to eat dirt as punishment for something or other.

In Mama and Papa's presence, it was a different deal. Good behavior and manners were enforced, especially at the table. You wouldn't catch any of us eating with our mouths open, slurping the soup, or grabbing the food with our fingers. Papa would have never put up with it. He even peeled and ate his oranges with a knife and a fork! The only exception to formal etiquette was the rare occasion when instead of fresh fruit for dessert we had a sweet dish, like strawberries with whipped cream and sugar, *brazo de gitano*, or chocolate mousse. Mama and Papa turned a blind eye if we licked the plate, and sometimes Papa, who had a sweet tooth, would lick it himself with a grin.

Our time together in the living room tended to be peaceful. We were all either reading a book, watching TV, or playing a board game. From time to time, if an argument got out of hand and shouting or tears were involved, Papa might intervene: "Enough!" It was so rare for Papa to raise his voice that one word was all he needed to make us fall in line.

By now the boys were on the third floor, which had only two terraces. My stomach tightened into a knot. A ball of air sat on top of it, stuck inside my chest. It wouldn't come out. Without warning, one of the boys grabbed Pablita, raised her above his head and threw her down with all his might. CLONK. Pablita fell in front of me, face down, arms and legs asunder.

"Noooooo!" I kneeled and picked her up.

When I pulled the cord on her back that made her talk, it didn't move.

"She doesn't speak, she doesn't speak!" I started crying. I untied her bow, unclasped her collar, and took off her dress. Her body was crooked. It had cracked on the side, and the front had slid off the back, exposing a round disc inside her belly.

The boys were downstairs by now, and when they saw the damage, they realized they had gone too far.

"Give her to me," said my brother. "I'll fix her."

"Don't touch her!" I yelled.

Pablita was the first doll I had truly cared about. I loved her platinum hair, her round blue eyes with long black eyelashes, her plump cheeks cushy like a real baby's, and her lovely babble: "*Upa, Mama, upa*," or "*¡Quiero un pirulí!*" She said eighteen different sentences, and her laugh always made me happy.

"We wanted to see how strong she was," whispered one of my cousins.

I was inconsolable.

Cradling Pablita in one arm and holding the broken-off belly in the other, I went to the living room.

"They broke Pablita, Papa." I could barely speak.

"Who broke Pablita? What happened?" I handed him the doll, weeping.

Mama hugged me and asked, "Who broke her? What did they do?"

"They threw her down from the terrace. She doesn't speak anymore," I stammered between sobs. Mama got up and went out to the hall, where she found the boys huddled. She ordered them into the living room.

"Why did you do such a thing?" said Papa sternly.

"It was an experiment," muttered one.

"You are grounded," said Papa. "Go up to your room and don't come out until I tell you. And you," he looked at my cousins, "stay down here until you are picked up."

They all filed out, crestfallen. My brothers went up the stairs without a word, and my cousins slunk into the family room.

I didn't care about their punishment. All I cared about was Pablita. I sat on Mama's lap, hugging my doll, unable to stop the stream of tears. Papa went out and came back with his toolbox and a roll of industrial scotch tape. He took Pablita and put her on his lap. He examined the two sides of her body, the nape of her neck where the cord was attached, and the disc. There wasn't a whole lot he could do. After detangling the cord, he dusted the disc with a soft cloth, placed the front on top of the back, perfectly aligned, and used the tape to secure the two halves. When he finished, he handed Pablita back to me.

"Try it now."

I sat Pablita on my knees, hooked my index finger in the round plastic tab and pulled the cord. It caught a bit in the middle, but after a soft tug it straightened to all its length.

"*Dame un besito*," said Pablita.

Static overpowered her voice. It was hard to decipher what she said, but I knew all her sentences by heart, so I recognized it. I pulled again. A crackling noise that might have been her laugh whimpered out.

"See?" said Mama. "All better. Now let's get her dressed."

I dressed Pablita in her short pink dress and took her to my room. Her sides felt crinkled with the strips of tape on it, not smooth like before. Her voice strangled, like mine. I combed her hair and put her down to sleep. I wanted to keep loving her just as before, but I knew she'd never be the same.

Road to Disenchantment

THE SECOND YEAR OF UNIVERSITY, the humanities department was moved to Plaza Universidad, close to Las Ramblas, and housed in the nineteenth-century building of the Universidad de Barcelona.

My college prep gang had survived the first year of separation in different colleges, but our friendship was petering out. The incident that sealed our separation happened when we returned to university after the summer. I turned eighteen in late September. I invited the gang to celebrate that we were legally adults with a formal evening party at home, in fancy dresses and suits. They had never been to my house. The only means of transportation to get up Avenida del Tibidabo was the last remaining cable car in Barcelona, *el tranvía azul*, which ran only every half hour, and a mile uphill on foot was not ideal for regular meetings.

The first thing Joan said when entering the house was, "Do you hang ham and chorizos from the beams?" Perhaps it was his way to cope with the high ceilings, the elegant wood staircase going to the second floor, the ample rooms, and the coat-of-arms tapestry hanging in the hall. Although my family didn't have accumulated wealth— Papa supported us solely on his earnings as a mid-tier lawyer—we were privileged to own this four-story house with a big yard he had inherited from his mother. To outside eyes we must have looked like millionaires.

During the party, a couple of drinks replaced my usual

earnestness with a brazen flirtation, but since Joan had reverted to coolness after our unfortunate sexual tussle and I knew he was never going to date me, I went for the next best thing. I liked the way Vicens treated his girlfriend. Perhaps he would treat me the same way.

I danced in front of Vicens, talked to him as if he were breathtaking, fixed him seductively with my eyes, and even fed him an hors d'oeuvre after taking a bite of it myself.

He stared at me, puzzled, not knowing how to react to this unwanted attention. I foggily noticed Remei's and Joan's searing looks from the other side of the room, but I didn't stop until the three of them left abruptly. The party fizzled out after that. I was left with the cleanup and a vague feeling of unease.

A few days later I visited Joan at his parents' house. He took me to his room without saying a word, closed the door, and faced me. I saw again Mama's eyes, her disgust pinning me to the bed like daggers.

"How could you behave like that?" he hissed. "You know Vicens is Remei's boyfriend. It was revolting. And you are a friend? You sicken me. I don't want to see you ever again!"

I stayed mute while he ranted, my chest flooding with shame. After the party, I had pushed my flirtation out of my mind, convincing myself that it was harmless. It certainly was out of character. I was too insecure to flirt and too prudish to interfere in a steady couple, but the frustration of Joan's inconstant attention, the elation of feeling beautiful in my dress, the thrust of a couple of drinks, and my bottomless thirst for love and attention had combined to bring out a side of me I didn't know I had.

I got up and rushed out of his house, so he wouldn't see me cry.

My engagement with this group of friends dissolved. What stayed was that forward girl I had just met. Several times over the years I couldn't resist the temptation to toy with men who were happily coupled. Even if I didn't find them sexy, I envied the tenderness they offered their partners, and I wanted to taste it myself.

I found out that the same men who showered their companions with kisses and affection would chew me up and spit me out with not even a cuddle, let alone a loving gaze.

The transition to democracy was showing progress, especially since King Juan Carlos named Adolfo Suárez as President of the Government in July 1976. Suárez was a striking man in his early forties who knew how to negotiate and moved swiftly. By September, he had put in front of Congress a Political Reform Act that proposed the legalization of political parties and opened the door to democratic elections. Congress approved it and a public referendum ratified it by an overwhelming majority. The election was set for June 1977. Millions of Spaniards would vote for the first time in forty-one years. It would also be the first time for me. I paid close attention to the news, the papers, and the political discussions at home to decide who I would vote for. My parents liked a centrist Catalan party. Several siblings, including me, leaned toward the socialist party. Guille joked that since his wife said she would vote socialist, he may have to vote communist, because he considered himself more progressive than her. In the end, Suárez's centrist party won, and the Socialist Party came in second.

Suárez's youth and efficiency could not disguise the fact that he and many other congressmen had held key positions in the Franco regime. The peaceful transition covered up their decades-long participation in repressing the voices they were now making room for. Likewise, the Amnesty Law we had clamored for in so many demonstrations passed a few months later, but it not only liberated the political prisoners that had fought Francoism, it also pardoned any crimes committed by people associated with Franco's regime.

The new government compensated for its political flaws by relaxing the iron grip on social customs. All of a sudden, women had access to the birth control pill. I was a virgin, and I had no plans to change that, but the pill became a hot topic of conversation among my girlfriends. Some wanted to use it, but it wasn't easy to get—many doctors still required that you be married before prescribing it.

The government also allowed freedom of the press and the right to associate and form unions. My parents had subscribed forever to the moderate newspaper *La Vanguardia*, but now my older brothers and I read the recently launched *El País*, which was left leaning. It was exciting to even have the option.

Just as I began to diverge from my parents in my newspaper choice, I withdrew from their Sunday visits to church. I told Mama I'd go to mass by myself in the neighborhood church at one o'clock instead of at ten o'clock with them so I could study in the morning. Instead, I walked down Avenida del Tibidabo and sat on a bench for an hour reading a book. Although I still believed in Jesus's teachings, organized religion and going to mass seemed out of touch with the times. Being well trained by then in the habit of silence, I kept my revolt secret.

Political and cultural changes rolled out fast, but not everything was rosy. Unemployment grew and the economy was in tatters. Dozens of people died in terrorist attacks. Hard-right groups added to the violence of ultra-left and independent groups who wanted to break Catalonia and the Basque country apart from the rest of Spain. Meanwhile, a legal right-wing group called *Fuerza Nueva* organized marches and meetings to revive Franco's memory and legacy. An undercurrent of vulnerability threatened the young democracy.

It seemed nothing could ever be simple. Social progress came hand in hand with bombs, just as Franco's "economic miracle" of the 1960s had come hand in hand with repression.

I felt unmoored. Demonstrations to protest terrorism and weeks of strikes to push for more reforms were common on my new campus. I duly participated but I was getting burned out, and I wasn't the only one. Newspapers discussed *el desencanto*, the disenchantment that was turning the young away from politics. The remainders of Francoism in Congress and the exhaustion of constant protests were taking a toll.

My classes, when they were not canceled due to strikes, were disappointing. Over a hundred students sat on bleachers in enormous rooms. Professors lectured from yellowing papers. There was hardly any discussion or interaction. The men in humanities were old-fashioned. I had only one close friend at university, Ingrid. The group of friends I had made during my college prep course had unraveled. I rarely went to San Julián anymore. My life seemed dull.

I chugged along, reading the assignments and studying the week before exams without feeling invested. The streets outside the university beckoned.

I often walked up and down Las Ramblas on my way to the city's main library, La Biblioteca del Carmen. On the wide promenade, flower stands were followed by pet stands. In front of kiosks bursting with newspapers, men gawked at the sudden explosion of boobs on every magazine cover, now that the strict censorship of the Franco years had lifted. Close to the harbor, street vendors with arts and crafts popped up. The street where I had marched arm in arm with fellow protesters teemed now with youth having fun and Inti-Illimani look-alikes playing flutes with colorful blankets laid on the ground to collect tips. Old couples sat on rented chairs lining the sides of the boulevard. For fifty cents you could spend an hour watching a colorful world go by. After so many years living above Diagonal, the crackling energy of Barcelona's throbbing heart dazzled me.

The chrysalid where I had slept during my adolescence showed some cracks, but it would still be a while before I fully spread my wings.

A Loud New World

IN THE SUMMER, I asked Mama if I could go to France to improve my French. Mama suggested we contact her cousin Carlos. He had a small hotel in Mâcon, close to Lyon, the hotel Terminus. Perhaps he would let me work there. Carlos agreed to take me in but warned I would have to work as hard as anybody else.

I arrived in Mâcon in June of 1977 to spend four months. Carlos, whom I had never met, showed me my bedroom on the third story of the hotel. He had transformed the whole floor into an apartment for himself, his wife Françoise, and their two kids. The children must have been away in boarding school or summer camps, because I never saw them.

I started working the next day as a *bagagiste*. I stood by the reception greeting guests, showed them the parking lot around the corner, and took their suitcases up to their room. The job itself wasn't much fun but witnessing the hotel gears shift throughout the day fascinated me.

Carlos's presence filtered into every corner of the Terminus. Small and wiry, his blue eyes sparkled with uncontainable energy and ideas. He couldn't sit still for more than ten minutes. You would find him reviewing the wine list with Jean, the young maître d', drumming up business for catered events, chatting up guests in the restaurant, planning a remodel of the bedrooms, or tweaking the dinner menu. To relax, he ran upstairs to our apartment, played a classical piece on the piano, and rushed downstairs to continue the battle. The lyrical melodies offered a surprising counterpoint to the brisk and booming ascent and descent of stairs.

His wife Françoise, by contrast, helped at reception in the mornings and took care of small jobs like arranging the flowers, but rarely interacted with the guests. Most afternoons, she sat in her small living room on the third floor watching soaps, a glass of red wine in hand.

One could still glimpse the delicate beauty she had been, with her small nose, arched penciled brows, light brown hair in a bouffant, and thin-boned wrists. She was elegant in a somber kind of way, always in black from head to toe, a loose cotton top with two pointy bra cups, rigid like a suit of armor, giving her shape, a pencil skirt that ended above her knees showcasing her lovely calves, and black kitten-heel pumps.

Her relationship with Carlos was tense. From my bedroom, I heard a couple of big rows.

"Go downstairs, *dis donc*! We need your help!" Carlos yelled once.

Françoise yelled back, "Why don't you call one of your girlfriends to come and help you?"

Their fiery arguments shocked me. My parents never raised their voices.

Although Françoise was reserved, she treated me kindly. My name was difficult to pronounce in French, so she came up with a nickname I loved: Maya.

My new name seemed to bring with it a lighter personality but sandwiched between this busy owner and his withdrawn wife, and stuck by the reception all day, I didn't have a chance to test it. I felt lonely. Carlos, Françoise, and I rarely ate together. Most days I ate at the bar alone, as my job schedule allowed.

I asked if I could work in the restaurant or the kitchen. Almost all the staff were between sixteen and nineteen, because Carlos recruited them from a restaurateur school in the area. I longed to be part of that group, but Carlos hesitated. Maybe he thought an eighteen-year-old bourgeois girl from Barcelona wouldn't be able to handle the fast-paced rhythm of service.

He changed his mind literally by accident. The crew was getting ready for a catered wedding. Jean Pierre, the sous chef, was carrying a huge covered tray with meat to the van when he slipped. The tray veered to one side and the sauce fell on his leg, scalding him badly. Carlos had to rush him to the hospital. But first, he ran into the hotel and recruited me on the spot to help at the wedding.

My job was to serve ice cream. It sounded simple enough but after a few dozen servings, my hand threatened to fall away from my aching wrist. My palm had a bright red round mark where it held down the metal scoop, and blisters developed on my index finger and thumb from pressing the lever. I wanted to either hit on the head with the scoop the umpteenth kid that came for seconds and thirds or roll into a ball behind the stand so nobody would find me, but I kept asking with a frozen grin: "Chocolate or strawberry? One scoop or two?"

Jean, the maître d', took over for about ten minutes to give me a break, but he couldn't stay longer because he was managing the crew, serving, and organizing the cleanup. When Carlos arrived, we were almost ready to leave. He complimented us because the event had run like a well-timed show. My raw hand elicited an admiring whistle and convinced him that I was ready to work hard in the kitchen.

He assigned me cleaning duties, like washing wine glasses or getting the restaurant ready once guests had left. Every day, from crumbs and wrinkled napkins I restored order to the world, each piece of flatware in the exactly right position over tablecloths freshly laundered and pressed. The chaos of the mundane dissolved in that perfect harmony.

The passage from this quiet space to the boisterous kitchen, where pots and pans clanked on the sides of the sink, and waiters and cooks cracked jokes once the tense speed of service was behind them, created a flawless balance.

I soon graduated to prepping, but I wasn't fast, or good, except when I peeled tomatoes and used the thin red ribbons to make rose-buds for each plate. Jean Pierre teased me: "*Alors*, Maya, are you singing a lullaby to the carrots while you cut them? Let me help."

I asked to be a waitress, and Carlos agreed to give me a try. Françoise took me to the flea market, where she bought me a form-fitting black lace blouse. I had a black mini skirt, which I covered with a dainty white apron.

For that group of young waiters and cooks it must have been a sight to see, that young Spanish woman in her sexy outfit, alone, and eager to learn the trade and make friends. But I was also the *patron*'s niece, so I didn't know if they would dare get close.

The restaurant was the crown jewel of the hotel Terminus. Carlos ran it as if we expected a visit by a Michelin judge, due any minute of any day, incognito.

The tables flaunted thick white tablecloths, and lavish flower arrangements bejeweled the room. An ornate cheese table lured you from the middle.

The waiters wore tuxedos and stood at attention with white napkins folded over their left arms. Jean stayed close to the door, straight as a rod, and received each guest with the deference owed to majesty.

He showed them to their tables and motioned a waiter to approach, launching the delicate ballet that left the guests of that mid-rate hotel awed with the superior service of its restaurant.

The food was even more dazzling than the ambience. It was there that I first saw a waiter deboning a fish tableside. The dish was *sole à la meunière*. The waiter expertly pushed aside all the bones on the edges of the sole with a knife, then ran it right down the middle of its flat belly. Delicately, he picked up the top of the fish with a silver spatula, one side at a time, and rested them on the borders of the plate. Next he carefully lifted the center spine, from tail to head, not even a morsel of flesh adhering to it, and tucked it away on a little platter, where the fish side bones already lay. After that, he replaced the two top halves of the sole over the bottom. The fish looked as if he'd never even touched it. He drizzled it with a buttery sauce and toasted almonds and placed it in front of the guest.

It was a small work of art, performed daily, in the anonymous restaurant of a humble hotel frequented by traveling salesmen and tourists en route to Lyon or Paris. This daily reverence for excellence and beauty appealed to me.

The chef, Lucien, in his late twenties—ancient compared to the waiters—was fat and unkempt, his butt cheeks showing over his checkered black-and-white pants when he bent to pick up a pan. He was also drunk by mid-service because he finished each glass of wine that came back to the kitchen half full. If there was wine left in a bottle, he would tip it up and drink long swigs between stirring a pot and flipping a steak. But he cooked like a god.

One of my favorite dishes of his was the soufflé Grand Marnier, a dessert, which I tasted when Carlos's mother, *Tía* María Josefa, came for a visit and we dined at the restaurant. It was magical how the mixture of eggs, butter, sugar, flour, and liqueur, flat half-way up the sides of a white porcelain container, rose like a fluffy yellow cloud and became an airy chef's hat, perched two inches over the rim.

One night, a customer who had ordered the soufflé glimpsed Lucien through the briefly open kitchen door. He was licking the sides of the white container to clean up the batter before setting it in the oven. What a scandal the guest stirred up! It took all of Carlos's powers of persuasion to convince him that Lucien had prepared that soufflé for himself, not for a client. The free bottle of wine didn't hurt. Carlos's yells when the kitchen closed could be heard all the way to reception. Not that they noticeably changed Lucien's attitude.

For a first experience in a work environment, I couldn't have fallen into a livelier place. It was endlessly captivating to see relationships forming and people pushing and prodding each other, the collaborations and deceptions, the emotions exposed and dealt with on the spot.

Carlos loved chatting up the guests and offering them experiences they would never forget, but sometimes his unbounded energy and flair got him into trouble.

Once a dinner guest ordered a steak tartare and Carlos decided to prepare it himself. The steak was always assembled next to the guest's table, so one of the waiters rolled the cart in with the raw meat and a dozen ingredients, including Worcestershire sauce, Tabasco sauce, Dijon mustard, anchovy bits, capers, and chopped herbs. Carlos mixed every condiment into the ground chuck with exaggerated flourishes, raising his hand a good two feet from the bowl every time he added one. Then came the final and most spectacular part: he flattened the meat into a patty and threw it in the air pizza-style. The steak flew up like a dazzling, fast kite. The whole restaurant held its breath, waiters and guests alike admiring the virtuosity of the owner.

Unfortunately, he missed the catch and the succulently spiced tartare fell on the floor with a big flop.

"*C'est pas vrai!*" exclaimed the dismayed guest as Carlos, his face burning red, had a waiter pick up the mess and come back with more raw meat. The second steak was swiftly prepared without ceremony while each of us carefully avoided looking at his table. Back in the kitchen, there were muffled laughs, but nobody dared comment lest Carlos fly into one of his short-lived rages.

Before I waitressed, Jean had to train me. We spent an afternoon alone in the restaurant.

He made me practice going in and out of the kitchen with plates in both hands, pushing the door with my shoulder and hip or opening it with an almost soundless kick.

Then he had me sit at a table and showed me how to pick up the dirty plate from the left and place the clean one with food from the right. His body behind mine displaced a current of air that warmed my spine.

I had marveled at the imposing towers the waiters balanced on their left hand while cleaning up the plates with the right, and I wanted to learn how to do it. As Jean taught me, guiding my hands with his, my gut somersaulted.

Opening a bottle of wine and serving it was the pièce de résistance. He used a sommelier corkscrew, which, once mastered, helps you uncork a bottle quickly and with style. The sight of it gave me a cold sweat. I had never handled one before and I was scared to make a fool of myself.

Jean removed the foil using the blade hidden in the handle, sank the corkscrew into the center of the cork, and twisted it down with his right hand, while holding the bottle in the air with his left hand. He bent the handle down and locked the metal lip on the bottle rim to pull out the cork.

It came out smoothly with a rewarding pop. He unscrewed it and put it away in his pocket, together with the corkscrew.

"Now it's time for the tasting. Serve a sip of wine to the person who will pay the bill, usually the oldest male. Twist your wrist to the right after pouring, to avoid a drop of wine sullying the tablecloth." He served a glass and used the white napkin folded on his arm to caress the bottle's neck and dry the cheeky drop that slid down its side.

I observed his elegant movements, imagining he was serving me that glass in a bistro, seated across from me at a tiny table with a checkered red-and-white tablecloth and a lit candle in the middle.

The first time I had to uncork a bottle in front of guests, my hands shook. To mask my nerves, I went through every step as slowly as possible. It was a table for two, and the couple followed my moves in silence. When I finished pouring the wine, the man said, "I have never been served wine so beautifully before."

I wanted to twirl and jump like an overexcited toddler. Instead, I looked at Jean, who had been eying me discreetly and he gave me a quick nod.

I loved working at the restaurant. The focused care that service required, the endless repetition of flawless rituals, and the immediate gratification of satisfied guests reminded me of the contentment I felt as a five-year-old filling page after page of well-rounded letters in my calligraphy notebooks. This quenched thirst for perfection was enhanced by the daily challenges I felt compelled to master. Could I carry that huge heavy platter and serve a table of thirty? How many dishes could I pile up into the tower I balanced on the palm, thumb, and pinky of my left hand? Could I entice guests to order cheese and dessert?

Waitressing also gave me a social life. The first weeks in Mâcon, I had spent my free time walking aimlessly in town or holed up in Carlos and Françoise's apartment. Now I wasn't lonely anymore.

As soon as I started in the kitchen, Jean Pierre, the sous chef, treated me to a beer on his first night off. It was fun, but it didn't lead to more. I had my eye on Jean.

Jean was about my height and had straight brown hair, a broad nose, and thick, inviting lips. He wasn't classically handsome, but the quiet pride he walked with and his irreproachable professionalism made him charismatic. On the surface, I didn't have a lot in common with a small-town French youth, almost two years my junior, who had never gone to college, but it didn't matter. I found him attractive, and I enjoyed his company.

One night we went for a drink. He waited for me outside, dressed—as always when he had time off—in a tight black silky t-shirt, black jeans, and a black jean jacket. This rocker uniform was inspired by his idol, Elvis Presley, but it also suited him, the dark color highlighting his blue eyes and fair skin.

We had a beer, and then we strolled in the park along the river Saône. It was balmy but late, and the park was deserted. Jean held my hand and we wandered for ten or fifteen minutes until we reached a large, canopied elm by the river, its thick trunk providing shelter from prying eyes. Jean placed his jean jacket on the grass. We lay on it and embraced. When he slid his hand inside my pants and caressed me down there, he wowed me. I didn't know a boy could do that to you. In my limited experience, boys wanted to get off or get it in, not make a woman swoon. I closed my eyes and kissed him, while I recited a silent prayer: thank you God, thank you, thank you, thank you, thank you.

After that night, Jean and I were inseparable, though we didn't have much opportunity for privacy. I couldn't bring him to our apartment, and he shared a bedroom with Jean Pierre. During our free hours in the afternoons, we sat in the hotel bar, a room at the left side of reception, where guests rarely went. We played Chinese checkers, watched movies on the small black-and-white TV, and discussed our plans for the future. I had no idea what would become of me, but Jean knew exactly what he wanted: to manage one of the magnificent castles in the Loire region as a luxury hotel.

We stayed up late once dinner service was over. The hotel was quiet. We cuddled on a sofa in the reception, keeping an eye out for the night guard, who would come at unexpected moments, a lascivious look betraying his quest to catch us having sex. But we didn't dare do more than kiss in the hotel's public spaces, and only when we were alone. Other times during the day, we would press our bodies together behind the bar counter when nobody was around or take the elevator without rhyme or reason, stopping it in the middle of two floors to kiss in peace, while the customers waited for their lift.

Although we were trying to keep our relationship discreet, it was soon obvious to the hotel staff. Carlos wasn't happy about our romance.

"What have you done to Jean?" he grumbled once. "He's distracted, half asleep, and making mistakes he's never made before. You have to tone it down. No going to bed past midnight!"

Every couple of weeks, Jean Pierre left for a night to visit his family, and we had the bedroom. The tiny room on the fourth floor had two single beds, a small closet where Jean kept two changes of clothes for work and one for holidays, his motorbike helmet, and Elvis Presley posters covering every inch of his side of the wall.

The first time we lay naked in bed, after weeks of foreplay, we could hardly wait to make love, but Jean asked for permission before he entered me. I told him I was a virgin, and he promised to be careful. We were both surprised when I didn't bleed, until I remembered what had happened when I went horseback riding at eleven, during my first trip to France.

Mama had sent my older sister and me to Dunkerque, to the home of her cousin Hélène (Carlos's sister) so we could practice French over the summer. Trying to keep us entertained, Hélène dropped us off at a riding school once a week. From the first day, the teacher made us ride without a saddle. The horses had a belt cinched to their bellies, with an iron handle on top. Round and round we'd go, grabbing that handle with all our might, white-knuckled and sweaty. Three or four men—the barn manager, the stable grooms, and the teacher— laughed and talked incomprehensibly in French while we tried to steady ourselves, cramped legs tightened around the animal's flanks.

My sister slid down on the first turn. Hoots from the men, followed by a quick push to remount her, clothes rumpled and terracotta colored. I stayed put for a couple of laps, my crotch hitting the horse's backbone with each bouncing step, before I fell in the same uncontrollable slide.

One day after class, I found blood in my panties. I had been longing to get my period with the hope that my breasts would fill out and Mama would get me a bra. I told Hélène and she gave me sanitary pads. For the next few days, I walked with that big white napkin between my legs, worrying that everybody would notice the bulk. I went to the toilet every hour to check if it was drenched, but I only found scattered brownish spots. Hélène said it was normal to have pre-menstrual scares, and that a heavier period wouldn't be long to come, but it took many months to start again.

When Jean entered me, it didn't hurt. It felt like a blessing. It dawned on me that I had been deflowered by a horse's backbone.

It felt safe and natural to be nude in Jean's warm embrace, even though, only a few months before, making out and having my breasts groped by Ramón had paralyzed me with fear because I thought I would be forced to marry him. It may have been because I was in France. Here there were no obligatory Sunday church services, perfect marriage role modeling, or feelings of guilt. There were no talks about sin or shame over a body's needs.

Jean and I knew in a few months we'd be apart, which made our time together ever more intense. He talked about continuing the relationship long-distance, but I was a realist. My life was in Spain and his was in France. Better to remain just friends after my departure.

"Maya, I don't know what you've done to me," he said one day. "I don't even want to go to the town's balls anymore, to have fistfights, to hunt rabbits with a stick while riding my bike in the mountains. All I want to do is be with you."

His devotion swaddled me in comfort. Perhaps I didn't fall as madly in love as he did, but I cared deeply for Jean. Even now, over forty years later, I remember him fondly, and I fantasize about seeing him again.

Carlos's mother, my great-aunt María Josefa, came to stay at the Terminus for a couple of weeks. She was a tiny lady in her seventies with short white hair, a wrinkled face like a well-ploughed field, and vivacious blue eyes.

If France's moral compass was light-years away from Spain's, even though the two countries were neighbors, just as far was Tía María Josefa's life from the lives of the rest of my family—at least the façade they presented to the world.

Tía looked conventional with her plaid skirts below the knee and her silk foulards, but she'd had her children, Carlos and Hélène, out of wedlock, both products of a decade-long relationship with a man whose first wife wouldn't grant him a divorce.

Her parents—my great-grandparents on my mother's side—had emigrated from Spain to Argentina in the 1920s when finances were tight, taking with them their unmarried children. They opened a small hotel in Buenos Aires that was frequented by artists. There Tía, a single girl in her twenties, met an older French-Catalan painter, and they fell in love.

He was married and had five kids, and she came from a proper Catholic family, but that didn't stop them. They left Argentina together and settled in Paris. When they had Hélène and Carlos, the painter gave them his last name even though he couldn't marry my aunt. He passed away when the kids were still young.

If that wasn't enough, Tía married another man later on, and when her husband passed away, she discovered he'd fathered a boy with a lover. Learning the mother didn't want the toddler, Tía took him in and raised him as her own.

Even though Tía María Josefa's behavior was scandalous to my very Catholic family, they didn't turn their backs on her. She often spent summers in Santa Margarita when her kids were young and she a single mother, but her past was swept under the rug, like so many uncomfortable truths. I didn't know about it until Hélène told me, quite proud of her mother's courage.

After I knew her story, I saw my great-aunt with different eyes. Here was a woman who looked as bourgeois as any other but had lived a passionate love affair with utter disregard for convention. Furthermore, instead of being angry at her husband's infidelity, she had taken in the other woman's child. Of course, she had been the other woman herself in her first relationship.

My clever aunt quickly figured out that I didn't always go to sleep after I closed my bedroom door. She waited up one night and caught me tiptoeing in the hallway at two a.m. after one of my escapades to Jean's room. She asked where I was coming from. I couldn't come up with a plausible lie in a split second, so I answered simply.

"I was with Jean."

"I figured as much!" she exclaimed. "I've seen how he stares at you and the way you brush against each other when you think nobody notices. Are you having sex with him?"

Coming from a family where sex was never, ever, mentioned, I was taken aback. Still, I had just turned nineteen, I was far from home, and she wasn't my typical aunt, so I nodded.

"I can't return you to your mother pregnant!" She had a note of real anguish in her voice. "Are you using protection, at least?"

"No, but I won't get pregnant. We're being careful." Her questions were so direct there was nothing else to do but answer them, no matter how embarrassing.

"Withdrawing is not a safe method. If you're going to have sex, at least use something safer."

"It is safe, Tía," I replied stubbornly while inside I wobbled, since that was precisely our birth control method. "I won't get pregnant."

She let me be, with another warning to be careful. And that was the last time she brought up the subject. What a relief that she was worried only about a pregnancy and not my morals or lack thereof.

A few weeks later Tía invited me to meet her in Paris for a few days and took me to all the tourist attractions. One afternoon, she suggested we go see *Emmanuelle,* a soft-core porn movie that everybody was talking about and that had drawn many a bus of pilgrims from Spain, where it was forbidden. I couldn't believe this old lady would sit unperturbed throughout the whole movie, which showed nude bodies, female masturbation, and lesbian and heterosexual sex. I still carried guilt about my own masturbation, now less frequent since I knew I wouldn't get relief. And here were these women, openly touching themselves on the big screen, closing their eyes and moaning, lost in their pleasure. If only I could do the same.

When we got out of the theater, Tía commented offhandedly, "What's all the rage about? It isn't that risqué!" I was speechless.

I wished my great-aunt lived in Spain. Maybe her guilt-free spirit would have rubbed off on me. It might have saved me many a heartache.

My bag was packed and waiting at reception, the sterling silver wine taster that Carlos had gifted me safe in my purse. I had said goodbye to everybody, except Jean, who wasn't around.

"Where is Jean?" I asked one of the waiters.

"He's in the cellar."

Of course Jean would be there, in the most private space in the hotel, where a guest would never venture. I went downstairs and found him with a paper in hand, reviewing the shelves.

"Jean, I'm leaving. Don't you want to say goodbye to me?"

I hugged him. His eyes were teary, his arms dead weights by his side. After a few seconds, he put them around me, and we embraced tightly.

His tears moved me, but my sadness was tinged with the

excitement of going back home, to my friends and my life, which I had always known would be waiting for me.

"I will write to you, I promise," I said.

Jean reached into the big pocket in the front of his apron and took out a small spiral notebook with a lime green cover.

"This is for you."

"What is it?"

"Poems. Don't laugh, you know I'm no writer, but they come from the heart."

I would have never imagined he'd write poetry, this young boy, with his motorbike, his practical dreams, and his pride.

"Don't read it until you're on the train," he said.

"I promise." I kissed him on the lips. We both got lost for a second in the spell of tender youth.

"Maya!" shouted Carlos from the top of the stairs. "You will miss your train!"

Extricating myself from Jean, I rushed up the stairs, my heart constricted by the melancholy of leaving behind the first boy who had ever truly loved me.

1966–67, San Julián and Barcelona
A Hike in the Dark

DO WE ALWAYS LEAVE BEHIND the things we love most? I must have been around eight or nine years old when I stopped going to Santa Margarita every afternoon.

Quica's youngest son, Rafael, came to San Julián with us after finishing the school year in a seminary. He didn't want to be a priest, but the seminary was a common option for low-income families to educate their children. Perhaps as a way to compensate for his upkeep, Rafael took us hiking to fun spots around San Julián. That's when I realized that there were more adventures to be had outside Santa's borders.

A couple of years later, a public, Olympic-sized swimming pool opened in town. It had temperate water, a thrilling ten-foot-high diving board, a bar with snacks, and a sound system that broadcast the musical hits of the year. Santa's freezing pool became less attractive and we stopped going there in the mornings.

Around that time, I became best friends with Gemma, a girl a year older than I was, whom I had known forever but hadn't had a chance to spend much time with when I was going daily to Santa Margarita. Every afternoon we rode our bikes to town to buy candy, then read comics together, or played ping-pong and swam in the pool at her grandpa's house, Can Serra.

Gemma's mom was always changing the furniture, the drapes, or the wall color. One afternoon there were three or four half-full pots of paint, left over from one of her latest projects, in Can Serra's family room in the basement. Gemma suggested that we use them to decorate the walls. "Are you sure we're allowed?" I asked. "Of course," she answered. "Nobody cares about this room!"

We got to work painting flowers and butterflies, suns and moons, all over the wall. Gemma's sister came by after a while, "Uh oh," she said, eyes round as platters. She bolted out the door, shouting: "Moooooom . . . Gemma and María Isidra have made a mess in the family roooooom." When Gemma's mom saw the wall, she yelled her head off, and everybody came running. Mary, the maid, said it had surely been my idea because Gemma would never have come up with such a prank.

I walked home crestfallen, upset at the injustice of it all. The hardest part for me was Mary's malice. Why would she blame me for something she didn't know was true? To add insult to injury, my dress had a big fat red stain on it. Fortunately, the multicolored print disguised it. When I got home, I ran to the bathroom to wash it, and it went away.

After this incident I avoided Gemma's home for a little while, but we still were as good friends as ever. It wasn't her fault that Mary was such a liar.

One day Gemma and I were playing Parcheesi in my bedroom, when I gathered the courage to ask her something that had been on my mind for a while.

"Have you ever touched yourself between your legs?"

"No. What for?"

"There is a little button, and when you touch it, it tickles your tummy."

"Really?" Gemma's big round blue eyes got even bigger and rounder.

"Yes. Do you want me to teach you where?"

"Okay."

I guided her finger.

"There. Now rub yourself." Gemma moved her finger a little bit, while I watched her. "Do you feel it?"

"I think so . . ."

She didn't sound enthusiastic, so I left it at that. It was clear we wouldn't share this secret, as I had with my cousin Sylvia.

I also initiated a couple of school girlfriends in the tickle game, but we only did it once or twice. It excited me to do it with others, but nobody seemed as eager to play it as I was. When I did it alone under the covers, the steel legs, the scrunched forehead, and the tense arm left me panting but utterly unsatisfied.

"*¡Dibujos animadooooooooooooos!*" Diego sprang up from the couch and ran from the living room yelling "Cartooooooooooons!" at the top of his lungs, so the rest of us would come to enjoy our daily dose of Bugs Bunny.

After the cartoons were over, my brothers went downstairs to play foosball. They had drawn a soccer field on a thin blanket and placed it on a table in the basement. They glued round pieces of paper inside twenty-two bottle caps, and painted them with the colors, name, and number of each player, forming two teams. With pellets as soccer balls, you had the National League of soccer.

They spent hours playing a parallel League in the basement. I usually stayed upstairs reading or playing with my dolls. I had tried to fit in when I was younger. I know because Dr. Udaeta, the family dentist, told me once that he'd asked me what I wanted for Christmas when I was about four, and I said I wanted a gun so my brothers would let me play with them.

By eight, I'd given up. I couldn't muster any interest in soccer or most other games my brothers played. My dolls, my books, and my girlfriends filled the void.

We did have fun family times. When we all sat around the table, a cacophony of voices competed for attention, fiercely vying to wedge a word in edgewise, like meerkats zooming in and out of the conversation's smallest gaps. Animated talk and delectable dishes went hand in hand. The car rides singing, playing games, and attempting tongue twisters were treasured moments. So were the family outings in San Julián to cook a *paella* or a big pot of *chocolate* in the woods, but as time went by, playful children devolved into disconnected teenagers, and the distance between us became a chasm.

I often thought that the two-year gap between me and my nearest older brother and the three-year gap between me and my nearest younger brother caused my estrangement. The first six siblings had come one a year, and two of them were only eleven months apart. I later realized we all endured our own kind of solitude. Several of my siblings inherited my parents' reserved natures and hardly ever uttered a sentence away from the dinner table. I wondered if they found comfort in their own private islands or if they felt bereft, like me, with words and emotions trapped inside. Since we didn't speak about personal matters, there was no way to know.

The long Christmas season started as usual, its path lit by the sparkling garlands on the street, and the string of parties that Mama hosted with impressive reserves of energy.

Christmas Eve we all went to *misa de gallo* at midnight at my school, the Sagrado Corazón. Abuelo passed a sonorous fart, but since he was hard of hearing he didn't notice. He kept asking, "What are the children laughing at?"

After mass, the whole Pascual clan came to our house, where Mama and Quica had prepared *el resopón*, the second supper. The dining room table, enlarged with two extra leaves, was covered with big platters of canapés, mini croissants with sweet ham and cheese, cold salads, Mama's famous pheasant pâté, made with Papa's own catch if possible, and, of course, *turrones.*

Wine and champagne flowed freely, in contrast with their absence from the family table during everyday meals.

There were around sixty guests, and nobody left the house until two or three in the morning. Even the youngest kids were allowed to stay up as long as they wanted.

By the time we got up the next day, the house already smelled golden thanks to the hen broth that Quica had going in the kitchen for the traditional *sopa de galets.* A turkey stuffed with sausage, dried prunes, and dried apricots would follow.

Christmas lunch was for our immediate family only; it was a day of rest and recovery from Christmas Eve's party. Every year the news after lunch began with Franco's speech celebrating "twenty-five years of peace," "twenty-six years of peace," "twenty-seven years of peace . . ." and was followed by the movie *Marcelino, pan y vino.* I knew I was supposed to like it, because Marcelino was a saintly kid who brought a statue of Christ to life when he offered it bread and wine, but I couldn't enjoy it. The conversations between Christ and Marcelino were boring and his death in Christ's arms morbid, even if he did ascend to Heaven right after that. I much preferred adventures such as *Veinte mil leguas de viaje submarino* or movies about odd heroes like *Mary Poppins* and *El Libro de la Selva* that we had gone to see in a theater.

December 26 was the day of San Esteban, the first Christian martyr, who had been stoned to death for defending Jesus, as I found out by reading a book on martyrs somebody had gifted me for my First Communion. We celebrated the holiday with lunch at Abuela Mercedes's home. *Abuelita* was always sitting on her dark green couch, dressed in black and white, with her short white hair impeccably coiffed and surrounding her head like a halo. I always felt self-conscious in her house because it was more formal than Santa Margarita, but I looked forward to being with Sylvia. Since she had been kept behind a grade in school, I saw her less often.

All these celebrations were the opening act for the big day, *Reyes*. It was January 5, the day *los Reyes Magos* arrived in town. We all piled into our two cars. Papa had some of my siblings with him in the blue Renault 6, while Mama drove the white SEAT 600 with the rest of us. We went downtown to Plaza San Jaime, where, from the balcony of Papa's office, we would watch the parade of the Three Wise Men as they ended their slow stroll from Barcelona harbor to City Hall. As we entered the building, the doorman gave each of us a little package with four *teas* wrapped in transparent cellophane bags with red string tied on top. *Teas* were hard and overly sweet four-inch sticks that stuck to your teeth for ages if you bit into them, but I liked the orange and white vertical stripes and the fact that we only got them once a year, on the eve of Reyes.

We went up on the ancient elevator that shuddered as if it would explode any second and piled onto the balconies sucking on the *teas* and waiting for the carriages. Melchor came first, all white hair and beard; then Gaspar, with bronze beard and hair; and last, Baltasar, who didn't have a beard but looked regal with his blue turban, resplendent against his black skin. Baltasar—or, as we always said at home, *Va a saltar y se cayó* (He jumped, and he fell off)—was my favorite king because he looked different. We also had a closer relationship with him because Mama told us that when my oldest brother was a baby, Baltasar had gone up to his bedroom and kissed him on the cheek while he slept. That's why his skin tanned so dark in the summertime, like Mama's.

After the parade was over, we returned home and had dinner. Before we went to bed, each of us left one shoe in front of the French windows that opened to the garden, a neat row of twelve shoes, from Dad's big brown boat shoe to a tiny white bootie that Mama had knitted for the baby she was expecting. She placed one card with our first name inside each shoe. We went to the Nativity that was set up in the fireplace and moved the big clay figures of the Three Kings and their pages close to the stables where baby Jesus slept.

The next morning, we were up at seven, but Mama and Papa didn't allow us to enter the living room until we all were dressed and had eaten breakfast. It was torture to wait, but around nine we were all ready. As we did every year, we got into a long line in the foyer, from the youngest to the oldest. Papa unlocked the door and peeked inside.

"Mmmm . . . I'm not sure the *Reyes* have left any presents this year. Are you sure you've all been good?"

"Yes, yes, yes, we've been good!"

"Let me see," said Papa.

He cracked the door a tad, slipped inside, and closed it behind him. A strip of light appeared under the door as Papa opened the shutters. We all shuffled from foot to foot, and pushed each other forward, talking excitedly. "Hey, don't squash me!" complained Jorge, who was right behind me. Papa came out again, and said, "There are a few things in there. Maybe you have been good, after all. Let's see!" He opened the door wide, and in we rushed.

Every couch, armchair, and chair was covered in packages, books, and action figures, a wondrous sight that left us dizzy. There were gifts for all of us and also for our parents' godsons and goddaughters, for

Quica, and for a few other people. We ran from one pile to the next in search of the card with our name on it. Mama held my younger sister by the hand because she didn't read yet, so she needed help to find her presents. I found my pile: two volumes from the *Los Siete Secretos* series, a board game, a cowgirl costume, a brand-new case of colored pencils, a pink journal with a little lock and its own little pen, and a lovely lemon chiffon top—a thin jersey, sleeveless but with a turtleneck. I heard my siblings' excited shouts around me. "We got the Scalextrix!" "I got Chutes and Ladders!" Mama and Papa went from one to the other, helping open packages, and we put on our new costumes. Their sixth-of-January smiles were always the widest of the year.

For me and my two younger siblings, there was still another surprise waiting. The Three Wise Men made a detour to the lower floor to bring the presents that Quica had requested for the youngest ones. It was always a small trinket, delightfully unexpected. One year I got a little peacock mounted on a mother of pearl seashell; another year I received a glass ball with a shimmering castle inside and snowflakes that swirled when you turned it upside down. This time I got a mini popcorn maker. It had an aluminum pot, five inches in diameter, which you filled with hard kernels of corn and heated on a little stove. A few minutes later they popped and pushed up the pot cover. It made only a handful of popcorn, a perfect snack. I felt proud that Quica trusted me to cook. Of course, I was already eight.

A couple of nights later I woke up sweaty and nauseous. It was pitch dark. I got up from bed, feeling faint. My body was hot, but a cold shiver made me shake. Putting my arms in front of me, I found the corner of my sister's bed and followed it with my hands to the other side, where the door was. Our bedroom was right near the staircase. I grabbed onto the banister and went down the eighteen stairs, which were divided into three flights. Once my feet touched the cold tiles of the foyer, a little bit of clarity coming from the street-lights showed me the way to the kitchen. Another staircase went to the lower floor. This one had fourteen narrow granite steps and a thin iron banister that I held onto with one hand while I put the other on the wall to my right. It didn't occur to me to turn on the light. I was almost sleepwalking. I landed at the ironing room, and from there it was a short walk through the basement to reach Quica's bedroom. I opened the door and walked toward the small and luminous Virgin Mary on her bedside table, a white and blue plastic figurine that glowed in the dark. I touched Quica's shoulder.

"Quica, Quica!"

Seeing the dark figure at her side, she shot straight up.

"Who is it? What's going on?"

"It's me, María Isidra. I don't feel well."

Quica put her hand on my forehead.

"You're burning!"

She had me lie down on her bed and went to get an aspirin and a cold compress. She stayed by my side, caressing my hair until I fell asleep.

In the morning, I woke up and heard Quica and Mama talking outside the bedroom. Mama came in and touched my forehead. The fever had gone down, but I still felt kind of woozy. "Let's take you to your bed," said Mama, "and I'll call the doctor." She helped me go up the two floors all over again and put me to bed. Once I lay down, she asked, "Why did you go to Quica's room? You could have fallen down the stairs and hurt yourself! Next time, come to mine."

I had no idea why I had gone to Quica's. It didn't make sense. Mama's bedroom was right next to mine. It was scary to walk through the house in the dark, but I wasn't thinking. My body had its own will, a will that had nothing to do with my mind. It had taken me to Quica like a lighthouse brings boats home.

La Torre

"MARÍA ISIDRA, GET UP. It's seven thirty." Mama walked in the room to open the shutters and she huffed. "You've been there again. It stinks in here!"

I could never hide when I had visited my new friends in the commune because every time I went, my clothes were saturated with a smoky smell that permeated my bedroom.

My friends were squatting in an abandoned house on a side street of Avenida del Tibidabo. They sucked electricity from a public line and kept space heaters in the bedrooms, but to warm the common areas they had a metal stove where they burned branches from the surrounding trees. Although it had a big pipe attached to the cover that stuck out the wall, it wasn't properly sealed, and smoke leaked through all its joints.

I had met this gang on Las Ramblas. Ever since humanities had been moved from Diagonal to Plaza Universidad, I spent most of my time there and in the old neighborhoods surrounding it. I fell in love with a city I never knew existed. Weekdays, I frequented the main city library, la Biblioteca del Carmen, which was on a side street of Las Ramblas. Weekends, I jumped on the Ferrocarriles Catalanes, the underground rail system that linked the city's north to the south, came out in Plaza Cataluña, and walked all the way down Las Ramblas to Rambla Santa Mónica, the stretch right by Barcelona's harbor.

There the authorities allowed a crowd of misfits to set up tables or spread blankets on the ground and sell handicrafts on weekends. It may have been an escape valve to keep at bay the Latin American immigrants who fled dictatorships and financial crises en masse in the seventies. Many highly educated exiles traded their white-collar lives for peddling junk jewelry or knitted scarves to scrape a meager living. Side by side with the *sudacas*—the diminutive for *sudamericanos* used at the time—Spanish bohemian types who yearned to live outside "the system" sold their wares.

America's hippie era was in full swing in Spain, ten years after it had peaked in the United States. At home, my brother Diego showed up with a daisy behind his ear framing his long hair and bushy beard and dropped out of university, while Guille, also long-haired and bushy-bearded, launched a weekly paper named *Underguía* that listed the city's leisure activities in witty language. A devil graced the cover, its long tail twisting around the promised fun. I admired his gumption. I kept all the issues and silently rooted for his creative venture until lack of funds derailed it.

During my weekend expeditions to Rambla Santa Mónica, I befriended many of the sellers and hit it off with the guys that squatted close to my house. I met Fernando first, a Chilean who earned tips by playing the guitar and singing mournful songs. He was a prettier version of the protest singer Víctor Jara. Everything in him seemed made of honey: his soft voice, his caramel eyes, his curly golden-brown hair and beard, his friendly laugh. Small-boned and lyrical, Fernando opened for me a nonthreatening path to a new world where an artistic inclination seemed a must.

Through him I met Joe, a tall, coarse guy with a long bristly beard and a bull's determination, the oldest of the gang at around thirty; Juan, a pint-sized mystical prophet with two women hovering around him—his current girlfriend Marisa and his previous one, Lucía, with their baby of around six months; Toñi, an affable girl with long black hair parted in the middle and an enormous crooked nose a la Rossy de Palma; and a few other guys and young women happy to experiment with bohemian living. My high school girlfriend Pilar joined in, as did Ángela, a Bellas Artes student who had also met the gang at Rambla Santa Mónica.

I had been back from France for about two months when I fell in with this group. I was corresponding with Jean, who sent poems with each letter, but as I became more entrenched in my new environment, I cut our communication. Our worlds were diverging too much.

La Torre, as we called the house where the commune sprouted up, became my second home, and this tribe my best friends. It helped that they were my neighbors and going to their house was on my way to anywhere, but I was also itching to meet somebody more adventurous than my college classmates; other than my good friend Ingrid, the philology crowd seemed nice enough but fastidiously earnest. I was tired of being earnest myself.

The commune was predicated on the utopian premise of sharing everything, from work to money to food and, occasionally, lovers. There wasn't a whole lot to share, however, especially in the money and food departments. I will never forget a lunch when all that Joe could buy with their scant earnings were radishes, which were in season and on sale. He plopped a huge bowl on the table, with a small plate of salt at the side, and they all sat around it, picking at the radishes without much enthusiasm, while Joe grabbed one after the other and ate them methodically. He stayed seated after everybody had left, and went through every single radish, biting and dipping in salt and biting again, crunch, crunch, crunch, aware that it was all they had until the next day, and being fed was the priority.

This gang's idealism and unorthodox ways captivated me, but their contradictions puzzled me. Juan, for example, was soft-spoken and peace loving, but thinly veiled conflict swirled around him. Once Juan, Marisa, and Lucía sat around the table for an hour in tense silence while the baby wailed in Lucía's arms. They didn't make any effort to comfort her. I don't know how the quiet confrontation ended or what it was about.

I talked to Marisa about their amorous triangle. She was careful not to voice any complaints, but she confided that Juan had fathered another baby with his wife that was only a month older than Lucía's baby. The fact that in the space of two years Juan had bounced around between a wife, two girlfriends, and two babies was stunning to me, but Marisa explained it matter-of-factly.

I listened and refrained from criticizing. After two decades in a world where everything had its place and every relationship its name, first the freedom of France and now the jumble of La Torre had crumbled the walls that enclosed my reality. The world beyond them was spacious and rumpled. I couldn't get enough. I wasn't a craftsman, artist, or musician like most of my new friends, but I was a sucker for a good story. It may have been this thirst for stories that made me open to people from all walks of life, even people whose love lives I couldn't comprehend. I didn't judge. I absorbed.

I wasn't the only one embracing a more casual attitude about sex and relationships. The whole country had tilted at enormous speed from repression to *el destape*—literally, taking the lid off. This term referred to the end of censorship in movies. For decades, censors had banned naked body parts and transformed many American classics by cutting out kisses or changing the script when dubbing a movie. During the first years of Francoism, it was even forbidden to subtitle foreign movies, lest any Spaniard who understood the original language be perverted. Dubbing allowed for manipulation. A famous case was the transformation of the adulterous Ava Gardner and her lover Clark Gable in the movie *Mogambo* into a brother and sister in the dubbed script, which made for weird incestuous innuendos.

The term *destape*, however, came to symbolize the transformation of Spanish culture as a whole. All of a sudden, boobs and butts were everywhere. They screamed at you from every magazine, they crowded a whole generation of Spanish movies in the second half of the seventies, and they filled TV screens with the pronounced cleavages of well-endowed hostesses, who became the main attraction of variety shows.

In a matter of months, as the young democracy was still flexing its muscles, Spain metamorphosed from a little old lady dressed head-to-toe in black into an oversexed teenager whose raging hormones didn't allow thoughts of anything else but who they could fuck next. Sex, for many of the young, became an innocuous social ritual, like grabbing a coffee at the corner bar during a work break.

Connections at La Torre reflected the new consciousness. Toñi alternated having sex with Joe and Fernando, and when she got pregnant neither she nor anybody else knew for sure who the baby's father was. It didn't matter, because she didn't have a steady relationship with either of them. Joe became my friend Pilar's lover for a while, but when Sara, an old flame of his, visited from France, he also hooked up with her, even though she came with her boyfriend, Joseph.

I got along with Joseph, a handsome young man in his early twenties, ten years younger than Sara. A couple of weeks after they arrived, as we were walking up Avenida del Tibidabo with two bags of groceries for the commune, he told me he liked me. I said that made me feel weird, because he was with Sara, but he assured me it was okay because they practiced an open relationship. We made out.

The next day, I went to visit as usual, and met Joseph in the garden. We walked into the kitchen to help with dinner preparations and sat beside Sara, who was cutting vegetables. She turned to me and planted her big kitchen knife on my neck.

"Don't you dare hook up with Joseph," she hissed. "He's mine."

"But, but . . . he said it was okay." I didn't dare move.

"Sara, please, let go of the knife." Joseph grabbed her arm and jerked it backward, but Sara shook it free.

"Shut up, Joseph!" she yelled. "I'm talking to her." She put the tip of the knife on my chest.

"Please, leave her alone. We haven't done anything, just a kiss." Joseph's voice sounded plaintive, as if he were begging for alms.

Sara pressed the knife a little harder onto my chest. She didn't take her eyes off me.

"Better keep it that way or I'll kill you," she said, her eyes hard, her voice hoarse. She threw the knife to the ground and stomped out.

"I'm sorry," said Joseph, taking my hand. "Are you okay?"

"I'm fine." I was watching the room from above, frozen, unable to feel a thing.

"I have to go see her," said Joseph.

"Fine."

I sat in the kitchen for a long time. My legs couldn't hold my body. My mind swirled. Why did Sara hook up with whomever she pleased but Joseph wasn't allowed to? As modern as everything seemed, the double standard I had soaked up since childhood still existed, only in this case it was the woman imposing it.

That was the end of my fling with Joseph. We both knew it wasn't worth the risk. He and Sara left a couple of days later and went back to France; they were planning to buy land for a permanent commune, where Joe would eventually join them. I never saw them again.

I led a schizophrenic life, continuing my studies and having most meals at home, but stopping at La Torre on the way in or out of the house and immersing myself in new experiences, not always agreeable but all interesting.

The first two years in college, I had coasted. I attended the classes, I read the books, and I studied the week before an exam, but that was the extent of my commitment. I had passed with seven Cs and one B. Now I made a conscious effort to reconnect with my passion for literature. When assigned *La Celestina* or *Les fleurs du mal*, not only did I read the books, I also dove into the gothic vaults of Biblioteca del Carmen and spent hours reading other books *about* them, branching out into additional authors of the period, copying quotes, and writing reflections in a notebook. The more I dug in, the more I got out, the homework leading me on bewitching journeys.

This renewed interest in intellectual work may have been a way to balance the emotionally charged and sometimes unnerving world of La Torre. I compared these people my age or a few years older, who were braving a poverty-stricken but independent life, with my nineteen-year-old cocooned self, and I felt ashamed.

I longed to leave my parents' home, but I wanted to graduate, and I knew that wouldn't happen if I were living in such precarious conditions. Although I had babysat and tutored for years, I didn't make enough money to rent a place by myself or even with a friend. There was also the fact that Mama would be livid if I left the house. She expected, like most every parent in Spain, that I would stay put until I got married.

I kept hobbling along, one foot in each world, trying to expand my universe's boundaries without exploding them for good.

When I was at La Torre, I became one of them, helping polish the engraved copper dishes they crafted, gathering wood for the stove, or lending a hand in the kitchen, but even in those humble tasks my confidence lagged. As soon as I left France, the aplomb with which I had carried myself vanished, as if crossing the border had smudged my freshly drawn outlines.

Once I was peeling potatoes side by side with a friend, and I noticed my peels were so thick that I was wasting a third of each potato.

"I can't even peel potatoes right," I said. "I'm not good at anything."

"Don't worry," he assured me. "I peeled a lot of potatoes during my military draft. That's why I'm so fast. Everything comes with practice."

I kept peeling, hoping that I would soon show improvement.

As much as I wanted to fit in, I set boundaries. When they got hold of acid, I didn't try it. The stories I'd heard of bad trips scared me. When Fernando flattered me with sweet words about my eyes, I didn't let him seduce me because, as pleasing as he was, I wasn't attracted to him. (I found out later that he had tried to bed my friend Pilar using the exact same words.)

After a few months with hookups happening left and right, I still hadn't had sex with anybody. The one time I went beyond my usual physical reticence was when two guys wanted to massage me in the nude.

We smoked a joint, which was the only excursion into illegal territory I sporadically allowed myself. I took my clothes off except for my panties and lay on the mattress on the floor of their bedroom, face down. They kneeled on each side of me and massaged me from top to bottom in soft, long strokes.

A couple of friends sat by us, talking, as if in the front row at a show. It was strange, coming from such a prim background, to be on display almost naked, but I tried not to think about it. That sensuous twin touch let me sink into my body.

When they got to my lower back, they suggested that I take off my panties so they didn't get oily. I was so relaxed that I slid my panties down my legs and gave myself over to their stroking of my buttocks, my hips, and the backs of my thighs. By the time they got to the soles of my feet I was, perhaps for the first time in my life, oblivious to my nakedness or, better said, grateful for it. I understood why Pilar felt comfortable opening the door to Joe's room in the nude. That had felt foreign to me, but I could see now that it was only skin, flesh, and bone, skin that could be seen and touched without any demands, skin that could receive without being forced to give.

I don't know if the guys saw the massage as a prelude to sex, but if they did, they didn't impose it. They spent a whole hour stroking my body, back and front, gifting me a time of innocent bliss. My anxious mind lay forgotten and pointless, displaced by a fleeting abandon into the trusting and sexless carnality of the present moment.

Mama and I traveled alone to Barcelona one September evening. I was ten. I had flunked math and I had to take a makeup test. By eleven a.m. I had finished the test, but Mama had a few things to do. She said we would have lunch with Papa when he came from work, and we'd leave for San Julián right after. Around one p.m., I went up to her bedroom to ask her something. As I went in, the door of her bathroom opened and Mama came out, butt naked.

"Aaayyyy!" She yelped like an injured animal, one arm flung

across her chest, covering her breasts, the other hand covering her privates.

"Why didn't you knock?" she bellowed, backing into the bathroom. She banged the door shut.

I don't know who felt more humiliated, Mama or me. I turned what had just happened around in my head over and over and my embarrassment shifted to anger. How could I ever have guessed Mama would take a shower in the middle of the morning? She never did that! And why did she walk out of the bathroom naked? She could have put a robe on! As for knocking, that was a first. She had never spelled out this rule.

I didn't need to be reminded again. Mama's reaction reinforced what I already suspected: naked bodies had to be kept hidden.

When she took me to buy bras a few years later and came into the dressing room, I felt myself blushing and my blood boiling with rage. She had the audacity to tighten my straps and clasp the hooks. How did she dare even brush my skin? Hadn't she taught me to recoil in front of a nude body? I fumed in silence.

Although I didn't know it then, my anger didn't spring from her presence in the dressing room. It came from when I was five and my innocent pleasure disgusted her, from when I was ten and her wrath when I caught her naked branded me with shame. Shame and prudishness had sunk into my subconscious as deeply as a stake through the heart of a vampire. They sucked the life out of me. I couldn't forgive Mama for that ever-present death, even if she hadn't intended it.

In December, an Italian guy who had been living in France moved into La Torre. He had met the gang at Rambla Santa Mónica and they invited him to join in.

Marco took over one of the abandoned bedrooms upstairs and built a bed with recovered wood, elevated two feet above the ground. It was the only room that didn't have a mattress on the floor. He spent hours drawing intricate designs with a black thin-tip pen and transforming the thick bamboo stalks that surrounded La Torre into engraved containers. Both sold well.

When he courted me, he didn't need to try hard. He was a tall, broad-shouldered man eight years my senior with a head of black wavy hair, bushy eyebrows, and kind brown eyes. I found him handsome and fun, and he made me feel protected.

I wrestled a prescription for the birth control pill from a gynecologist a friend had recommended, swearing that I was about to get married. Every afternoon after classes were over, I joined Marco at La Torre, but I never spent the night with him because that would have caused a rift at home. At two or three in the morning, Marco threw on his coat and walked me the ten minutes to my house.

One night, as I opened the door of my bedroom, Mama came out of her room, tightly wrapped in her long blue cotton robe.

"María Isidra," she said, "I found this in your nightstand."

She showed me the box of birth control pills that I kept in the first drawer.

I gulped and hovered at the door, not knowing what to say.

"It's late now, but we have to talk about this." Mama handed me the box and left.

I went into the bedroom, unsettled. I wasn't used to discussing anything personal with Mama, much less anything related to sex. I didn't want to have that conversation.

A couple of days went by and she didn't broach the subject. I relaxed. I thought she had decided to avoid the confrontation, her usual modus operandi. But on the fourth day, she came to my bedroom when I was about to get undressed and said, "We need to talk."

She closed the door.

"I was disappointed when I found those pills in your drawer. You know I never snoop, but I've been concerned about you. You come home at all hours of the night. You are always with that group of weird people in the abandoned house. Don't think I haven't noticed them going up and down the avenue. What are you doing? I can't understand it. Sex is so important and so meaningful. How can you treat it with such carelessness?"

"I'm not treating anything with carelessness." I tried to keep my voice firm, even though my stomach was jelly. "I don't see it the same way you do. I don't think you need to be married to be with some-body, but that doesn't mean it's not important." In reality, intercourse with Marco was a side trip included in the package deal. I enjoyed the cuddling and the kisses; the rest didn't leave much trace.

"How can it be important if you are not in a committed relation-ship? If there is no love?"

"Who said there is no love? I know what I'm doing, Mama. Nobody is taking advantage of me. I'm in a relationship."

"If you're in a relationship, why don't you bring him over? You don't spend any time in the house with us; we hardly ever see you."

"Why would I spend any time in the house?" I raised my voice. "When I'm here, nobody even notices. Everybody is busy reading a book or watching TV. Nobody talks to anybody. I spend my time out of the house so I can be with people who at least acknowledge me, people I can talk to and who do things with me, because at home I feel like a ghost. We are not together. We are only sitting in the same room." I had a knot in my throat. The pills had vanished from my mind.

Mama softened her voice. "We may be reading or doing something else, but of course we know you're here, and Papa and I are concerned."

"Papa? Ha!" I snorted. "Papa doesn't even know I exist, or any of us for that matter. He cares more for his dogs than he cares for us."

"That's not true." Mama sounded more anxious than angry. "He cares for all of you. A lot. He's reserved, but when we are alone in the car, he asks me about you. He is worried."

"What good does it do that he talks to you in the car? He doesn't ever talk to me!" My voice broke and the tears I was trying to contain spilled out freely.

Mama stayed quiet for a moment, as if she were searching for words. She shuffled a little but stopped short of making contact. "I'm sorry you feel this way." Her voice was low and composed. "We care about you, and we are concerned. Please, think carefully about what you're doing."

She left the room without any more mention of the pills. I sobbed, my chest heaving with the pain of the truth I had spoken, but a little part of me felt triumphant: I had dodged the bullet regarding the pills, and I'd also let Mama have it. Concerned about me? Ha! Now she knew that if I never spent time with them it was their own fault.

Our shared living, in which we had only the space in common, made me suffer. We still talked only during lunch and dinner. I didn't know much about my parents or my siblings, aside from the little I'd gathered from occasionally prying into their drawers when I was younger: a few photos of our childhood, a handful of letters from my oldest brother's girlfriend, now wife, in his nightstand . . . not enough to give me a clue about who they really were or what they cared about. Neither did they know about me. On the other hand, being in the house while giving as little of me as possible had its advantages. I put up with some rules while doing my best to eschew the rest and subjected myself to my parents' impositions while sneering at them.

Little did I know that coexisting with the most important people in my life, all of us remaining in our own little bubbles, had become an entrenched way of being in the world for me. I would replicate it in my later relationships. I trained my boyfriends to set up their own impenetrable island so they wouldn't access mine. It was easier to stay safely confined than to bridge the chasm. I attributed our distance to their many faults or to the circumstances while failing to consider the stubborn walls of my own heart.

Marco infused new life into La Torre thanks to his occasional but expert shoplifting, which kept the troops fed when the pantry was empty. He had a specific raiding technique. Dressed in a light gray designer suit, a beautiful powder blue silk shirt, an elegant leather belt with a silver buckle, and shiny black loafers, he'd walk into a store with his head held high and his step confident, grabbing chorizos and cheeses, bread and pasta, and shoving them under his jacket without hesitation. Nobody suspected this suave man.

I would wait outside and, when he came out, marvel at his booty, but my Catholic upbringing tugged at my conscience.

"You shouldn't steal, Marco."

"I'm only taking what we need to survive, and I only grab products from wealthy stores that rob people blind anyway."

He would go home, prepare an enormous spaghetti dish with tomato sauce and sausages, and happily yell: "*¡A comeeeer!*"

Everybody appeared within seconds, like moles burrowing out

of their holes, scurrying toward the infrequent pleasure of a cozy warm meal.

One of Marco's favorite hunting spots was El Corte Inglés, a big department store in Plaza Cataluña. He once walked out with a fancy acoustic guitar, black and gold, slung over his shoulder, with the price tag still attached. I was dumbfounded.

"How did you do that?"

Marco laughed his "caw, caw, caw," soft laugh, a sparkle in his eye.

"It was easy; I walked in, put it on my shoulder, and walked out. Nobody believes a thief would do something so blunt, so they assumed I had paid for it."

"But you don't need a guitar; you don't even play!"

"I can learn," he said cheerily, "and we need it to lift our spirits."

It was true that the atmosphere at La Torre hadn't been a happy one of late. The bitter cold, the scarcity of food and money, and the lack of direction were piling up, and there was always the threat of eviction. The building had been expropriated by the city to build an urban highway, and it was a matter of months until they would knock it down. Some at La Torre had a clear idea of where to go next; others, none. They clung to the present, but as time went by, the end of this temporary reprieve loomed, and the present wasn't enough.

Marco did have a plan. Every year, when the weather turned warm, he traveled to a long-term camping site in Colliure, a small town in the south of France, where he and a group of friends set up tents and lived on the cheap for five or six months until it got too cold to stay outdoors. While there, he survived by selling his art to tourists. He didn't need much.

He invited me to go with him, but I couldn't do it. I wanted to finish my studies, and besides, living in a tent for months on end didn't appeal to me. Knowing our relationship would be short-lived gave a melancholic tinge to its easygoing rhythm.

Marco left in late spring. La Torre kept fraying at the edges. Tension built between Joe and the rest of the gang, who didn't work as hard as he wanted them to. Money continued to be an issue, and now that Marco wasn't around, communal meals were rare. Each person dug deeper into their own den.

I kept visiting out of loyalty, more anguished than happy. I obsessed over their problems as if they were mine. My friend Ingrid got fed up listening to the saga of La Torre's tribe and its dysfunctional behavior: the new babies, the old arguments, the jealousies and the scarcity, the confusion about where to go and what to do. I was almost crazed, going back and forth between trying to support them and feeling guiltily eager to evade their dramas.

This tension resolved when a cousin who was living in London called to offer me a summer job as a nanny for a wealthy family. Mama was ecstatic that I would be far from the commune, but I didn't need her prodding. I had started studying English a year before at the North American Institute, and I jumped at the chance to learn the language better.

When I returned from London four months later, La Torre was in its death throes. Juan, Marisa, and Lucía had left to find more stable living quarters close to Madrid. Others soon followed them. Everybody was seeking an escape route.

The week before the eviction, we said our goodbyes and went our own ways.

Rhythm and Emotion

AFTER I GOT BACK FROM LONDON, I didn't want to share a room with my older sister any longer. I appropriated Quica's old bedroom in the basement. I furnished it with cast-off pieces from the rest of the house: a single bed placed in a corner, the heavy wood table on which my brothers used to play foosball as a desk, and a square trunk covered in thirty-year-old tags from Paris and Vienna, where my parents had honeymooned, as a makeshift dresser. An antique folding screen—handsome with its carved wooden frame and red damask three-piece body—hid two strips of wood hammered onto the wall, crammed with clothes on hangers. I painted the walls white, the baseboards burgundy to match a potted azalea in a corner, and the pipes on the ceiling black.

Mama wasn't happy when I moved downstairs because that exiled me even further from the rest of the family—I even had my own entrance—but she admitted the room looked good. My three older brothers had married and moved out, but they came to lunch every Sunday. There were still plenty of us, and plenty of housework. A cleaning lady came three mornings a week, but the brunt of keeping the house rolling, the clothes ready, and the meals on the table fell on Mama, and she didn't accept much help. (*La señora Francis*, whose radio program Quica and I used to listen to, would have approved.)

That winter I learned that several of my friends from La Torre didn't end up well. Juan, who had fathered a third baby, this one with Marisa, hanged himself due to some philosophical belief. He announced his intentions calmly the day before and asked his girlfriend and the rest of the friends who lived with them to respect his wishes. I'm not sure if they didn't believe he would do it or simply followed his orders, but he went through with it, and that was that. A few months later, another friend from La Torre also killed himself. The police found his car parked on a deserted beach on a gray winter morning and his clothes on the sand. Marco, whom I visited a few times in France, survived a suicide attempt. He ended up reconciling with life when he became a father. Toñi got hooked on heroin for a few years, one of the myriad addicts of the seventies and eighties in Spain, some of whom died of AIDS.

I've come to think of those of us from La Torre, and others like us, as the lost generation, a generation that harbored much hope and idealism but was bulldozed by the lightning speed of change. We had grown up ensconced in a repressive dictatorship and a strict Catholicism. After Franco's death, the pressure that had been boiling under the surface sent the lid flying and we burst into the air with irrepressible energy.

Drunk on freedom, we abandoned the political fights that had given us direction and made life about play and experimentation. An unbounded desire to try it all, to risk it all seized us, but a new fragility arose from the fracture between the rigid structures of a past that didn't fully represent us and a present that both elated us and bewildered us with its tangled shape.

Some of us who were more traumatized, more confused, or simply played harder fell through that crack. Others ended up exchanging their rebellious ideals for a comfortable if disappointing bourgeois life. A few, over time, integrated passion and survival.

Now that I had lost my Torre gang, I redoubled the emphasis on my studies. I knew books would never let me down. My fourth year of university had begun. Classes, as we branched out into our majors, were smaller and more interesting. Ingrid, immersed in her Arabic studies, didn't share any with me, so I pushed forward by myself on my literature exploration.

For the first time in four decades, Catalan entered the university curriculum. The new Constitution of October 1978 rescued the non-Castilian languages from their Francoist jail and started the process of creating *Comunidades Autónomas*, the regional governments that gave a voice to Spain's cultural diversity. I enrolled in Catalan even though it didn't belong to my field of studies. At twenty years old, I learned to write a language that I had heard and spoken in San Julián since I was a child. It was a rightful homecoming.

The Constitution also made official the transition from the long Franco dictatorship to democracy. That settled, most youth, already turned off by politics due to *el desencanto*, set aside activism and concentrated on enjoying their new freedoms, as did I. Voting in elections would always be a sacred duty, but other than that, I was content to leave politics to the politicians. Barcelona's underworld drew me in like a siren song.

Every day after class I trekked down Las Ramblas to the Biblioteca del Carmen, embedded like a jewel in the middle of the *barrio chino*—a confounding name, since no Chinese lived in the neighborhood. Chinatown in Barcelona meant a red-light district, a low-income area that was also the territory of whores and transvestites, the latter a novelty just beginning to emerge. It was a luxury to move from the uncontainable vitality of the narrow streets adjacent to Las Ramblas to the quiet and austere refuge of the library and the treasure hidden under its tall gothic arches. I dove into the books as I dove into the neighborhood, eager and happy, as if joining a party.

I was at the library one afternoon a few months into the course, sailing good-humoredly through the cryptic archives, which sent me round in circles from one reference number to the next, when a girl with long, straight brown hair and coffee-colored eyes asked me if I was working on Valle Inclán's *Sonatas*. I looked at her, surprised.

"I'm also in the nineteenth-century course," she said. "My name is Mar."

"Oh, hi. No, I'm not working on the *Sonatas*. I'm reading about the troubadours."

"The troubadours? But we don't have to write an essay about the troubadours."

"I know; I'm not reading about them for an essay."

That sentence opened the door to everything else that happened between us. We couldn't be more different—she from Madrid, me from Barcelona; she living with her boyfriend in Chinatown in the lower side of the city, me living with my parents in the affluent upper side; she upfront and almost insolent, me cautious and yielding—but all our differences melted when the first line of a poem intoxicated us and we recited it in unison, when the exquisite decadence of Valle Inclán's Marqués de Bradomín prompted us to write him a love letter, or when Borges's doppelgangers sent us into a prolonged fantasy about our other selves, living mysterious lives on the opposite side of the hemisphere.

We became inseparable, sitting side by side in the classes we had together and spending hours every afternoon in the library, with coffee breaks to share our enthusiasms.

Some mornings she came late to the first class or skipped it. After several of those incidents, I asked her, "Don't you have an alarm clock?"

"Yes," she said, "but last night I didn't go to bed until five, so I didn't even hear it."

"What were you doing on a Tuesday night up until five?"

"I went for a couple of drinks with my boyfriend, we ran into some friends, and one thing led to another. I couldn't get up this morning. I had a horrible hangover. I still have it, but I took a couple of aspirins and it's getting better."

Her confession surprised me. I'd gotten tipsy occasionally during a party, but I'd never gotten that drunk. At home, alcohol was invisible except during the holidays, and even then it was scarce. One whisky or sherry with appetizers, two bottles of wine for lunch that served a dozen people, and a glass of cognac with coffee for anyone who wanted one. After lunch, the liquor disappeared again until the next holiday. Neither my friends from the college prep course nor those from La Torre had been big drinkers, the first too clean-cut, the latter too poor. Booze consumption had ramped up in San Julián as we got older, but I hardly went there any longer.

"You should go out with us sometime," said Mar. "You'd have fun."

"Sure, I'd like that."

One afternoon, after a few hours in the library, she suggested we grab dinner.

"Let's go by my house first, so we can leave our books."

We walked fifteen minutes to Calle San Pablo, right off Las Ramblas. Her apartment was on the first corner, in a dilapidated building. There was no lift. The stairs smelled like piss and Clorox. The paint was crumbling off the wall.

As soon as Mar opened the door of her place, a nauseating stench punched me. A tabby meowed and rubbed himself against Mar's legs. She hung her corduroy jacket on a coat hanger whose arms were heavy with garments.

"Don't you want to take off your coat?"

"No. We're leaving soon, right?" I wrapped myself in my green loden coat, which looked out of place in her apartment, like a Swiss chalet dropped in the middle of an alley.

We walked down a short hallway to the living room, sparsely furnished with a chaise longue, the springs coming out at the feet; a cheap round wood table without a tablecloth, showing an empty enclosure at the feet for a nonexistent brazier; and two chairs, one with the wicker on the seat coming undone. Mar threw her books on the table and herself on the chaise. I sat on the chair that was in one piece.

"Did you forget to clean the cat's litter box?" I asked, hoping that she would get rid of the offending smell.

"I haven't forgotten. It's my boyfriend's turn to clean it, and I won't do it for him."

"Doesn't the smell bother you?"

"I don't care about the smell. I care more about him doing his part."

As we were talking, we heard the door open. A moment later there was a bang and a string of swearing.

I jumped on my chair.

"What was that?"

"It must have been the coat hanger. It's always falling down. Once Pol came in at four a.m. so drunk that when it fell on top of him, he wrapped himself on the coats and went to sleep right on the floor."

As if waiting for his cue, a guy entered the living room.

"Hey," he said.

Before he had a chance to add anything else, Mar snapped, "Clean the litter box! The house stinks!"

"What a welcome. Aren't you going to introduce me to your friend?"

"No! Clean the box, you pig!"

He walked toward me as if he hadn't heard her.

"Hi, I'm Pol." He extended his hand.

"Hello," I said, shaking it. "I'm María Isidra."

Pol had disheveled black curls falling past his ears, enormous green eyes like a cat's, and thick eyebrows joined in the middle. His face seemed somewhat too big, with full cheeks and lips, the latter now open in a smile that revealed slightly crowded teeth, but his eyes were unforgettable.

"What are you guys up to?" he asked.

"YOU are up to cleaning the litter box. WE are going to dinner," said Mar. "Come on; let's go," she added, getting up from the chair.

"Can I go with you?" asked Pol.

"No," said Mar.

I got up and walked after her toward the door.

"Bye," said Pol.

I raised my hand to wave goodbye.

"Let's go to El Egipto," said Mar, "It's right here, behind the Boquería market."

While we ate dinner, I asked her about Pol. She said they had been together a couple of years. When they met, Mar was still mourning the death of her first boyfriend. He had killed himself before turning twenty for no other reason than the belief that you should give up life when you were at your peak of youth and creativity instead of languishing through a slow decline.

That loss had changed her. I knew how much when, a few months later, I saw a photo of Mar at her parents' home in Madrid, taken days before her boyfriend jumped to his death from a skyscraper. She had the same big, expressive eyes, small round nose, and rosebud mouth she had now. The jaw, however, belonged to a different woman. In the photo, it was supple and smooth. Now it was thick and square, its heaviness obliterating the freshness of her youth. Something had been broken in her, something that could never be repaired. Perhaps it was this unspoken brokenness that tied me to Mar, aside from our passion for literature. I'd also had a few cuts and bruises.

As I got to know Mar and Pol better, I realized their relationship hung by a thread, like an almost severed thumb. They shared a boundless imagination, a love for rituals, and a passion for popular culture and beauty, but clashed on most everything else.

Pol came from a working-class neighborhood in Madrid and didn't have any education beyond high school or any ambition except following his whims. He worked a menial job at Telefónica, the only telephone company in Spain, just for the salary. Half the time he was on medical leave, for alleged depression or any other forged illness. The other half he arrived late and hungover. The famous director Pedro Almodóvar had also worked at Telefónica before breaking into the movie industry, the steady salary and three p.m. quitting time allowing him to take risks. But Pol didn't have goals beyond enjoying drinks, meals, travel, music, dancing, poetry, and friends. I came to think of him as *un artista de la vida*: fully dedicated to the art of living pleasurably. I had never met a person so invested in the present moment.

Mar looked a little rough with her insolent attitude and washed-out clothes—faded jeans, amorphous sweaters, big red handkerchief covering her head at the slightest sign of rain. With that handkerchief on and a hand on her waist as she examined you from head to toe with squinting eyes, she was the spitting image of a crude and seductive *maja*, straight out of a Goya painting. But in reality, she came from a wealthy bourgeois family who lived in a plush house on the outskirts of Madrid.

When she decided to study philology at the University of Barcelona, her father assigned her a generous allowance so she wouldn't have to work. The vulgar tone from the 'hood that she often resorted to was a thin varnish. As I would eventually find out, she changed colors as quickly as a chameleon, even though her iron will and her inner strength remained.

A few weeks later, on a Friday, I was sitting on the university patio enjoying the sun during a break when Mar, who had missed class again, approached me.

"Hey! I was looking for you. We're going for a beer at El Zurich. Will you join us?"

El Zurich was a bar with a big terrace right in front of the beginning of Las Ramblas, a common spot for meeting friends. It was a five-minute walk from the university.

"The next class is about to start, and I . . ."

"Who cares about the next class? Ask somebody for the notes on Monday. Come on! It will be fun! We have two friends visiting from Madrid and they want to meet you."

She gestured toward the three guys standing a few feet behind her. Pol was talking to a tall man—the spitting image of a Madrid preppy, black hair combed back, V-neck navy blue sweater with a light blue shirt collar sticking out, navy slacks and navy *sebago* penny loafers—and a short, chubby man dressed in brown corduroy pants, a flannel shirt, and a brown faux-leather jacket. Older, unshaven, dark circles under their eyes, they stuck out among the young students like a red wine stain on an immaculate white tablecloth. Pol raised his hand and waved at me. His lips opened in a big Cheshire cat smile.

"Don't you want to enjoy this beautiful day?" said Mar. "Or are you going to throw it away, like the rest of them?" She pointed to the students scattered around the patio, now getting up and heading to class.

Pol whistled and jerked his head to the side, pointing to the exit, while motioning with his hand to come along. I hesitated for a second, then got up and said, "Okay, let's go."

Mar laughed and grabbed my arm, walking with me toward the odd trio. She introduced me to Juanma, the tall one, and Blanes, the chubby one. We left the university building and walked down toward El Zurich. Juanma and Mar kept running after each other, playing some type of silly catch, laughing.

"They're like little kids. Worse! It's impossible to get anywhere fast with these two," complained Blanes.

"Let them be," said Pol. "Let's go ahead of them."

We arrived at the bar and grabbed an outdoor table. By the time the others joined us we already had our beer. I wasn't much of a drinker, but I ordered a half pint so they wouldn't think I was too stiff.

"You could have waited for us, couldn't you?" Mar stood up above Pol defiantly, as if ready to pick a fight.

"You could have come faster," said Pol, in an indolent tone.

They exchanged barbs like expert swashbucklers going for the heart while I looked at them, awed by their verbal agility.

In the end, Pol laughed and conceded with a comical curtsy. "You win."

Only then did Mar push back a chair and sit down, satisfied.

After the first beer came a second. I relaxed, sitting back on the chair, the sun on my face, the quiet classrooms receding from my mind.

"Let's go have lunch," said Mar.

Around three, the time when at home we would have finished lunch and Dad would be dozing on the sofa with the news blaring on the TV, we walked down Las Ramblas and took a left at Calle Fernando, ending up at Plaza Real, a big square in the middle of the Gothic neighborhood, its arched corridors housing restaurants and nightclubs. We ate a shawarma at a Middle Eastern restaurant and walked a few more blocks to the Borne neighborhood, where the hippest bars and the renowned music club Zeleste were always jam-packed at night. We had coffee and cognac. At six, Blanes announced that he had to take a nap.

"Let's go home to rest. Tonight, we can go dancing. You are staying, right?" said Mar.

"Sure," I said, dizzy and sleepy myself after all that booze.

When we got to San Pablo, the guys took a nap while Mar and I talked in the living room. I was relieved to learn they'd given their cat to a neighbor because Juanma was allergic. No more litter stink!

That evening after dinner we went back to the Borne neighborhood and hopped from bar to bar until they closed at three. We came out of the last bar and walked toward Paseo del Borne. Mar, who had drunk quite a bit, threw herself with all her might against the metal shutter of a closed shop. CLANK! The loud clatter resonated up and down the street.

"What the hell are you doing?" said Blanes. "Are you crazy?"

Mar laughed and threw her body against the shutter again. CLANK! The crash reverberated, a loud explosion in the quiet night. A light came on at the balcony above.

"Stop it right now! You're going to get us thrown in jail!" hissed Blanes, furious.

Pol and Juanma snickered from afar. I didn't say a word, stunned at Mar's impulse to rebel for the sake of rebelling. She didn't care about consequences or whom she was bothering. She wanted to infuriate Blanes and fill the darkness with a booming imprint of her energy. I envied her recklessness, her confidence.

Blanes grabbed her arm and attempted to drag her away. Mar stayed put, her mouth a twisted smirk. She freed her arm and threw herself against the shutter a third time. CLANK! The balcony window opened, and somebody yelled.

"I'm calling the police, assholes!" A hand holding a pot appeared over the rail and a stream of cold water showered down. Mar laughed hysterically and we all took off running, adrenaline pumping as we disappeared into the labyrinthine streets, howling. When we were sure nobody had followed us, we slowed down and walked toward Las Ramblas.

"You guys are all mad," said Blanes. "I'm going home."

"Yes, go home, you party pooper," said Mar, "you're making a big deal out of nothing. Can't we have a little fun?"

"You call fun waking up half the neighborhood?" said Blanes. "Good luck, *macho*," he said to Pol. "Your girlfriend is crazy." He took off, hands in his pockets.

"Well, what shall we do?" said Juanma.

"Let's go dancing," said Pol.

"It's three thirty," I said. "Is there anything open?"

"Sure there is," said Pol.

We walked down Las Ramblas until we reached the last street on the left, Calle Escudillers. On the right side of the street, toward the end, there was a door with the name *Tabú* above it in red neon cursive letters. Pol pushed the door and we all went in.

The club was a little dump: a dark corridor about eighty feet long and twenty feet wide, running along a bar. The corridor was divided in two by a fringed plastic curtain, thick and black. When we came in from the street, the place looked empty, and the music was muffled, but as I parted the fringes, trumpets leapt at me like a tongue of fire. I entered and let the curtain close behind me, a shiver running through my spine.

It was my first time hearing salsa, but I knew right away this was the music I had been waiting for my whole life. Dancing to pop music, I'd always felt awkward, but the drums, the brass, and the voices filling up Tabú were blistering my veins. My hips swayed and my feet moved spontaneously. I didn't know the steps, but I was in sync with the beat.

"What do you want?" asked Juanma. "My treat."

"I don't care. A gin and tonic," I said. Juanma ordered the drinks and came toward me with a glass. I was already dancing. I put the drink on the table where Pol and Mar were sitting and looked around.

Four rectangular tables covered by checkered green-and-black vinyl tablecloths sticky to the touch were flanked on one side by benches set against the wall, sporting a few rips in their vinyl upholstery. The DJ booth was at the end of the long and narrow dance floor. To the right was the counter bordered by tall stools. A gorgeous woman served the drinks. She had a luxurious mane of black hair down to her waist, enormous black eyes, olive skin, and a voluptuous body, which she showed off in a tight dress. Other than us, there were only a few men seated at another table. They looked Latin American. The glorious sounds of the Fania All Stars dissolved the grimy surroundings into fire and light.

I couldn't sit down. I danced with Pol, Juanma, and alone, lost in Pedro Navaja's tale of woes, the swinging *azúcar* of Celia Cruz, and the vigorous riffs of Eddie Palmieri. I had drunk enough to crack open my usual shyness, and now the music transported me to a place deep inside myself where there were no thoughts, only rhythm and emotion.

I noticed the men at the other table staring at me, whispering. After a while one came and asked me to dance. I said yes. The sheer joy that filled me as I tried to follow his turns was intoxicating. I stepped on his toes a couple of times, but the locked eyes, my beaming expression and the heat emanating from our bodies brought along its own kind of forgiveness.

I danced with all the men from the other table, one after the other. Each had his own style, his own flourishes. I followed the best I could, laughing when a step surprised me, giving myself to the subtle pressure of a hand on the small of my back, letting the music put a shake on my shoulders.

There was a new freedom in this fluttering from man to man, briefly united in our quest to honor the deep thumps of the *tumbadoras* and the centering one–two, one–two–three of the *clave* while sashaying to the playful accents of a *trombón* or the improvised *soneo* of *el cantante*. For a few minutes we were one, in the now, all senses engaged in the moment.

When the song was over, it was thanks and goodbye, and a different man offering his hand. I took it and stepped onto the floor, ready to learn a new, unique vocabulary. There were no fears, no confusion. Each tap on a drum was a crumb marking my way home, to a haven where my body beckoned bliss, only now that bliss was public—and proud.

At five in the morning, the DJ announced the club was closing. We walked back up Las Ramblas. I was flying high, the new rhythms reverberating in my bones, every cell fizzling and flaring. I had never felt so alive.

"Do you want to stay overnight?" asked Juanma. "We can share the bed; no hanky-panky, I promise."

"I'd rather go home. I don't have toiletries or clothes for tomorrow. I'll grab a taxi."

I arrived home exhausted and happy, my flesh knowing—even before I knew—that my life had forever changed.

A New Birth

I WOKE UP LATE AND A LITTLE HUNGOVER. As I lay in bed remembering the night before—the verbal fireworks between Pol and Mar, her street games with Juanma, her rough duels with Blanes, the clatter of the shutters in the quiet night—it dawned on me that Mar wasn't the right name for my friend. Mar meant *sea*, but she wasn't wide and flat like a calm sea, nor was she turbulent like an ocean during a storm, condemned after it exhausts its violence to quiet down. She was an uncontainable tide, a *marea* that rose and seized everything around it with unavoidable strength, a wave of vitality that ate up the beach and made it disappear, like she made people around her appear lackluster and washed-out. I decided from that moment on I would call her Marea.

We had made plans to meet again for lunch. I almost ran down Avenida del Tibidabo on my way to the subway, wondering what we would do today. When I got to their apartment, Pol opened the door.

"Hello, gorgeous." He kissed me on the cheek. Did he mean it? I didn't think of myself as gorgeous. I had grown up as one of ten kids, an indistinguishable mass of elbows, legs, movement, and ruckus that with time had mutated into silences. My parents had never told me that I was special, beautiful, or destined for great things. Practical and austere was our family's style, hardworking and responsible our way to move in the world. Being a good person was paramount; being average, a tacit corollary.

I stepped inside and found Blanes nagging everybody.

"It's two thirty already! Are we going to eat lunch or what?"

It was another half hour before everybody was up and ready to move. Pol offered to prepare a salad, and Juanma said he'd boil some pasta. There was a rustic clay bowl on the kitchen counter with limp lettuce in it. Pol threw the leftovers away, wiped the bowl out with a paper napkin, cut a clove of garlic in two and rubbed it all over the inside of the bowl.

"You're not going to wash that bowl?" asked Blanes.

"Nah," said Pol. "Salad tastes better if you let the leftover dressing marinate the bowl. It's like espresso coffee pots; you're never supposed to wash them, just rinse them with some water."

"You're crazy—and lazy. You'll get us all sick," said Blanes. "I'm not eating your salad," he added.

"Your loss," said Pol.

When we finally sat down to eat, it was past three thirty. Used to the two o'clock sharp lunchtime at home, I was starving, my stomach grumbling. I served myself some salad, a little apprehensive. With the first forkful, taste exploded in my mouth, the garlic bouncing off the richness of the olive oil and the acidity of the red wine vinegar, the plump tomatoes bursting and contrasting with the crunchiness of the romaine and sliced onion, the saltiness of the anchovies, and the bitterness of the green olives dancing on my tongue. As simple as it was, the salad had a depth of flavor that couldn't be explained by the humble ingredients on the plate. Even Blanes ate some after hearing everyone's compliments to the chef.

As I ate quietly, I reflected. Perhaps it was okay to let things get a little dirty, the gritty layers of time and change accumulating as the secret ingredient to make them interesting.

Midway through lunch I gathered the courage to say what I had wanted to say since I first set foot in the apartment.

"Mar isn't the right name for you," I announced, looking my friend straight in the eye, my voice firm even as my insides trembled. "I'm going to call you Marea, because you're like a tide that rises and covers up everything else."

"You mean a tide that lays waste to everything else, right?" said Blanes.

"Ha, ha, ha," mocked Marea, eyes blazing. She turned her attention to me. "You can call me Marea if you want." I released the breath I'd been holding. "We also found a new name for you," she added, smiling.

"Really?" They had been talking about me!

"Yes; we've decided to call you Isadora because you're a passionate dancer, like Isadora Duncan."

"I love it!"

I had never liked my name. It was too long and old-fashioned. To make matters worse, it was the same name my mother had, and I wanted to be my own person. Isadora sounded romantic and unique. It left my Christian name behind, which seemed appropriate now that I had abandoned Sunday masses and confessions. Plus, Marea and I had renamed each other at the same time without even knowing it. That alone anointed us as priestesses of a new religion, one that didn't require disciples or rules but would be populated by our own sacred scriptures and rituals—the books we loved and the games we played.

From that day on, I introduced myself to new friends as Isadora, tracing a deep line on an invisible stretch of sand that separated the person I had always been from the person I wanted to become. Out was the good girl who colored within the lines. In came the young woman who wanted to tear up the paper and throw big gobs of paint on Barcelona's medieval cobblestone streets.

As soon as Blanes and Juanma went back to Madrid, I packed a bag most Saturdays and stayed overnight in the room at the back of Pol and Marea's apartment, where they had a mattress on the floor. Marea and I were always together, spending weekday afternoons at the library and hanging out with her friends on weekends.

Literature ruled our days, bars our nights, but they met in the middle. We talked for hours about the books we were reading over drinks and cigarette smoke, analyzing metaphors and hidden meanings as if solving the puzzle of life. Nothing excited us more than getting into the mind of an author we admired. Discovering that the protagonist of Juan Goytisolo's *Señas de identidad*, Álvaro, drank a wine that happened to be made with albariño grapes—a variant of his first name—seemed all-important, another sign of his identity that would make it into the paper we had to write for class. We invented backstories for the characters in a novel, discussed a plot for hours on end, and devoured books as if they were candy. I had always loved reading, but this was the first time my passion for words and stories had transcended the boundaries of my own mind. As a shared adventure, it was infinitely more fun.

Poetry linked us to Pol, who read aloud the poems he loved, poems that stayed forever etched in my mind. We might not understand every verse of T.S. Eliot's "The Love Song of Alfred J. Prufrock," but it didn't matter. The melancholy of this old man, who wondered if he dared to eat a peach or wear the bottom of his trousers rolled, shook us to the core. Life's changes had a way of sneaking up on you. Some people couldn't weather them, as I had learned from the fate of many friends now lost to time.

Marea never ceased to surprise me. It wasn't only her playful take on high culture or dramatic embodiment of low culture. It was the ravenous hunger with which she devoured life and her comfort in her body. She changed her clothes in front of me in the middle of a lively discussion—her torso naked since her small breasts didn't need bras—and even inserted a tampon, as if it were the most normal thing ever. I still shivered with shame whenever I remembered the day I opened Mama's bedroom door without knocking and caught her coming out of her bathroom naked, and here was Marea, without an ounce of modesty, oblivious to how odd her nudity seemed to me.

This brilliant, original, and fearless woman had chosen me as her new best friend. I couldn't believe it. What on earth did she see in me? It was hard to comprehend. She opened a new era in my life at the same time that transformation swept the country.

In March, new elections had confirmed the centrist UCD as the governing party, but the left had won many small and mid-size towns' city halls. The new mayors immediately tackled quick symbolic changes, like the removal of names that celebrated Franco and his exploits in public spaces. Plazas and avenues were rechristened with hopeful beacons like *Plaza de la Constitución* or *Calle de la Libertad* at the same time that "Isadora" was bringing out a new me. (I would later learn that varnishing the surface doesn't repair the cracks.)

I had spent my childhood and teen years in the upper side of the city, my home in Avenida del Tibidabo up on a hill, my school in Sarriá, a solid middle-class neighborhood at the foot of another hill. Even my incursion into the hippie life through my friends at La Torre had centered on the abandoned house where they squatted on a street adjacent to Avenida del Tibidabo.

Now I hardly left the lower side of the city, from Plaza Cataluña down to the sea. The long promenade of Las Ramblas and the neighborhoods to its right and left became my home at heart. Back then, Barcelona wasn't packed with tourists. It was ours. Walking up and down Las Ramblas, you ran into the odd guy selling American cigarettes by the unit, young couples strolling hand in hand, old men with felt hats or tweed caps and a stub between their lips sitting on the chairs lining both sides of the promenade, families with squealing kids delighted to buy their first pet at the birds stands, matrons buying carnations for Sunday lunch at the flower stands, long-haired guys offering brown bars of hashish while mumbling "Chocolate, direct from Morocco, best you've ever tried"; young people meeting at the Canaletas fountain right at the top of the Ramblas, whose water, according to legend, had the mysterious ability to bring you back to the city once you drank it. On each side of Las Ramblas, restaurants from long ago, vintage businesses with art nouveau signs proving their storied pedigree, and venerable buildings like the Liceo, the opera house, gave it character. Dime stores with plastic souvenirs in rows of identical cheesiness, fast food restaurants, and innumerable living statues hadn't yet transformed the promenade into a cheap circus.

We liked to sit on the terrace at Café de la Opera in the afternoons to drink coffee and cognac, time passing by as we watched the lovebirds strolling down to the sea with eyes only for each other; we also walked, lost in conversation, from the top to the bottom of the promenade. In a photo from that time taken right by the statue of Cristóbal Colón, Marea is dressed in tweed pants and manly spectator shoes, smoking a cigarette, while I wear a light sweater with a handkerchief around my neck and my hair cut pixie-style, perhaps unconsciously trying to play the part of boyfriend to my muse. From time to time we'd venture above Plaza Cataluña, to marvel in front of Gaudí's Casa Batlló and La Pedrera, up in Paseo de Gracia, or to play like little kids in the Tibidabo amusement park.

A mandatory stop before any new adventure with Pol and Marea was the minuscule bar on the corner of San Pablo and

Las Ramblas—a four-foot counter directly on the sidewalk with a wall of liquor behind it—where we gulped a shot of *cazalla*, moonshine that burnt your throat as it slid down. We ended a night of drinking and dancing at a cheap restaurant, all Formica and primary colors, that we renamed *La Ruina*, the Ruin, because it opened at five a.m. and only drunkards and bohemians frequented it at that ungodly hour. After the last few drinks at La Ruina, we crossed to the other side of Las Ramblas into La Bouería, the most beautiful open market in the city, where we sat side by side with construction workers at small counters and ate hearty stews for breakfast before stumbling to the nearby apartment and to bed at eight o'clock.

I rediscovered my city step by step, hour by hour. A little Romanesque church from the tenth century hiding in plain sight on Calle San Pablo, its quiet and diminutive cloister offered to us like a jewel. A hole-in-the-wall deli and bar close to Las Ramblas, packed with Serrano hams hanging from the ceiling, cramped like a row of scrumptious soldiers. Only two small round tables fit in the tiny, dark space. Plates of ham, manchego cheese, and cured olives paraded in front of us, accompanied by a robust Rioja and crusty bread. A handful of sunken tombs from Roman times in a small square to the left of Las Ramblas doubled as impromptu seats where we lingered at four a.m., reciting poetry.

Every day was laced with art and play. A game of spoof would keep us bragging and laughing while we drank pints. A Kavafis poem filled us with longing for Greek gods, long voyages by sea, and voluptuous bodies. A Concha Piquer record had us singing along with her Andalusian *coplas*, popular folk songs where sailors, prostitutes, gypsies, and star-crossed lovers displayed their heartbreaks and dramas with abandon and cockiness.

Icons of Spanish popular culture that at home had been frowned upon as coarse—from popular flamenco dancers to matadors—became objects of my admiration, their exuberant expression modeling a way of being in the world that didn't apologize for its brashness. On the contrary, brashness was something to cultivate. As if I had taken a pair of scissors to an oppressive girdle constricting my body and shortening my breath, I expanded with a sigh of relief. Freedom!

Being expressive and excessive was an overdue correction after decades of proper and contained behavior, not just for me but for my whole generation. A passion for shock value took over music, movies, theater, graphic arts, and books. In Madrid it had an official name, *la movida madrileña*, the Madrid Movement, and it gave birth to punk rock bands, graffiti artists, and Almodóvar's first films, which introduced raunchy characters and melodramatic plots that relished scandal. In Barcelona, this cultural movement went unnamed but had similar strength.

We were touching the eye of the hurricane, but not fully overrun by it. Pol and Marea's friends were at the epicenter. We hung out with actors from a famous alternative theater group, a graphic designer who published some of the most significant underground comics of the '70s and '80s, bohemian poets of the New Generation, all booze and art.

As fascinating as this crowd was to me, I tended to stay quiet, observing without participating much. I had always been better in one-on-one relationships or in small groups where I could have deep conversations. Perhaps big groups took me back to the original big group, my family, where I often felt unseen and unheard.

Only at Tabú, after a few gin and tonics, did my shyness fall aside. I begged Marea and Pol to go there every night we went out so I could find again the daring girl who hid somewhere inside me.

The one–two, one–two–three rhythm of the *clave* inevitably moved my feet and my spirit. Those two simple sticks of wood tapping each other produced a sharp staccato pattern that despite its simplicity, or perhaps because of it, supplied the bedrock from which the vibrancy of the winds, the ardor of the drums, the lushness of the voices, and the heat of the bodies erupted without ever being fully consumed or transformed into ashes.

Summer Awakening

"HI; WOULD YOU LIKE TO PLAY volleyball with us in the pool?"

The boy pointed to a group of three guys and one girl who were huddling behind him. I hesitated.

"We need one more player to be equal teams," he added.

I didn't know any of them, but I said yes. He introduced me to brothers Salva and Tito, to their cousin, and to their neighbor and friend, Maite, a blond, blue-eyed girl about my age. We spent the morning playing ball, doing cannonballs, diving from the high plank, and racing each other in the crawl and breaststroke.

I wasn't used to so much activity. My summer girlfriends never came to the public pool because they had swimming pools at home or they came much later than my family, who even in the summer kept the two o'clock lunch. I usually lay alone on the concrete bleachers and sunbathed, slathered in Nivea cream, while listening to the music the bar owners played. Occasionally, I swam a few laps.

The boys invited me to join them for a hike in the afternoon, and we made plans to meet at Salva and Tito's. Their home was on a picturesque pedestrian street. Neat little houses with windows full of potted red or pink geraniums flanked both sides. The stone pavement was uneven, as if someone had roughly cut and clumsily thrown on the ground big slabs of the limestone that surrounded the town. It was carved with horizontal grooves to prevent decades-ago carts pulled by donkeys from slipping down the slope on their way to Las

Siete Fuentes, the Seven Fountains Park, one of my favorite spots in San Julián.

At five o'clock, as planned, I rode my bike to meet my new friends. I wished Gemma could have come with me, but she was spending the month of July in England.

This group was a mix of summer vacationers like me—*los veraneantes*—and San Julián natives—*los del pueblo*. Usually there was an invisible border between the two. Even the bars were spontaneously segregated. Barcelona folks sat at Bar Nuria, and most townspeople sat at Bar Joan, which was right in front, or up the street at Can Cuca.

San Julián had become a fashionable destination for upper-middle-class Barcelona families in the 1890s due to its temperate climate and medicinal waters. They built beautiful summerhouses in the art nouveau style, like Santa Margarita and Can Madirolas, the house we rented for our vacation. Even though the *veraneantes* brought business to town, the divide between us and *los del pueblo* seemed difficult to breach. The two groups kept their distance, crossing paths mainly as customers and clerks or employers and employees.

Language opened another gap. In Barcelona you didn't hear much Catalan, at least not among my family and their close circle of friends. It was forbidden to use it in official documents or on street signs, and you couldn't learn it in school. In San Julián, however, you heard only Catalan everywhere. Abuelo spoke it perfectly, but Mama and Papa spoke it with an accent, just as older San Julián natives, when they spoke Spanish, had marked Catalan accents.

Papa's family came originally from the north of Spain, which may be why he grew up speaking Spanish and so did we. Some upper- and middle-class families, however, spoke Spanish simply to reflect their politics. If Su Excelencia el Jefe del Estado said Spanish was the only language in the country, that was how it "should be."

The Saturday night folk dance *sardanas*, which we danced in the middle of the crossroads right by Bar Nuria, was one rare occasion when townspeople and vacationers mixed on equal footing. You joined any circle of dancers you wanted as long as you respected the boy/girl/boy/girl order. Old people, young people, and kids held hands, and expert dancers who counted the steps out loud and did fancy footwork welcomed novices who attempted to imitate them as best they could.

I had grown up surrounded by people who were summer visitors, like me. It happened organically because our parents knew each other and were friends. Up until that day I had never hung out daily with a "mixed" group of friends. This gang was my first foray into a different territory, one that I had chosen myself.

When we got together that first afternoon, we quickly decided on a plan: we would ride our bikes to a tiny town five miles away and have a soda at the only restaurant. I feared I wouldn't be resilient enough for the bike ride, but Salva said he'd help me. Sure enough, he rode beside me and pushed my bike with his hand on my seat when I lagged until I caught up.

I developed a crush on Salva almost right away. A tall sixteen-year-old, he looked half gypsy and half gazelle with his black curly hair, dark brown eyes, well-formed eyebrows, and tanned olive skin. He appeared to do everything in slow motion but always arrived first wherever we were going. Salva talked unhurriedly, dropping his words as if with a measuring spoon. When he was amused, he drew a breath and waited a few seconds before letting out a deep, long laugh, showing small, even teeth strangely childish in his thin, mature face. Always even-tempered and friendly, he was nevertheless surrounded by a certain remote air, as if he lived on another planet and was visiting us only temporarily while part of his brain remained in this other, unknown world.

I enjoyed everything about my new friends: our pool play, our bike rides, our hikes to beautiful spots a few miles away from San Julián, and the frankness of our talks. Once we had a conversation about puberty, and the boys wanted to know if we girls already had our periods. We didn't yet, and one of them remarked, winking, "Just as well; you still have a lot of growing up to do, especially Maite." He didn't say it in a mean way. We all laughed, including Maite. She had barely turned twelve and was still quite flat-chested, but I was almost thirteen, more developed, and already wore a bra. That probably had a lot to do with the attention the boys lavished on me.

The last few summers I had loved spending time with Gemma and my other girlfriends, but we mostly talked and laughed, never venturing farther than our homes and a few spots in town or close to it. Going on these longer excursions with their variety of activities was an exciting change. I fantasized about introducing the gang to Gemma in a few weeks. What fun we'd have . . .

One day, the boys suggested we throw a party. I put on my favorite outfit: a turquoise jersey ensemble of short shorts and a sleeveless top with a scoop neck, ribbed with a navy blue band. The thin knitted fabric clung to my body and showed off my breasts.

We met at Salva and Tito's house. Their parents were not in. It was mid-afternoon but we closed the shutters. We switched on a small table lamp and threw a red shawl on top. We played a few rounds of *la botella*, spinning a bottle to see who had to kiss whom and giving each other kisses on the cheek. Then we danced.

Most of the boys held me respectfully at arm's length, awkwardly shuffling from side to side. Salva and another boy, however, pressed me against their bodies. I didn't like the other boy, so I moved away from him. When Salva asked me to dance, though, I let him hold me close. I wrapped my arms around his neck and buried my face on his shoulder, a mixed scent of chlorine and sweat sending tremors down my legs. I wished the song would last forever. His hand on the small of my back, my thighs embracing his, our bodies so tightly wrapped not even a needle could have come between, all conspired to loosen my consciousness of where I was, lost in our togetherness. I tingled from head to toe. I would have kept dancing with him all afternoon, but Salva was the slippery kind, teasing without committing. I had to dance again with everybody else before he and I took a turn again.

When the party ended, something had been altered in me forever. I now knew what desire was, the urge to give myself to a male body, the unspoken language of the flesh.

That evening I went home holding close to my chest the secret of my grown-up senses and the glow of having been wanted by those boys who were also my friends. My parents sat reading in the living room, waiting for dinner to be served. I approached the coffee table, still savoring the sensation of Salva's body tightly pressed against mine.

Papa looked at me and remarked, "You're getting a little plump, aren't you?"

He bent his head again and kept reading his newspaper. I went to the bathroom and looked at myself in the mirror, turning this way and that. I had a little potbelly, yes. Was that the reason Salva didn't want to dance with me more often? I sucked in my stomach to flatten it, but I couldn't hold it in for more than a few seconds.

Quica called us to dinner, and I went, trying to forget Papa's comment and focusing instead on the fun I'd have tomorrow. I served myself fewer fries, though.

Soon the parties happened more frequently and became more sophisticated. Other San Julián teenagers joined the group. One of them had a room that he'd fixed up as a proper disco. Empty egg cartons covered the walls floor to ceiling, making them soundproof. There were big speakers and even a disco light. We called the room *la huevera*, the egg basket. Our core group still spent some days hiking and biking, but many afternoons veered into dance marathons. I felt a little uncomfortable. There were a lot of boys I didn't know and didn't care about. I liked the music and the chance to dance with Salva, but now he was spread thin among more girls, so I had fewer chances to offer up my body to his embrace.

August came around and Gemma arrived in San Julián. I rushed to her house the first afternoon and told her about the friends I'd met, about the hikes, the bike rides, the games at the pool, the talks and, of course, the dances. I introduced her to the gang that same day, but she hardly talked to them.

The next day we went to *la huevera*. Gemma was pretty, with light brown hair in a bob, bangs, and enormous blue eyes. She was in demand, but she didn't enjoy the attention, all those boys from town ogling her like birds of prey, lining up to squeeze her between their arms. The next day she told me she wasn't interested in this group.

I didn't understand why Gemma didn't like them, but she had been my best summer friend for a few years, and I didn't want to lose her. My loyalty to her outweighed my excitement about the boys and girls I had just met. I still played with them at the pool, but when they made plans for an afternoon, I told them I was busy. They realized it was over when they asked me to go with them one evening to the rackety itinerant circus that set up once a summer in a field close to town. I said I was going with Gemma and other girlfriends instead, and they didn't want to be with them. After that, they never asked me out anymore, and even in the pool they kept their distance. I moved on reluctantly.

Gemma and I would join a different group of boys and girls

the next summer, but things never got romantic for most of us. The girls had crushes on older boys, while the boys had crushes on older girls. The fact that no one pursued me reinforced my feeling that I must not be anything special. When my high school girlfriends and I formed our mixed-gender group in Barcelona and I realized I was popular with those boys, I felt relief. It seemed that a condition of being noticed was to place myself in a world as far away as possible from the one I grew up in. Since all I wanted was to be seen, at around sixteen I stopped going to San Julián most weekends, staying instead in Barcelona with some of my older siblings. Later, my trips to Mâcon and London kept me away two whole summers. Once I met Marea and Pol, I left San Julián behind for good. I still felt affection for my summer friends, but I had become a different person, with a different name to match.

That winter, Quica retired. I missed her, but my visits to the ironing room had been less frequent the last couple of years. Building relationships with my girlfriends had become my main concern.

Mama tried a girl in her early twenties as a live-in maid, but it backfired—she spent more time listening to our records than doing chores and fainted when a cousin bled profusely after an accident. Luckily Mama arrived home at that moment and took him to emergency. After that fiasco, we had only a woman who came on weekdays from nine to three to help clean and cook.

With less help, Mama kept everything running smoothly for all of us, but it might have been then that her character started to turn. She had always been busy chauffeuring, grocery shopping, planning, and doing the light cleaning. Now she also took over the never-ending laundry and cooked dinner every evening and both meals on weekends. She didn't ask for help, considering it her duty to keep the household humming. The only exception was that after dinner, my older sister and I cleared the table, loaded the dishwasher, and helped wash the pots and pans while the boys and our younger sisters filed upstairs. Certain things never change.

One evening, I went to the kitchen while Mama was cooking dinner to ask for advice about my latest girlfriend drama. I blabbed and blabbed while she stirred the soup in the pot and fried the croquettes. At one point she offered a suggestion, which I quickly dismissed, and she resorted to her go-to answer to most every question or doubt: "*No sé qué decirte.*" ("I don't know what to tell you.")

Confidences and intimate chats were not Mama's cup of tea, but ramming them down her throat while she tried to put a meal on the table at nine o'clock sharp for twelve demanding diners made them even less welcome. She had a thousand thoughts competing for her attention, from the next day's menu to the gift she had to buy for the birthday party one of us would attend that weekend to where the heck we would spend the summer, now that the owners of our summer home had decided to take over the house and vacation there themselves. I didn't notice that she was busy and exhausted. Instead, I concluded that she didn't care about my problems. That was the last time I tried to have a heart-to-heart with her. I retreated even further into the privacy of my mind and relationships with my school friends.

School had changed a lot in the last few years. The nuns now dressed in long tweed skirts, modest twin sets, thick stockings, and flat brown shoes. They didn't cover their hair anymore, but kept it closely cropped. Most classes were taught by lay teachers, Mass was consigned to one day a week, and veils were exiled. Guitars were added to upbeat hymns. When the New Testament readings talked about the wealthy having a hard time getting into Heaven, the sermons veered into social justice. The priests abandoned their cassocks, wearing instead black pants and black sweaters with white collars. Our priest during the last two years of high school wore green aviator Ray-Bans and drove a motorcycle.

He seemed a bit too handsome and fashionable to be a clergyman. His closeness with a girl in my class, the one who wore makeup and mid-high heels and always found a way to let her socks fall to her ankles to show off her calves, made me wonder: could her frequent confessions and meetings for spiritual guidance conceal a less holy purpose? I quickly put those impure thoughts out of my mind.

That same year, a movie by director Manuel Summers, *Adiós cigüeña adiós* (Bye-bye stork), told the story of two teenagers—a boy of fifteen and a girl of thirteen—who in a moment of passion have sex. The girl gets pregnant. Scared to tell their strict Catholic parents, they hide the pregnancy with the help of their friends and prepare for the birth.

The movie was a hit. All my girlfriends saw it, but Mama forbade me to join them, thinking I might get the wrong idea.

In truth, having sex couldn't have been further from my mind. My high school girlfriends and I met with boys in cafés to drink sodas and go to the movies, and we had parties with music and dancing, but it was all very proper. A boy would tell you he liked you, dance only with you while pressing his body against yours, and hold your hand while walking, but it didn't go further.

I was fourteen when the nuns invited a doctor to come talk to us about sex. He showed colorful slides of the uterus, the ovaries, and the inside of a penis and summarized how humans reproduce. The Q&A promised to be interesting, because the doctor gave us permission to write our questions anonymously, with no topic off-limits.

We had to throw them in the basket a nun passed around. I asked if masturbation was a sin and if it would harm me, as rumor had it, but the little piece of paper stayed crumpled in my pocket for fear the handwriting would give me away. When I got back home, I ripped it into tiny pieces and flushed it down the toilet. By that point, I wasn't sharing my dirty habit with anybody, especially not my new girl-friends, and I was too ashamed to mention it during confession. But no matter how much I tried to kick it, I couldn't, even though after a few minutes, my legs tensed, my stomach contracted, and the red balloon flew up and out of my reach.

Other girls may have similarly repressed their curiosity, because the questions were directed to "safe" topics like periods and preg-nancy, the only obvious consequence to intercourse. *Orgasm* was a word that had not yet entered our vocabulary or even our consciousness.

This tame class and a conversation I had with Mama when I was around ten taught me all I knew about sexual relationships.

Mama sat with me on a sofa by the fireplace and asked, "Do you know the difference between boys and girls?"

It seemed an easy enough question.

"Girls have long hair and boys have short hair."

"Very well. What else?"

"Mmm . . . Girls have earrings and boys don't."

"Yes, that's true. What else?"

"Girls wear skirts and boys wear pants."

Mama was getting impatient.

"Yes, yes; all of that is true, but the other thing that makes them different is that boys have a willy and girls do not."

"Oh . . . yes." I remembered the doctor game I'd played a few years before with my brothers and cousins.

"Boys use their willy to plant a seed in girls and that's how you can grow babies."

I had no idea what she meant, but I didn't say anything. Mama sighed, as if she had gotten rid of a big weight, and said, "Okay, go play now!"

A few years later, talking with girlfriends about where babies came from, I remembered that explanation. As confusing as it had been, I was the only girl who had gotten one at all. I'm not sure why Mama did it. Perhaps she wanted to plant a seed about seed-planting to warn me about the dangers of unwed pregnancy later on.

Danger Zone

"YOU'RE MUCH MORE ATTRACTIVE than you think," said Marea. "Heck, even Pol would be at your feet if you gave him a chance!" I had been complaining about my looks again, and Marea had finally had enough.

"Pol? What do you mean? He's with you. How would he have eyes for anybody else?"

"Don't be naïve. Of course he has eyes for other women! We have an open relationship anyway."

Their open relationship was news to me, but it didn't shock me. It was common among bohemian youth at the time, while marriage was rare. Marea's playfulness with Juanma assumed a different shape. Had they had an affair during his visit?

I'd had flings myself with various partnered men in our crowd, but these entanglements left a bitter taste in my mouth. A typical scenario would be me admiring the tenderness a man displayed for his partner, accepting his advances when we were alone, thirsty for that affection, and feeling cheated when all I got was a mechanical quickie.

Men who gawked at you hungrily for days became blind to your presence as soon as they got their dicks out of your body. I, on the other hand, never went into casual sex without the hope that it would lead to something more. I wasn't in it for the pleasure. In fact, I rarely enjoyed it. As soon as it was clear that the man on top wouldn't look me in the eye or caress me with care, I retreated to a place inside myself, seeing what was happening as if floating from above. I could feel anew the bristles of the sofa pinching my cheek, my body moved and prodded and then discarded like a flower with a broken stem.

Still, after Marea mentioned that Pol liked me, I saw him with different eyes. His ability to abandon himself to the present moment had always enticed me—the way his arms moved with such ease while he danced, his full lips opened in a mischievous smile, his carefree laugh, his utter abandonment to bliss. He emptied his mind of thoughts at will, letting his body take over.

I wanted that. I wanted to be skin and guts, trembling with anticipation. I wanted to live in the freedom of my sensations. I wanted that triumphant joy I accessed only through the thumping of the drums and the fire of the winds. I wanted it now. I wanted it always.

Perhaps I wanted Pol also because he was Marea's. His attention elevated me. If he saw something special in me—he who had landed Marea—it might mean I actually had it.

The next time we all went out, I danced with Pol a little closer, and I looked him straight in the eye for a tiny bit longer. We were at a friend's house. Around three a.m., Marea announced she was going home. Pol and I stayed behind.

That night we made love for the first time, but I don't remember it. I can't pinpoint the exact moment when our bodies connected in memorable ways. Although we hooked up occasionally, I didn't fully give myself to him until his relationship with Marea was over. I put loyalty to my friend over lust for my lover.

The water fell slowly, in a small rivulet from up high. He didn't cover his head with his arms. He didn't complain. He didn't look up. He stayed seated on the mattress on the floor, his back against the wall, his head slightly forward, his eyes closed. When the glass was empty, she let it fall. It bounced on his head and rolled off, first on his chest, then onto the sheet. It stayed there, inert, as still as I was, lying to his right.

"You're an asshole," said Marea. She was wrapped in her short red kimono, barefoot, her eyes flashing, her jaw rigid.

"If you say so," said Pol nonchalantly, a smile curving his lips.

Before he added another word, Marea left the room.

I didn't dare speak. Pol got up and went out, naked. He came back a few seconds later with a hand towel. He sat on the edge of the mattress, his feet on the floor, his back to me, drying his black curls. Then he turned around to dry the sheet. He caressed my cheek and said, "Are you okay?"

"You said she didn't mind about us . . ."

"That's what I thought."

After a moment, he added, "I'm sorry. I have to go see her."

"I understand."

He put on his pants and left, turning the light off on his way out.

I lay back down in bed. I heard them talking in their bedroom. Shit. Marea must have heard us making love, even though we tried to keep it hushed. Should I go home? I decided against it. It was four a.m. and I was tired.

I understood why Marea got mad. But hadn't she done the same thing with others? I tried not to think about the fact that hooking up in Marea's own house was taking the open relationship concept a step too far, but it nettled me like a deeply buried splinter on the sole of my foot.

I slept fitfully and woke up at eight. The house was quiet. I dressed and left the apartment on tiptoe. When I got home, I went to the kitchen to fill a glass with water. Mama was already up, emptying the dishwasher.

"Weren't you away for the weekend?" she said.

"I wasn't feeling well."

She didn't say anything else. These days we didn't talk much. Not that we'd been chatty before. After our heart-to-heart when she'd found the pills in my bedside table, we'd gone back to our usual routine of not talking about anything personal and maintaining a façade of normalcy.

I kept up appearances as best I could. During the week, I rarely went out at night because I had to get up early in the morning, and I wanted to do well in school. Also, I was a morning person, so two or three long nights out a week were all I could handle. But on the weekends, if I didn't stay overnight at Marea's, I often made it home after nine in the morning, wasted. When I ran into Mama or Papa, they averted their eyes and didn't say a word. Silence followed me around the house like a thick fog for a couple of days, after which they went back to addressing me as if nothing had happened.

I had become a rebellious teenager in my early twenties. I had even rejected the name I shared with my mother and my great grandmother, which branded me as part of our family. When friends called and asked for Isadora, Mama, Papa, and my brothers said there was no Isadora living in the house and hung up. I took refuge in my room and within the high walls of my life, suffering from the isolation but relishing the feeling of being "different"—a difference that wasn't always in my best interests. As long as there were no blow-ups—and there were never any blow-ups because no one acknowledged the tension—I slid along, stubbornly fastened to my mute defiance.

I spent that Sunday anxious about seeing Marea in class on

Monday. Would she talk to me? Or would she ignore me as well? Maybe she would slap me in front of everybody. She certainly didn't mind causing a scene.

My fears were unfounded. Marea missed the first class, but when I met her on the patio between classes, she was less upset than I had imagined. She made it clear that her house was out of bounds for my hookups with Pol but also confessed that they were pretty much done as a couple.

We were now in the fifth and last year of university. In the following months, their relationship continued to disintegrate. They led independent lives.

Marea and I kept doing things together and even talked about studying for a PhD and writing a joint dissertation. We hung out less with Pol and the rest of the gang. We took a few weekend trips with a friend who had a car. Up to that point, when I traveled, I had a definite purpose: I was camping nearby, visiting some monument, or going to work in a particular city in a particular country. With Marea, trips were different. You had a landmark, perhaps a fortress on top of a hill in a certain tiny town, and the rest was left to mood, the weather, and the unexpected. It made for marvelous discoveries, some boring stretches, and a few alarming situations, sometimes of our own making.

One night, Marea and I riled up the men in a small rural town, visiting the only club and dancing provocatively. Marea flirted and played with them, and I followed suit. The men surrounded us, getting more excited and aggressive with every lascivious turn. They boiled up to the point of explosion. At a certain point our friend urged us, "We have to leave. NOW." He dragged us out the door and into the car while a mob closed in on us. We escaped unharmed but were followed by yells, the car rattling with a couple of stones the men threw at us. Fearing a gang rape, we drove around town a few times so they wouldn't know where we were staying.

On another trip, this time by train with a different friend, we shared a hotel room. Marea and this guy made love in one bed while I masturbated in the other, my back to them, feigning sleep. I had left behind my compulsion to touch myself since I started having lovers, but when I resorted to it, I still tensed up, the bright red balloon flying out of reach.

Not so that night. Hearing the moans and rumbles of Marea's lovemaking was exciting. It seemed I could let myself go only when I was part of some transgression.

Toward the end of our last year of college, Marea began dating a man who was the opposite of Pol. Serious, sober, intellectual. The vulgar attitudes and slang from the popular boroughs of Madrid disappeared as if they had never been anything more than a costume she eventually outgrew. At the end of the academic year, she moved in with him, while Pol stayed at the Calle San Pablo apartment. Marea and I slowly fell apart. Her distance opened the door for me to resume and intensify my encounters with Pol. There was something about him that bewitched me—his green eyes, his languorous ease, his ability to simply be. With Marea gone, I was all in, and so was he.

At least that's what I thought.

1980, Barcelona and La Escala

Finding Paradise

WE WALKED, JOKING AND LAUGHING, stopping to kiss every few steps, our hungry hands pressing the half moons under our back pockets, Pol's cock pushing against my lower belly, his tongue dancing, teasing, exploring, a matador's cape inciting my desire. Everything else fell away like an old theater backdrop that crumbles under the weight of time. Only he remained, and the streets of Barcelona opening up like a flower.

Books, booze, and life bled into each other as we carved rites to honor our heroes. We drank tequila and mezcal while reading Malcolm Lowry's *Under the Volcano*, the writer's binges absolving our own benders. We frequented Bar Marsella in Calle San Pablo, the oldest bar in Barcelona, which was rumored to have been a favorite of Picasso's. There we sat among bottom-rung prostitutes, semi-indigent old geezers, and a smattering of artists at precariously tilted small tables with round marble tops. We ordered absinthe, the drink par excellence of the decadent nineteenth-century French poets. The elaborate ritual of balancing a flat spoon full of holes on the rim of the glass, placing a sugar cube on top, and pouring water on it from a glass decanter had its own charm. The dissolved sugar pared down the blast of the absinthe, its green color muddying in tandem with our minds. Here we were, brother and sister in arms to Baudelaire, Verlaine, and Rimbaud and, like them, over one hundred years later, walking a city for hours on end, capturing its ragged beauty—if not in written verse, in spoken word. Each author blessed a particular brand of drunkenness.

A pocket-sized bar called Pastís on a side street at the end of Las Ramblas was a favorite hangout. The owner played only Edith Piaf songs and we drank *pastís* exclusively, the sweet anise-flavored liquor becoming palatable only because it paid homage to the tragic French singer.

I adapted to Pol's routine, forgoing my natural tendency toward early mornings to soak into his long-drawn-out nights. Before lunch it was beer; with lunch, cheap red wine mixed with seltzer water. The afternoons were perfect for sitting on a café terrace sipping a cognac and watching the world go by, the slow burn in my throat warming up my outlook. Sometimes Pol got into an almost catatonic state—not a word, an occasional cigarette, an occasional sip. We spent an hour or two hardly speaking. I don't know if he thought about anything in particular during those times or if he just existed. I was content to exist alongside him.

In the early evening, I switched to tequila straight up, not only because I liked the taste but because I loved placing grains of salt in the fold between my thumb and index finger, licking it, quickly downing a shot of tequila, and immediately squeezing a slice of lemon between my teeth. Late evenings were for mixed drinks.

I didn't care where we went, what we did. Sometimes we met with friends; other times we ran into friends. I followed Pol's lead in our nightly pilgrimage to bars in the Borne neighborhood, always popping with writers, actors, and musicians standing in front of the counter, talking shit. I was replacing the Catholic rituals of my childhood with the ceremonies of cultivated barflies.

Pol never looked drunk. The slow drip of booze throughout the day allowed him to maintain the same deceiving decorum that

Malcolm Lowry treasured. He became a little quieter, his step a little slower, with every drink. I became loquacious, more daring. I leaned on Pol a little harder when we retraced our steps from the Borne to the Ramblas and San Pablo.

Sometimes on the way home our kisses escalated to fondling, his hand inside my shirt, inside my pants, on my crotch. Once the urge was so acute that we stepped inside an apartment building's lobby, tearing our clothes off in the dark, him pressing me against a wall. He was already inside me when the street door opened and a guy yelled, "Get out of here or I'll call the police!" We pulled up our pants and ran out laughing, eager to get home, where the thrust of his body against mine would end up with a thousand exquisite deaths and a lingering in a space out of thought, out of time, out of place.

I had never felt this way before. I'd felt anticipation, tenderness, excitement, and even some pleasure with previous lovers, but I'd never been able to let myself truly go. Now, with every fuck, I got suddenly tossed into a black hole and landed in paradise. Our bodies dissolved into one, and everything righted itself in the world.

Foreplay was poems recited, songs sung, dances danced, laughs shared, driving to Pol's kisses, the weight of his body over mine, his soft skin, his long limbs and narrow chest, his shoulders already a little hunched, as if he mixed adolescence and old age in the wisdom of his flesh. Looking at me without flinching, his wide mouth grimacing, his green eyes tying me to the now, nothing hidden. Him always on top, no frills or flourishes. There was something about our builds that made them fit like a perfect puzzle, something about the vibrancy of our touch that brought me to climax by his hand stroking my arm or his lips brushing my neck while we stood in a bar.

I was now finished with my BA. It was 1980, I was twenty-one, and I had no idea what to do next. Most of my classmates planned to become teachers in private schools or, after taking the entrance exams, in public schools—not much else to do with a BA in literature. A few would continue studying for a PhD. Now that Marea and I were not going to study together, I had ruled out that option. I wanted to work and become independent, but for now summer was here, and I didn't have a care in the world except what to plan next with Pol.

For the San Juan holiday on June 23, he had a three-day weekend. We decided to spend it at La Escala, a little seaside town. It was our first trip together. We didn't do much and didn't need much. Eat, drink, contemplate the sea sitting at a harbor café, walk, and make love. Everything went smoothly, as if the world had rolled down a red carpet so we could glide into a never-ending party.

On Saturday night, we enjoyed the fireworks—on the horizon, coming from another town—from the front-row seat of the beach, alone. As we were returning to the hotel, we heard music. We followed the sound and ran into a little *verbena*, an open-air dance festival celebrating San Juan, with colorful garlands hanging from trees, a table set with *sangría*, wine, olives, cheese, and cold cuts, and a few metal tables and folding chairs in a circle around a small stage on which was a five-piece band playing *paso dobles*, *chotis*, and other popular danceable Spanish music. It looked like a private event for the elders of the town, but Pol and I joined the couples serenely marching and twirling and drinking punch. They accepted us benignly, perhaps too surprised to scold the city youngsters who had crashed their party and were enjoying tunes from long ago alongside them. Sometimes an open smile is all you need to be forgiven for minor sins.

After a few dances we walked back to the hotel. That night, as we made love, Pol's slow, deliberate, rhythmic motion seemed to crash like waves over my whole body, taking me with irresistible force to that hidden world only we could enter.

"You are the sea," I said, caressing his back, bringing him deeper into me with my legs wrapped around his body. "You are the sea, you cover me all, you bring me life, you bring me death, you are the sea."

"I'm just a man," he said, bemused.

"No, you are the sea; you are MY sea."

I gave myself to him, letting the waves crash and cover me, lost in the salt of his sweat, the sounds of our moans, his eyes open wide, his buttocks hard under my palms, the smell of the Mediterranean on his curls, disappearing into that rich blackness where everything made sense.

The day we returned to Barcelona we ran into Marea on a street close to Las Ramblas. She looked shocked when she found us walking arm in arm.

"Where are you coming from?" she asked, surveying us from head to toe.

"We just came back from La Escala," I said.

"You went there by yourselves?" She sounded a little bewildered.

"Yes; we spent the weekend there. It was great, we ran into a *verbena*, and . . ."

Marea's face went white with anger.

"I don't have time to listen to your stupidities," she blurted. She turned around and walked rapidly in the other direction.

"What's the matter with her?" I asked Pol, genuinely shocked.

"Who cares? Don't worry about her."

But I couldn't let it go. Marea was already living with her new boyfriend. She knew Pol and I had hooked up occasionally in the past. Why get upset that we were together now when she was with another man?

Perhaps what bothered her was our trip. Marea and Pol had traipsed around Spain like insatiable vagabonds, visiting not only the big landmarks of Castile and surrounding regions but also all the little towns in between, searching for the extraordinary around every corner. Pol was the perfect companion for adventure trips with loose itineraries.

When we talked next, I discovered that was not what had bothered Marea. The same cruelty she had displayed when anybody angered her, she now directed to me.

"How can you date Pol knowing he was my boyfriend?" she asked. "That's disgusting. Do you like to play second fiddle? That figures, since you can never get the first." She smirked, her eyes like daggers.

After that, our friendship was over.

Soon after our encounter, her boyfriend got a job as an interpreter somewhere in Africa and they married so she could join him. Years later, my friend Angela ran into her at Las Ramblas, pushing a stroller with a baby and watching a toddler.

I never saw Marea again, but I'm grateful to her for teaching me that a woman could be strong and fearless and show every part of herself without apologizing. I was not yet as brave, but through her, Pol, and encountering salsa I had reclaimed a part of me suppressed over decades that savored pleasure and play, even if it was still embedded within a fractured mind.

It didn't escape me that Marea's strength and energy echoed Mama's, though for Marea rebellion was a favorite sport while Mama rebelled only when she was mad or she felt her territory threatened.

The first time I witnessed Mama's defiance, she was driving us to school. We came up on a big line of cars. The traffic light was not working, and the cars crossing perpendicular to us kept zooming through while the drivers on our street, either timid or distracted, stayed still.

"We're going to be late. Why aren't these people going forward?" Mama was a stickler for punctuality, and she got impatient when others didn't move as efficiently as she did.

After a couple of minutes, bursting with frustration, she honked twice. Very long honks. "Move already! We're going to be late!" More honks.

Suddenly a policeman on a motorcycle stopped at Mama's side and knocked on her window.

"What does this one want, now?" Mama rolled down the window.

"Ma'am, honking is forbidden. I'm going to fine you for disturbing the peace."

"What? How come you're fining me instead of the drivers in front? I'm trying to get my kids to school and they're making us late. You should fine THEM!"

"I'm sorry ma'am, but the drivers in front are not breaking the law. You are."

"That's not fair! You're going to fine me for honking a couple of times when these guys are creating a bottleneck? And of top of that, now YOU are making us late! Why don't you do something useful and manage the traffic at the intersection instead?"

Mama's voice rose like milk boiling over, but the policeman didn't bother answering. He finished writing the slip and handed it to her.

"Here is your fine, ma'am."

"Well, this is what I do with your fine!" Mama tore the paper in a dozen small pieces and threw them on the pavement. We gasped. The policeman gasped. Mama rolled up her window and, seeing that the line of cars had disappeared, flew across the intersection.

I looked back. What if the policeman stopped us and took her to jail? But he was staring at our car rushing up the street, his mouth agape.

A notice of the fine still arrived at our home and Mama had to pay it, but I never forgot the mix of pride and terror—wrapped up in incredulity and adrenaline—that rocketed through me that morning.

Mama's indomitable spirit was legendary in our family. A few years later, she was struck by a motorcycle and was taken to hospital by ambulance. An old friend happened to be out on the street when she had the accident and went with Mama to the hospital. Mama hated ambulances and always said they went too fast. She refused to lie on the gurney, alleging that she was perfectly fine and nobody would force her to lie down as if she were an invalid. There was no convincing her. In the end, her friend had to lie on the gurney all the way to the hospital. Mama sat on a bench complaining that they were making too much of a fuss, that there was nothing wrong with her, and she demanded that the driver didn't go too fast and didn't turn on the siren. At the hospital, an x-ray revealed she had a broken pelvis. She spent the next two months lying immobile on her bed, which must have been torture.

When she was in her late eighties, she forgot a pot on the stove and the kitchen caught fire while she was dozing in the living room after lunch. A neighbor saw smoke coming out of the house and alerted the fire department. Firemen broke a window to enter the apartment and rescue Mama, who had slept through the commotion. When a fireman picked her up so he could take her outside the apartment in a hurry, this diminutive lady kicked him and punched him until he put her back on the floor. She was perfectly able to walk out on her own, thank you very much.

In and Out

I RANG THE BELL WITH ANTICIPATION, remembering that day, almost two years before, when I had rung the bell of this same apartment for the first time. After a few seconds, Pol opened the door.

"Hello, gorgeous." He kissed me lightly on the lips. Then he saw my suitcase. "Are you going somewhere?"

"I'm coming here to live with you!"

"Oh! That's a . . . nice surprise."

I beamed.

"I told my parents I'd spend the summer with you and, if everything worked out, I'd move in permanently."

"And what did they say?"

"They weren't happy, but what could they say? I'm of legal age."

I saw again Mama's worried face. I heard the disappointment in her voice. I was almost twenty-two years old, but in Spain children did not leave their parents' house until they got married, whether they were eighteen or thirty-five. My three older brothers had followed that pattern, staying home until their wedding days, and my older sister still lived with my parents. A young woman leaving her family's home to live with a man without being married was unheard of in our circle.

Mama tried to convince me to stay.

"Why do you need to live with him? Can't you just date him?"

"I love him, and I want to see if our relationship can work."

"But how are you going to support yourself? You don't even have a real job. Babysitting and tutoring won't be enough to pay the bills. Does he make enough money to support you?"

"I'll find a full-time job."

"Who is this man, anyway? We haven't even met him!"

"I'll introduce him to you later on," I said, although I had no plans to introduce Pol anytime soon. I couldn't imagine him in the same room as my parents. They were from different planets.

"I can't force you to stay, but I think you're making a mistake," said Mama.

Papa didn't talk. He kept shaking his head, his eyes trained on the ground.

I waited until they left for San Julián that weekend, the beginning of summer vacation, to pack my bag. I yearned to be with Pol. I hadn't asked him if he wanted to live with me. I wanted to surprise him. His tenderness, our passion, our intimacy, our constant play and wonder had surely weaved an airtight net to catch us if either of us faltered.

I unpacked my bag while Pol looked on. It was hard to believe my clothes now hung on the same hangers that had held Marea's shirts and pants. I hugged Pol and we fell on the bed. We made love hungrily, still half-dressed. When we finished, Pol stayed on top of me for a few minutes. I moved my body against his, getting him hard again. We climaxed a second time, which was as perfect as the first. We always went for doubles. I couldn't get enough of him, his scent, his voice, his touch.

That month of July we spent weekends in a little town where Pol's friends were working on a new play. They all lived together in a house and wrote the play collaboratively, as several theater troupes did at the time. It was a fascinating process, but as much as I enjoyed observing it, I noticed that whenever we got there, Pol spent more time with them than with me.

As the days went by, he pulled away. His catatonic state, which up to then had flared up from time to time, perhaps as a way to battle a hangover, invaded longer stretches of the day. His silences drowned me. I wasn't sure what was going through his mind, but I tried to ignore it. It was easier to focus on the unexpected adventures of every day.

The same unease I felt was overtaking the country. The majority party in Congress, the centrist UCD, was falling apart. As the right and left parties teetered to the center, many UCD members abandoned ship and joined them. Adolfo Suárez, UCD's leader and the president of the government, had fallen in disgrace. The Socialist party had presented a motion of censure in May, alleging that he was negotiating with terrorists, and almost gotten him impeached. An undercurrent of discontent from the extreme right and the armed forces brewed in the shadows. Spain was sitting on a ticking time bomb. So was I.

One night, Pol and I were coming back from our usual barhopping when I felt dizzy. I had drunk a lot, and I could hardly walk.

"Let's sit at Las Ramblas for a while," said Pol. "The air will do you good."

We sat on two chairs on the right side of the promenade, in the front row. It was five o'clock on a Sunday morning and nobody was collecting chair-rental money. Two guys and a girl seated in the back row were talking loudly. I turned my head slightly. They seemed young, around seventeen or eighteen. The girl had a ring in her nose and a mobile, expressive face.

"What are you looking at, blondie? Are you spying on us?" she said.

"Not at all." I looked away.

"Did you guys see that? Blondie is spying on us. What the hell! Who does she think she is?" She spoke in a piercing tone.

"Yeah, who does she think she is?" said one boy.

"She's going to get it!" said the other.

"I wasn't spying on you." I looked back and saw one of the boys put his hand in his pocket. He briefly showed a knife's handle. I grabbed Pol's arm.

"We should go," he whispered.

"I'm too woozy to get up," I whispered back.

We remained seated.

"You don't know who you're messing with, missy!" said the girl, pushing my back.

"Why are you pushing me? I didn't do anything to you," I complained with a furry tongue.

"Ah, no? And how about spying on us, eh?" She pushed me again.

Pol turned around. "We don't want any trouble. She's drunk and can't walk right now. I'm sorry if she bothered you."

The girl examined Pol critically for a moment. He sounded like her, like a guy from a popular *barrio* of Madrid, and he looked the part too. Her friends kept jeering and mocking me.

"Shhh, shut up, you idiots," the girl said. They fell silent. "Don't you see the little princess drank too much and can't hold her liquor?"

They all laughed.

"I like your earrings," said the girl, changing tactics. "Can I try them on?"

I brought my hand to my ear. These earrings were my favorite pair: long, dangling brass pendants, with a complicated pattern opening up in a teardrop shape, the filigree set with amethysts. I had bought them at a craft stand on Las Ramblas a couple of years before and I wore them often.

"Well, are you going to let me try them or not?" insisted the girl.

Her friends heckled me, as if I were a wayward sheep they were trying to bring to the pen. Their voices made me queasy.

"Don't be so selfish!"

"Come on!"

"Do it, blondie!"

I turned around. "These are my favorite earrings and . . ."

Suddenly, the girl reached for my ears and pulled my earrings out. They didn't have studs, so they were easy to remove.

"These are your favorite earrings?" said the girl. "They're trash!" She hurled them on the pavement in front of me.

Right at that moment the city cleaning crew was coming down Las Ramblas with a high-pressure water hose, erasing from the ground the empty wrappers, the cigarette stubs, the stinky pools of vomit, so the Sunday crowds would enjoy their leisurely family walks. The jet hit my earrings with full force. They disappeared down the street, pushed by the torrent of water.

It happened so fast that I froze on the chair, shocked.

"She threw my earrings away!" I said to Pol as if he hadn't seen it. The words had trouble coming out of my mouth. I heard the hoots and laughs of the gang muffled in the background as if I were underwater, trying to come up for air.

"Let's get the hell out of here," said Pol. He grabbed me by the arm and dragged me away while the gang continued hollering and mocking me.

We were a couple of blocks from home. I walked beside Pol, hanging on to his arm so I could walk straight, my skin covered in goose bumps. I kept repeating, "She threw my earrings away. Why did she do that? Why?"

"What were you thinking?" Pol groaned. "Why did you even

engage those hooligans? Didn't you see they were dangerous? You don't know how to handle these thugs. You could have gotten us both killed."

Tears poured down my face as torrentially as the water that had swept my earrings away. I couldn't see the ground in front of me. Pol softened his voice,

"Don't cry. We're okay; that's what matters."

But I couldn't stop crying. I was crying for the anger in his voice and for my lost earrings, but also because I couldn't comprehend that there were people who found pleasure in hurting others, people who harmed you because it made them feel powerful.

I thought darkness was something you fought against even though it was a part of you, as it was a part of everyone. But that girl had reminded me how vulnerable we all are, how we all can be mistreated for no good reason. No matter what Pol said, I knew that she hadn't taunted me and thrown my earrings in the street because I'd done anything wrong. She did it only to gain the admiration of her buddies. For her, I was a zero, a non-being, a nobody. And we could all be nobodies for another person under the right circumstances. That's what truly hurt.

We arrived home and went to bed. Pol tried to console me, with no success. He gave up and fell asleep. I kept sobbing. Sensing the imminent loss of our relationship, despair overtook me. I would again be facing the somber side of life alone. All the instances of wickedness and misery I knew about came to my mind, from the smallest of faults to the purest of evils: Mary the maid who blamed me to save Gemma when we painted a wall; my body crushed at six years old against my will; me pressing a young child for a few seconds against my crotch; the men laughing at me and my sister during horseback riding lessons; the thoughtless boy who forced my hand on his cock; my thoughtless pull to seduce partnered men so I could gain their tenderness; my friends lost to suicide and to heroin; the dissidents executed by the Franco regime, which had first awakened my political conscience; the kidnapped, tortured, and murdered bodies in Argentina and Chile that my buddies at La Torre had known firsthand; the innocent victims of the terrorist group ETA; the women raped, molested, punched, and harassed everywhere.

I remembered Primo Levi's book *If This Is a Man*, which I had read as a teenager. He detailed the atrocities he had witnessed and suffered himself as a Jewish prisoner in Auschwitz. The horror of his experience was attenuated by an Italian civil worker, Lorenzo Perroni, who every day risked his life to give Levi a piece of bread through the metal fence of the concentration camp. When I read that scene, I vowed that I would always try to be like Lorenzo Perroni and bring a little light and kindness to those around me. I often failed, but at least I strove to do, and be, better.

The unbearable knowledge that some people don't give a damn about hurting, abusing, and killing whoever gets in their way and that, in spite of my best intentions, I too could hurt others ripped my insides.

I fell asleep at close to eight a.m., exhausted. I woke up three or four hours later, when I heard Pol stir.

"How are you?" he said. He was sitting on the bed, his pants already on. "You look awful."

I felt awful. My head was exploding, and my limbs weighed a ton.

"I'm going out for breakfast. Do you want to come?"

I didn't want to get up and face the world, but staying alone in the apartment with my misery seemed even worse.

"Give me a minute to wash my face."

I got up slowly and walked to the bathroom. My reflection in the mirror said it all. My eyelids were so swollen that my eyes were slits, with dark circles underneath and boogers in the corners. My hair was tangled, my lips chapped, my skin dry, pale, and suddenly aged. I stank. I washed old sweat from my underarms with a hand towel and soap and old booze from my mouth with toothbrush and toothpaste. Too bad I couldn't wash away the dread that filled my chest.

I splashed some water on my face, bunched up my hair in a ponytail, and peed. Sitting on the bowl, lifeless, I thought I would not be able to get up again. I forced myself to stand and walk back to the bedroom. Pol was sitting in the living room smoking a cigarette. I put on a pair of jeans and a T-shirt.

"Let's go," I said.

We walked to a café in the small square that was close to the house and ordered coffee. I wasn't hungry, but I ordered a croissant anyway, hoping it would settle my stomach. Pol read the paper. I didn't say anything or do anything other than slowly force bites of the croissant down my throat and drink the coffee.

After about twenty minutes, Pol looked up from his newspaper.

"How are you doing? Hungover?"

"A little." That was an understatement. "I can't get over what happened yesterday."

Pol moved his hand as if trying to swat my words away.

"Let it go, won't you? They were punks. You're too thin-skinned, Isadora. You're not made for street life."

The tone of his voice put me on high alert. It felt like a definitive judgment that divided us, him the street-smart guy who handled anything that came his way, me the naïve dilettante who drowned in a drop of water.

Maybe he was right that I couldn't handle certain situations, but I could certainly handle being with him. I hoped he saw that, but I knew the distance opening between us had grown with last night's incident. Our relationship was disintegrating. Would I be kicked to the curb or barely survive an attempt as Suárez had survived the motion of censure?

The next day Pol went back to his job at Telefónica after a couple of weeks of medical leave. Since it was summer and everyone was out of school and on vacation, I had no tutoring or babysitting lined up. The money I'd been saving during the year was dwindling. I needed a source of income, but I couldn't focus on finding work. When Pol was away, I read and cleaned the apartment like a little girl playing house.

"I'm a bad influence on you," said Pol that evening.

"What do you mean?"

"You should be out there working at a school or a university. This life is not for you."

"But I'm happy here with you. There are no teaching jobs during the summer. I'll find something soon."

He shook his head but didn't add another word.

The following weekend, the last of July, Pol went out on Saturday night without me. He said he needed a night alone. He came back at dawn, drunk, and fell asleep right away. I got up on Sunday and tiptoed around, cooking. I wanted to have a nice lunch ready when he woke up.

He stayed mute while we ate.

"Why are you so quiet? Is everything okay?"

"I need to talk to you," he said gravely. "You're a great girl; I love being with you, but . . ."

When I heard "but" my heart started racing.

". . . it's been only a few months since I broke up with Mar, and I'm not ready to live with another woman yet. It's too soon for such a big commitment."

My throat closed and my sight blurred. I tried to contain the tears, but they slipped out. I couldn't find my voice.

"Isadora, please don't cry. I'm not ending our relationship. I just need to take things more slowly."

He caressed my cheek, and dried my tears with his thumb. A little voice inside me kept repeating, *I knew I couldn't compare to Marea! I knew you would never love me as much as you loved her!*

The fact that I had precipitated his retreat by showing up at his door with a suitcase a few months after we'd started dating didn't cross my mind. I was too used to my pattern of self-doubt, to interpreting every rejection as something I caused instead of accepting that the timing, the other person's needs, and the circumstances also weighed in. If he didn't want to live with me, it had to be because I wasn't worthy of his love and commitment, not because he wasn't ready to commit.

"I'm serious," he said. "I want to keep seeing you. I just don't want to live together yet. I'm going to move to my friends' house in a few weeks. I can't afford this apartment anymore, and I can't go there with you."

I still couldn't speak. Pol hugged me. I let myself be kissed, taken to bed, caressed, and undressed, like a rag doll. He made love to me slowly and tenderly. That powerful wave lifted me up, covered me, and laid me to rest, making me forget everything around me for a few minutes.

After we turned off the light, I whispered, "I'll leave tomorrow."

Pol hugged me and whispered back, "I'm sorry. I love you, Isadora."

We went to sleep as we often did after making love, him wrapped around me, his chest on my back, his legs following mine, his hand on my belly, his mouth on the back of my neck, in that tender embrace that made me feel safe, a safety that I now knew was not to last.

Test Time

AFTER POL LEFT FOR WORK, I packed my suitcase and returned to my parents' home in Avenida del Tibidabo. It was the first week of August, and the whole family was in San Julián. I decided to stay a few days in Barcelona to pull myself together.

That evening Pol called to ask how I was doing. He said he missed me, and we made plans to go to a play the next day. After the play he asked me to stay overnight. We made love, but I couldn't let myself go. I observed our bodies from that place inside myself where nobody ever found me. Pol didn't notice.

The next day I caught a train and a bus to San Julián. I arrived around one in the afternoon. My siblings were at the pool, as usual; Papa was out, perhaps painting or golfing, his new hobbies; Mama was alone in the kitchen preparing lunch.

"Hi," I said.

"What are you doing here? I thought you were in Barcelona."

"No. I'm coming home."

"Do you mean for the summer?"

"No, for good."

She opened her mouth to say something, then stopped herself. "Okay," she mumbled, returning to her pots.

Sometimes the lack of communication in my family came in handy. The last thing I wanted was to talk about what had happened. I was still trying to make sense of it myself.

I spent the next three weeks in a daze. I read Agatha Christie novels, went to the pool, and hung out with my summer friends, trying to distract myself.

Toward the end of August, Mama asked what my plans were for the year. I had no idea what I wanted to do with my life. Planning for the future was impossible when it took all I had to get up in the morning, but I couldn't tell her that. I said I would study for the entrance exams to get a permanent position as a teacher in public school. Most people in Spain considered landing a permanent government job or teaching position the ultimate success. The prospect of staying in the same job all my life didn't hold much appeal for me, but I lacked the energy and focus to figure out what else to do.

The exams were held in June in Madrid. They were very competitive. People studied for months and often had to take them two or three times. When we got back to Barcelona at the end of August, I teamed up with a girl I had met at university to tackle the enormous reading list and exchange notes. I also found a job as a nanny working from eight to three every day and a second job, through an agency, giving private English lessons. I chose to stay in my old room in the basement and save for a down payment on my own place. If I passed the exams, I'd probably get a position in a different city, so it didn't make sense to move out just for a few months.

I put on twenty pounds that winter. I started eating seconds with every meal, snacking between meals, curling up in bed on the weekends with Agatha Christie and a stack of cookies and chocolate. An hour after those were gone, I would get up to get a piece of bread, slather it with butter and add cold cuts. My lack of control disgusted me, but I didn't know how to stop. I had to fill up the emptiness.

In January, President Suárez, weakened by the internal dissension in his party, resigned his position. On February 23 of 1981, a session in Congress held to vote for his replacement transformed into a coup d'état. An army officer, Tejero, entered the House of Representatives with some two hundred guards and soldiers and held the congressmen hostage for eighteen hours. The discontent of the right wing, always brewing under the surface, had reached a boiling point. Our country had been bitterly divided—progressives versus conservatives—for almost two centuries. It seemed that fracture would never heal.

Like every Spanish family, we sat glued to the radio as one broadcaster from station SER kept recording and broadcasting, live, the sounds in the room, unnoticed by the assailants. All the other stations were playing military music. I was terrified, as if lost in the middle of a nightmare. Freedom was so fragile and complex . . . We had just gotten out of a dictatorship and now we were stumbling back in, just as I had been forced to retreat from my newfound independence.

Around one a.m., King Juan Carlos appeared on TV. He denounced the coup and upheld the continuation of the democratic process. We went to bed not quite relieved. Tejero and his soldiers still held the congressmen hostage. It would be noon the next day before they allowed them to leave.

As soon as they were set free, we watched a broadcast of the coup d'état on TV. The camera crews had been taping the congressional session so they could give a summary on the evening news. When Tejero entered the room, the TV crew kept filming for half an hour. They got everything: the yells of the guards; their orders for all present to throw themselves on the floor; the resistance that Lieutenant Colonel and Minister of Defense Gutiérrez Mellado and outgoing president Adolfo Suárez offered, confronting Tejero physically; the shots in the air; the panic. Watching the coup d'état on television, even the next day, shook us so deeply that many Spaniards remember it as if they had watched it in real time instead of twenty-four hours later.

After Tejero and the military officers who had plotted the coup surrendered, we all breathed easier. King Juan Carlos grew in stature. Spain kept making slow progress toward an imperfect, but functioning, democracy.

I also tried to make strides in rebuilding my life, but even though work and studies kept my days busy, in the evenings a persistent emptiness seemed to suck in my stomach. It needed filling.

Sometimes I called Pol, who now shared an apartment with his actor friends; other times I went for drinks in the Borne neighborhood, where I might run into him. Occasionally we spent the night together, but the spell was broken. When we made love, he went about it in his usual no-frills way. I kissed him, hugged him, and caressed him as if nothing had changed, but I didn't feel anything other than a longing for the magic we'd shared. I wondered what had ever been so arousing. I left his house in the morning promising myself that I wouldn't fabricate "spontaneous" encounters anymore.

I also picked up random lovers, one-night stands whose names and faces would soon blur. I'd go out, have a few drinks, and bring out Isadora, the confident, sensual girl who landed any man she wanted. I got a rush from inspecting the guys in a bar and deciding which one would be mine. I developed an infallible method. Look the man straight in the eyes, smile, ask a lot of questions, a hand on my waist to better flaunt my curves, hold a cigarette waiting to be lit.

For a few hours I felt powerful, in control, even though as soon as the clothes fell off, my walls came up.

There was the guy from Libya who insisted on positioning a

mirror to see me from all angles and who wouldn't stop calling me for weeks after that first night. I had no intention of seeing him again. The Catalan guy who yearned for his former girlfriend and said my short hair reminded him of her. I accidentally left a pair of earrings on his bedside table, but he never responded to my phone messages. The American guy who belonged to a strict church and was a virgin; his guilt after I deflowered him brought me more perverted pleasure than the sex. I happened to have my period and the red stains on his white thighs compounded his horror.

There was the chef I'd met earlier whom I seduced right at his restaurant, in the middle of dinner service. We had sex in the broom closet on the second floor while diners chatted downstairs, scarcely ten feet away: a thrilling turn-on. We met a few more times, but he pulled away when I tried to get closer.

There was the famous poet who insisted on keeping his undershirt on while we had sex. And my younger brother's friend, whom I pulled aside during a party at home, took downstairs to my bedroom, and had sex with while the party went on upstairs. It was this guy's first time, and he was smitten. We went on a couple of dates, but after the rush of conquest I lost interest. Since he liked fine wines, I sent him on his way with a parting gift, the silver wine taster my cousin Carlos had given me as a farewell present when I left his hotel in France at nineteen. I had a compulsion to leave meaningful things behind, as if attachment to objects were as dangerous as attachment to people.

There was also the Dutch guy I met dancing salsa who penetrated me forcefully, even though I tried to stop him, palms on his chest, too wasted to kick him in the balls. After a few minutes I let him do his thing. Hadn't it been me who drank too much, who approached him, who seduced him? Perhaps I deserved being unheard, being unseen, being unloved, being mistreated. It had always been my place. He confirmed it.

An episode of this kind got me off the streets for a month or two, but I soon went back love hunting. Two or three nights a week, I did the rounds of the Borne bars, got drunk, and went dancing at Tabú. Salsa was the only place I felt comfortable in my skin. The few hours I spent in that dark, run-down club were my slice of heaven. As soon as I heard the drums, the piano and the strings, the winds and the singers, I forgot everything that ailed me. I let myself ignite with the heat of my body.

Most times I came home curled in the corner of a taxi's backseat at four or five in the morning. I staggered to the kitchen, cut the tip off a baguette, slathered it with butter, added two slices of ham and forced it down my throat before falling into a dreamless sleep. The next day I had trouble remembering why I had a lighter I didn't own in my pocket, where the money I'd had in my wallet went, whom I'd met, and what I'd said. I considered myself lucky if I'd made it home in one piece instead of going to bed with somebody I didn't care about.

June came, and I traveled to Madrid for the entrance exams. My study buddy and I took a double room in a cheap motel. The exams would take place on two separate days. I had lost interest months ago.

The morning of the first exam, I must have been the only one in that humongous room without an ounce of nervousness. I answered the questions summarily and left the building before anyone else. I went to Plaza Mayor in Madrid's downtown, sat at an outdoor table at a bar, and ordered a beer and a couple of tapas. I knew my friend would go back to the motel to study, but I didn't plan to open a book.

I was on my second beer when a guy approached me. He was about my height, tanned skin, short black hair, an Alain Delon with dark brown eyes instead of blue. He was dressed casually but sharply in a fitted light blue button-down shirt with the first three buttons open, showing curly chest hair and a gold chain, tight dark blue jeans, and navy blue penny loafers.

"Hello," he said in English. "Are you alone? Would you like company?" He flashed the whitest teeth and put his hand on the back of my chair.

"Yes, I am, and yes, I'd like company," I answered in Spanish.

"Ah! You are Spanish!" he switched to Spanish. "You look British or German."

"I'm from Barcelona. I'm here to take the entrance exams."

"Did you finish the exams already?"

"No. But I don't care. I want to enjoy Madrid."

"Well, I'd love to help you enjoy it."

"That sounds promising."

He sat with me. I had always loved listening to people's stories, and his was fascinating. He was a playboy, a *real* playboy, who lived off European tourists who came to Spain on vacation to find sun, fun, and a passionate Spanish lover. He provided the fun and the passion, and they provided him with meals, luxury hotel rooms, money, and a good life. July and August, he cruised beaches along the Costa Dorada. The rest of the time he stayed in Madrid, looking for prey at the Plaza Mayor, a tourist attraction.

He had begun his career in the early seventies by chance. He wanted to have sex and the *suecas*—the Swedish girls who came in droves in the summer—were happy to oblige at a time when Spanish girls still kept their legs closed tighter than a strongbox. When he realized there was money to be made, he specialized in the trade. Even now that landing Spaniards was as easy as landing the rest, he kept pimping himself out.

He showed me around a few quaint neighborhoods of Madrid and later took me to dinner. He insisted on treating me, lest I think he was trying to drain my wallet, too. After dinner, we went to his home, and he displayed the rest of his professional arsenal: an ability to have intercourse four or five times a night. It was a question of letting enough time pass between one fuck and the next, he explained, and keeping his partner entertained in other ways while waiting for his mojo to come back. He told stories and jokes, did impersonations, and even sang. I would have preferred to catch some sleep, but he was intent on showing off his entire repertoire of amatory feats. It was exhausting.

The next day I showed up at the examination room half asleep. As soon as I read the questions, I knew it was hopeless. I tore the paper in two, threw it in the trash can, and left. On the way back to Barcelona, I swore I would jumpstart a new path. I was done with meaningless jobs and meaningless lovers.

Comfort Food

"YOU GUYS WANT TO COME TO MY HOUSE? I have homemade chicken soup."

I looked at my friend, then at Leo, who had made that kind offer. At five in the morning, after three hours of dancing, a comfort meal was tempting.

I had met Leo a week or two earlier at someone's house. He was from Colombia and had come to the city on a fellowship to take doctoral courses in communications. He wanted to meet again, but I didn't give him my number. We'd had a pleasant conversation, but my head was in a different place. I was applying for jobs at private schools and trying to stay focused.

When my college buddy and I ran into him at Tabú, I discovered that Leo was an excellent dancer. My friend didn't care much for salsa. I had dragged him to Tabú after dinner, as I did everyone. Usually, my pals would flee after an hour or so, bored to tears, but I remained, too entranced with the music and the dancing to leave before the last note.

That night, my college buddy stayed, perhaps hoping that we would end the night together. He spent most of the evening in his seat while I danced with Leo, delighted with his moves and his flexibility when I turned to the wrong side. Leo would laugh, change his step, and catch up with me. It tickled me how sometimes he got transported, let go of me, and did quirky things like pulling himself up with two fingers on the back of his neck, as if he were lifting a puppet, while sliding his feet from wide open to closed.

Now a bowl of steaming chicken soup shimmered between us. Before my friend opened his mouth, I jumped in.

"Sounds good to me! What do you say?"

"I guess . . ." said my friend.

We walked from Tabú to Leo's apartment, a twenty-minute stroll crossing the old neighborhood where I had lived with Pol, until we reached Ronda de San Antonio.

Leo lived alone on the fourth floor of an apartment building. Luckily, it had an elevator. That was not the only perk compared to Pol's living arrangements. The apartment was neat and tidy, and the furniture, though scarce and simple, was all in one piece. We went to Leo's bedroom, where he had a small radio, so we could listen to music while we ate. It had two single beds covered with thin blue-and-white bedspreads, a bedside table in the middle with several books piled on it, the radio on the floor between his bed and the window, and a cheap dresser in front of the beds with a small TV on top, the antennae precariously canted to the right.

Leo turned the radio to a jazz station.

"I'll bring the soup in a minute."

As soon as he left the bedroom, my friend said, "You're not planning to stay long, right?"

"Oh, no, we'll eat the soup and leave."

"Okay."

Leo came back with two bowls of soup. My friend didn't want any. I brought the first spoonful to my mouth. The broth was clear and fragrant, with tender chicken, carrots, potatoes, and pieces of corn. I detected onion and garlic, but there was also an herbaceous flavor I couldn't pinpoint. I had never tasted it before.

"It's so good! What have you used? There's a different flavor to it."

"It's *guasca*, an herb we use in Colombia to make *ajiaco*, a traditional soup. This is not *ajiaco*, but my mother sent me some *guasca* and I seasoned the broth with it."

"I love it!" Each spoonful bathed my insides with a feeling of well-being.

I looked around. There were several Latin American authors in the tower of books on Leo's bedside table, along with a smattering of European writers.

"How did you like Vargas Llosa's latest novel? I enjoyed his first books more," I said.

It was like opening a high-pressure faucet. We chatted away about Vargas Llosa, García Márquez, Cortázar, and other authors. The empty bowl of soup lay forgotten on the floor. My friend whispered a couple of times, "Shall we go? It's six already." Later, "It's almost six thirty." But I was immersed in that passionate back and forth about books that had first drawn me to Marea. At some point, my friend got up and left the room. I thought he was going to the bathroom, but I heard the front door open and close.

"Wow, he left without even saying goodbye," I said.

"Do you mind?" asked Leo.

I took him in: thick, black, longish hair swept back, exposing a wide forehead; soft brown eyes that slanted down at the corners, giving him an adorable puppy air; the nose shaped in a round, well-proportioned triangle; wide cheeks; full lips opened up in a radiant smile; and perfect white teeth. He looked warm and attractive, but more significantly, we spoke the same language, our conversation flowing as easily as our bodies had merged on the dance floor.

"No, I don't mind," I said.

I stayed with Leo the rest of the weekend. We spent Saturday walking around Las Ramblas and perusing books in various book-shops. Sunday afternoon, we went to the movies for a double feature. I noticed his eyes glued to my profile.

"You're going to miss the movie if you keep looking at me," I said a couple of times.

"I don't care. You are more interesting."

I will never forget the expression on his face. The tender smile, the surrendered eyes, the utter abandonment to his feelings.

That was Leo. From the first night we spent together he loved me without reservation and without fear of showing it. I wasn't used to being loved so fully, so openly, so tenderly, so steadily.

We were good for each other. We both loved reading, writing, salsa, and movies. We both loved Barcelona. We talked for hours, danced for hours, and stayed quietly by each other for hours, lost in books.

Two months after that first night, we were living together, begin-ning one of the happiest periods of my life, a happiness that seemed destined to last forever.

"Why did you let go of my hand?" I mumbled.

"Here, let me hold it again," said Leo.

Every night I fell asleep before Leo because I got up earlier. He kept reading and listening to jazz with the volume low until past midnight. We had moved the bedside table to one side and pushed the two single beds together. Leo always held my hand while I drifted off to sleep. If I woke up while he was still reading and noticed he'd let go, I complained.

We settled into our life together with marvelous ease. Leo was my beau, my reading buddy, my best friend. I was his muse, his com-panion, his beloved.

I had landed a full-time job at a Catholic high school teaching five classes a day. The school was in Sant Cugat, a town thirteen miles away from Barcelona; I had to take a train and a bus to get there. I left the house at seven a.m. and came back around four p.m. to correct homework and tests and prepare the next day's classes. Leo, meanwhile, stayed home reading and writing. He didn't need to work because the fellowship provided him with enough money to survive for a couple of years, but he rarely went to class. Instead, he read methodically, with as much insatiable thirst for words and stories as I'd always felt. I didn't resent his easy life. Coming home after the long commute and opening the door to find him lying in bed reading made me happy.

My teaching load was heavy, but I enjoyed it. I discovered I was good at making learning fun, and I delighted in my students' progress, but I raised a few eyebrows with my reading choices, especially when I commented on gay symbols in García Lorca and Cernuda's poems. A few students were novices on their way to becoming nuns, and they shot furtive glances at each other.

This school had stayed frozen in 1974, the year before Franco died. But it was 1982 and the PSOE—the Socialist Party—had won the general election with an overwhelming majority. It was the first time since before the civil war that Spain had a leftist government. The party's electoral slogan, "*Por el Cambio*" ("For the Change"), reflected this era of accelerated transformation.

The new president, Felipe González, and vice president, Alfonso Guerra, were in their early forties, and so were most of their ministers. Even if their politics were more center left than socialist, they offered a generational revolution. Power was now in the hands of the young.

There was an air of optimism in the streets that matched the excitement of my new adult life. While Spain still struggled in many areas—unemployment, terrorism, the closure of outdated factories demanded by industrial reconversion, and an epidemic of drug addiction and robberies to feed that addiction—Spaniards focused on enjoying life, the elite by speculating and amassing fortunes, the young by throwing themselves into music, movies, and nightly pilgrimages to fashionable bars.

Punk rock dominated the airwaves and TV programs, but I went in a different direction, plunging deeper into salsa with Leo by my side. We danced at Tabú two or three nights a week, going home early on weekdays and staying until close on weekends.

The club oozed passion and sweat, the perfect condiments for a sound born in the 'hood and corners of the Bronx and Manhattan, where Cubans and Puerto Ricans mixed their rhythms with jazz, R&B, boogaloo, soul, and disco. Salsa was a bastard music proud of its gritty identity, balancing on the fine edge of danger and excitement with sensual ease. It was not yet widely known in Barcelona, and Tabú's ambience was dicey. There were only a couple dozen people at the club most nights, only a few of them women. The majority were Latin American immigrants, with a sprinkling of Catalans who, like me, had fallen in love with the music.

These were not the white-collar immigrants who had come to Spain from Argentina and Chile in the seventies to escape dictatorships and state-sanctioned terrorism. They came from the rougher neighborhoods of Colombia, Venezuela, and Central America in search of a better life. A few looked shady, but it didn't matter. They loved hard-hitting salsa. We were kin.

Tabú's owner, Paco, matched the neighborhood, the locale, and his patrons. He was handsome in a vulgar kind of way, with coarse features and a mop of straight brown hair that he swept back with his hand regularly. He spoke little and hardly ever smiled. Locked in the DJ booth at the end of the narrow dance floor, he watched everything like a prison guard during yard time. He didn't need a bouncer. He was beefy enough, and he had a cold, dangerous look that made it clear you were better off not crossing him.

His girlfriend, voluptuous and dark with a luxurious mane of black hair falling to her waist, tended bar. I once asked her why she didn't dance when we were the only people in the club instead of standing behind the counter for hours doing nothing.

"Oh, no, Paco would never allow me to dance," she whispered.

"He doesn't own you," I said.

"No, no, I could never cross him. Don't worry about me; I'm okay." She shot nervous glances at the DJ booth.

Paco's brother was as loquacious and flighty as Paco was brooding. He once invited us to his apartment after the club closed to continue the party. The mound of cocaine on the table confirmed he was a dealer. His little white poodle yipped at his heels until he let him lick some coke from his finger. The tiny dog went crazy, running, jumping, and doing summersaults. A few minutes later it was back at his heels asking for more. He obliged.

At Tabú, Paco played what he pleased and didn't take requests, but they weren't necessary. He had mastered a fierce repertoire. Palmieri, Cheo Feliciano, Celia Cruz, Rubén Blades, Tito Puente, Ray Barreto, Héctor Lavoe, Willie Colón, El Gran Combo, los Van Van . . . those were his heroes—and mine. I knew the lyrics of most songs by heart, the way the timbales would peel off in a crazy improvisation or the trombones would blow off the roof with their deep voice. Leo and I often sang in unison with the *soneros* while we were dancing. When Rubén Blades listed Latin American countries at the end of the tune, "Plástico," we yelled *"Presente!"* after each one, as if every country were a part of us.

With salsa, my body was free, and I felt confident of my appeal. It didn't matter that I had a boyfriend. Everybody danced with everybody else. We were there to pay homage to the way the music torched our veins, swung our hips, and moved our soul.

We often went to Tabú with Enrique, Leo's best friend, who was also from Colombia. Enrique was a wiry, harsh, complicated guy with short brown hair, a slightly pockmarked face, a straight pointy nose like a ram, green pupils on yellowed irises as if a dissolute life had permanently tainted them, thin lips, and a broken front tooth. Despite his acerbity, we immediately hit it off. His sense of humor and raw honesty drew me in, and his affinity for the rugged lining of life resonated with me.

He didn't have a formal education, but his curiosity and doggedness pushed him to engross himself in books, movies, and music and consider them without prejudice, drawing his own conclusions—which he would relate as if they were gospel—and relishing a good fight with whoever had a different opinion. He spent months rereading a book, digesting it in such a deep way that he would never forget its lessons.

Despite our different upbringings, an instant familiarity took root between us—a mix of affection, respect, and annoyance such as close siblings experience. And there was also the dancing. Enrique pulled me close and guided me with a firm hand. The electricity running through our bodies lit a fire in my gut. It was fortunate I wasn't physically attracted to him off the dance floor; we would have broken Leo's heart. Still, I had a crush on Enrique, a personality crush. I loved his intellect, his confidence, his roughness, and his vulnerability—which few people got to see. I don't know what he loved about me, but we became fast friends, a friendship that would last until his death three decades later, and which overcame disappointments, betrayals, and geographical distance.

Little by little all of Leo's friends became my friends, some of them for life. One was Gloria Cecilia Díaz, a children's book author. She had briefly dated Leo back in Bogotá, and when she came to Barcelona and contacted him, we became close. Gloria Cecilia used to tell me that she had never imagined Leo being in such a committed relationship because he had been a player in Bogotá. I knew this was true because Leo himself had told me he'd never been faithful to his previous girlfriends and that he had learned to love by loving me. Perhaps it was because we were a match at every level: intellectual, emotional, and musical.

Our relationship was serious, so I introduced him to my family. Mama agreed to meet him, but she wasn't happy about it. I'm not sure if it was because we were living together without getting married or something else because she never told me, and I didn't ask. She treated Leo politely but coldly. The rest of the family greeted him pleasantly but detachedly, not making much conversation, as was their habit. We didn't go visit often.

It bothered me that Mama didn't make an effort to be warmer, but I was too happy to ruminate about it. I loved my life with Leo, our shared passions, our outings with interesting friends, many of them writers, and the immense tenderness we shared. I enjoyed living in a working-class neighborhood in the heart of Barcelona instead of in a tower atop a hill. This life felt real, as if I had finally met my destiny.

There was only one problem: as much as I adored Leo, I didn't much desire him.

From the beginning, sex with Leo, for me, was less important than the rest, but the first few months it excited me. After the initial sensual rush subsided, sex became a necessary ingredient in our relationship, like water is for boiling pasta, but not the spice that gave it flavor. Coming from my torrid union with Pol, the contrast was jarring.

I liked Leo's mouth, his long-fingered hands, his hair, and his lean, tanned legs. I liked hugging him and kissing him, but no matter how much I tried, I couldn't feel that tightening in my belly that would make my skin tremble and my heart race. We talked about it, I cried about it, but I didn't know how to change it. Love and commitment for me spelled domesticity and loyalty, not eroticism.

This lack of lust kept me up at night. I'd go to sleep holding Leo's hand at eleven o'clock, wake up at two, and toss and turn until five in the morning worrying about it.

Between the insomnia, my busy schedule, and moving from the typical three-course Spanish meals at my parents' home to the simplified one-dish meals we put together, I lost twenty pounds in the first six months we lived together and never put them back on. I was constantly nervous. I feared the relationship would disintegrate if our sex life didn't pick up.

One morning I was commuting to school with an old college girlfriend who took the same train. I was so exhausted from the lack of sleep and so anxious about the previous night's lovemaking, which had ended, as usual for me, in disappointment, that I couldn't keep it quiet any longer. I confided in her my dread that the relationship would peter out if I couldn't feel pleasure with the man I loved.

"The same thing happened to me and my husband," she said.

"Really?"

"Yes. We all grew up with a stigma around sex, believing that intercourse was for making babies and that pleasure was dirty. It screwed most of us up. My husband and I loved each other but when we made love, I was anxious, and it hurt down there."

"What did you do?"

"It took a lot of work, a lot of talking, a lot of patience, but I finally was able to break through my inhibitions. Now we still have off days, but most of the time I enjoy sex and we have a good time together."

This conversation gave me hope, but words couldn't quicken my pulse. In some subconscious part of my brain, striving for pleasure with Leo must have appeared dangerous. The impenetrable walls I had learned to build since I was a child, those that kept me from opening the door to intimacy so my most secret, vulnerable self wouldn't get smashed, went up automatically.

A few times the urgency in my gut awoke. One afternoon we made passionate love while Leo's uncle and his wife—who had come to live with us for a few months—napped blissfully in the other bedroom. It was that old pull of the transgression. Their closeness and the need to be hushed made it seem as if we were doing something forbidden behind their backs. That aroused me beyond my usual reticence.

When "mischief" wasn't part of the equation, the effervescence fizzled out like the gas in a bottle of Coke left open too long. It was sweet but it didn't thrill. I took to faking orgasms to avoid disappointing Leo.

Although the mismatch of our bodies tormented me, the meeting of our minds and the merging of our feelings were strong enough to pull us forward. We pushed each other in areas that mattered to us, like reading and writing. I had been a voracious reader since I was six, like everyone else in my family—books giving us the perfect way to remain isolated while together. Throughout my studies I had gained a robust knowledge of Spanish literature from medieval times to the present and a good command of modern Latin American writers and Ancient French literature. Now I settled into my own course of study, reading new authors at length: all of Proust, all of Flaubert, all of Celine, Sartre, Camus, Marguerite Yourcenar, Henry Miller,

Faulkner, Flannery O'Connor, Steinbeck, Scott Fitzgerald, Thomas Mann, Joyce, Milan Kundera, Italo Calvino, and dozens of contemporary Spanish novelists from Javier Marías to Muñoz Molina.

I had also been writing on and off since I was eleven—from short stories for school to poems and, later, lyrical prose fragments. Leo's commitment to becoming a writer inspired me to do more. I lacked time and energy to launch a solid practice during the week, but I put in time on the weekends.

Whose Family Is This?

LA SEÑORITA ANA MARÍA ASKED US to write a story every week. Sometimes she provided the topic; other times it was open. I would sit in the family room to write and lose track of time.

The first draft of a story came out with ease, but then I obsessed about every word and detail, refining them until I was satisfied.

Most weeks, the teacher would read my story aloud in class, and my classmates would ooh and aah. She even shared some of them with the school's director. Whenever she ran into Mama, she told her I had a lot of talent.

I was flattered by the praise and attention, but they weren't the main reason I kept applying myself. I simply enjoyed writing more than anything else I had ever done. The real world vanished while I focused on the worlds I created.

One week, la señorita Ana María asked us to write about our fathers. I pictured Papa coming back home from a business trip. How I had missed him! I greeted him with a hug and brought him his slippers. We all gathered around the fireplace in the living room to hear his tales. I sat at his feet, and he caressed my hair while he talked.

La señorita Ana María handed me back the story with a big red A underlined two times. "Show this one to your dad," she said. "It's so warm and beautiful . . . He will love it."

No way. If I showed it to Papa, he would know I had lied. Papa never went on business trips. I never brought him his slippers. In fact, he never wore slippers around the house. We never gathered around the fireplace to hear him talk. He was a man of few words. I never sat at his feet or felt his hand on my hair. These displays of affection were overly sentimental for our kind. I had written a story about the way I wanted our family to be, not the way it was. Perhaps all writers are liars.

I wonder now how my parents would have reacted if I had shown them the story. Would they have found it tender or too syrupy? What if they had shared it with my siblings? The story may well have proven that I fit the label they often used to describe me: I was *cursi* (corny). I knew Mama was proud of my writing feats because she mentioned them to my aunt during a visit to her new home, but perhaps she wouldn't have appreciated this one.

My cousin Sylvia and her family had moved that spring from their elegant flat to a modern house in Pedralbes, the toniest neighborhood in Barcelona, where people lived in single, newly built luxury homes instead of apartments.

As her family climbed steadily up, ours slipped steadily down. We still lived in the same four-story house with a big, terraced garden, but our lifestyle was coming loose at the seams. Papa spent hours silently pacing around the table in the foyer, his hands interlaced behind his back, his sight focused on the floor in front of his feet. It was a miracle he hadn't opened a trench. I thought he was lost in his usual daydreaming, but years later I heard my oldest brother say that Papa was tormented about money—or the lack of it. The "M word," however, was never mentioned at home. I'm not sure if that was an attempt to protect us from worry or simply the last remains of the chivalrous mentality that money wasn't a worthy topic to bandy about.

Perhaps Papa made less money as time went by, or expenses grew as the children got older, or inflation got the best of us. I don't know, but around that time a few clues that our finances were tight cropped up. One year my younger siblings and I didn't get textbooks until the second week of school because Mama could afford only my oldest siblings' books the first week. When we shopped for winter shoes, she insisted on the cheap, ugly, flat ones that lasted forever. We started to have lunch at home when paying for the school lunch became too expensive. The steaks we ate became thinner, and we had them less often.

Mama never mentioned these changes or complained about money troubles, but once I heard her say that school fees were a burden.

"Why don't you apply for fellowships? The school offers them," I suggested.

"There are other families that need a fellowship more than we do. When the day comes that we have to ask for help, we will, but for now, we can manage."

The day we went to visit Sylvia's new home in Pedralbes remains etched in my mind. It was a modern building with a flat roof and wall-to-wall windows overlooking a vast span of grass, a swimming pool, and the tennis court below it. The furniture seemed highly breakable or soil-prone: glass tables, white sofas, elegant lamps. The children's family room had its own TV.

Mama walked behind Tía Lolita while she gave her a tour. At some point, as Tía pointed out this or that feature, Mama started talking about the stories I wrote for school and the A's they garnered. It was typical of Mama to never offer praise directly to us but to praise what we did when talking to others. Was she trying to even the playing field with Tía through my academic success? A paltry offering compared to her overwhelming display of wealth.

I often had the uncomfortable sensation that we didn't measure up to Papa's side of the family. They were genuinely affluent, mostly through marriage, while Papa's income as a lawyer was stretched to the limit supporting a family of twelve, and we lived from envelope to envelope—the envelope filled with cash that Papa would hand to Mama every Friday for the weekly expenses. Of course, those expenses included renting a summer home, which put us squarely in a privileged middle class, but the descent in our status was becoming noticeable.

Mama didn't waste time lamenting her new circumstances. She kept herself busy, perhaps deriving her sense of accomplishment from the myriad tasks she undertook. She ferried us to school four times a day; planned the lunch and dinner menus; did the daily grocery shopping in a string of stores, her list neatly written in a tiny spiral notebook with a blue or red cover; ran errands; and took us to assorted doctor and dentist appointments. She also tended to various volunteering projects, from teaching Catechism in our school to volunteering biweekly in a facility for disabled patients. While she occupied herself with daily chores and philanthropic work, Tía Lolita managed her real estate holdings.

But it wasn't only the money that set us apart from the rest of the Mencos clan. It was also the attitude. At Tía's house, maids wore black uniforms with starched white aprons and white gloves. They served the table ceremoniously, seen but not heard. The everyday china was fine and the silverware silver. We, on the other hand, used thick green Duralex dishes for daily meals, and our maids had never worn uniforms. My older sister or I passed the platter around the table, first to Mama, who served half the kids, and then to Papa, who served the other half.

Not only were the house and service immaculate at Tía's house, she was perfectly coiffed, her hair in an artful bun, her face tastefully made up in a natural look. Preening in Tía's house was a plus, unlike in mine, where it was a frivolity. *"Para presumir hay que sufrir,"* Tía often said. ("To doll up, with pain you will put up.") She urged Sylvia to brush her hair a hundred strokes in the evenings so it would shine, a ritual that would have fit me like a glove because I was a girlie girl.

Mama was the polar opposite. She never wore makeup except for coral lipstick when she went out. As the years went on and our finances got tighter, she wore secondhand clothes from our aunts for days at a time. Her weekly visits to the hairdresser for a wash and blow-dry ended. Now she washed her hair at home and, since she had neither the know-how nor the patience or the vanity to style it, she always looked a little unkempt, her short hair falling flat above her ears.

Even though Tía's perfect demeanor and strict ways scared me a bit, I admired her way of smiling directly at you, as if you knew an inside joke that made you part of a select clan, and the fact that in her home, every issue came to the surface. Given her family's hot temper this could make for fiery disagreements, which probably weren't much fun, but at least the anger and unspoken conflicts didn't wither their insides.

None of this mattered when it came to my friendship with Sylvia. We saw each other less often since we weren't in the same grade at school, but when we spent time together on weekends, we got along as well as ever. Under all the polish, Sylvia had a misfit streak that matched mine; hers was expressed in rebelliousness at home and lackluster results at school, while I continued to be a good girl, my insurgency concealed under sheets, my secret constrained to the dark of night.

Love and Betrayal

MY RELATIONSHIP WITH LEO approached symbiosis. His undivided attention and adoration spoiled me. I needed it like a junkie needs her fix. Going without it for even a few hours, except when I was working, made me anxious.

Now that I had a full-time job and a steady boyfriend, the alcohol-soaked weekday afternoons of my time with Pol receded, but weekend outings with Leo sometimes became fourteen-hour marathons. From Tabú, we went to an after-hours club and then to a friend's house to continue drinking and dancing until midday Sunday. Leo got bombed in his usual harmless way, becoming a little more animated when dancing salsa, laughing louder, and sleeping deeper, but without creating a scene or going crazy.

"You must be the only person I know who becomes more lucid when she drinks," Leo's aunt said to me once. Alcohol didn't make me smarter, but it made me less shy. My good-girl quiet demeanor dissolved with the ice cubes at the bottom of my second drink, and out came that fearless woman who declared her literary opinions with confidence and subjugated a man with a sway of her hips.

After a few months of living together blissfully, Leo took to going out with Enrique on Thursday nights. I hated to be left alone every Thursday, but I had to teach the next day and I couldn't afford to be out late.

"Come on, Menquitos," he'd say, using my last name as an

endearment, as he often did. "You're going to sleep anyway and I'm not doing anything wrong, just having a few drinks with my friend."

I kissed him good night grudgingly, knowing that it was important for him to have that sliver of independence. Since he left around eleven o'clock, which was my usual bedtime, his absence didn't sting much. But if I woke up when he came back, I couldn't go back to sleep for a few hours, while he fell into a deep slumber. Insomnia had become a nightly habit.

One week after the school year was over, I received a call from the Mother Superior. She asked me to come visit. I came ready to discuss the following year's class schedule, but when I got there, she laid me off. She said it had nothing to do with my teaching abilities and that I had been a wonderful addition to the school, but they now had a nun who could take over my position and they didn't need me anymore.

I was so shocked I burst into tears. The nun consoled me and explained that I would have a generous severance package. I left the school feeling defeated. I suspected the real reason for my layoff was my "subversive" commentary on the gay symbols in Cernuda and García Lorca's poems. I had been naïve, and now I was jobless.

Sitting in the train on the way back home, I read the letter that spelled out the terms of the layoff and severance package. My sadness lifted. It was enough to survive for at least six months.

That summer Leo and I had planned trips to the Costa Brava and to a jazz festival in San Sebastián. We went forward with them, and I postponed searching for a job to the end of August. It was great to relax after such a hectic year.

When we got back, I enjoyed every second of my recovered freedom. I was feeling it fully now. I had money, a solid partner, and time to write, but one incident a few weeks later threatened our relationship.

It was September 23, 1982, my twenty-fourth birthday. We went to lunch with Enrique and Gloria Cecilia to celebrate. After lunch, Enrique and Leo decided to go for coffee by themselves. I was upset.

"Are you going to leave me alone on my birthday?"

"It'll be quick, I promise," said Leo.

"What's the matter, Isadora? Do you always have to keep him on a short leash?" asked Enrique.

"It's my birthday. Leo should spend it with me."

"Don't be silly. We're only going for a coffee," said Enrique.

"Why can't we go with you?" I insisted.

"I can't," said Gloria Cecilia. "I have a migraine. I need to go home."

"Well, why can't *I* go with you?"

"You don't have to be with Leo at all times, Isadora. We have things to discuss," said Enrique.

"Don't worry, Menquitos," said Leo. "I'll be home soon."

They left. Gloria Cecilia and I walked toward the bus stop, I almost in tears. She comforted me.

"Try to relax, Isadora. It was shitty to leave you alone on your birthday, but he'll be back soon, and you can talk it over. I'll call you in a little bit to see how you're doing, okay?"

She hopped on the bus, and I walked home clutching the seven volumes of *The Diary of Anaïs Nin*, which had been her birthday present. Once home, I lay on the bed and forced myself to read. It was four p.m. I was going to get through this.

I soon was immersed in Anaïs Nin's life. Leo called after an hour to say they had run into some friends and were going for a beer, but he promised to come home soon.

As the afternoon went by, I got more and more agitated. Gloria Cecilia called every now and then, which kept me from going crazy, but every hour or so I threw the book aside and paced the apartment talking to myself, going from anger to desolation.

It was past ten o'clock when Leo finally showed up. By then, my eyes were swollen, my face was blotchy, and I had worked myself into a frenzy. When I heard the door, I jumped out of bed like a jack-in-the-box and went out to the dining room, in full drama mode.

"Now you're coming! You left me alone the whole afternoon on my birthday!"

Leo took a step backward, a bewildered expression on his face.

"Come on, Isadora, we can still go to dinner, it's only ten o'clock." He tried to take my hand, but I pushed him away.

"It's almost ten thirty! And I don't want to go out to dinner anymore! Why did you have to leave with Enrique, today of all days? You say you love me, but I begged you to stay with me, and you didn't care."

Leo tried to hug me, but I wouldn't have it.

"Leave me alone. You're so selfish! All you do is read, write, and have fun with your friends. Can't you even support me on my birthday?"

I had forged the illusion that Leo and I made an indissoluble unit. Now the first cracks were showing, and they terrified me. It was that terror that made me push him away and walk around the apartment sobbing like a two-year-old scared shitless by the volume of her own voice, which only makes her howl even louder. He had to pay. He had to pay not for a few hours of solitude, but for puncturing the bubble I had blown around myself. The bubble that protected me from ever again feeling unloved, unseen, or dismissed.

Leo kept trying to calm me down, but I couldn't be tamed with words. I walked out of the apartment with my robe wide open, stark naked under it, moaning like a madwoman, "I can't be with you anymore. I can't trust you. I'm leaving you!"

I pressed the elevator's button, my eyesight blurry, whimpering. I was vaguely aware that the racket may have brought the neighbors at the opposite end of the hallway to their peephole, and that they could open their door any second and find me there disheveled, exposed, and crazed, but it didn't matter. I wanted to escape the building as if that could help me escape my distress.

Leo came after me. For the first time since he'd arrived home, the mix of common sense, affection, and defiance in his voice became pure fear.

"Isadora, please come back into the apartment. I'm sorry. I shouldn't have left you alone. Please, I didn't know it'd hurt you so much."

When I heard the alarm in his voice, the sorrow in his tone, something broke in me. My knees buckled, and I crumpled in his arms. He walked me back to the apartment, his arm on my waist to keep me upright. I was crying softly, spent by the lack of control over my own emotions.

He walked me to the bedroom and helped me lie down on the bed.

"Are you okay? Do you want some water? Are you hungry?"

I curled up in the fetal position. Leo lay down beside me and smoothed my hair. He kissed my forehead, dried my tears. Little by little I relaxed, and I fell asleep.

The next day I woke up as if hungover, but the clouds that fuzzed my brain had nothing to do with booze; like an ear plugged from overexposure to high-decibel noise, my brain was a little muffled, as if the intensity of the night before had depleted its capacity to register emotions. The shame of having lost control was counteracted by a sense of safety. I had been loud, wild, and excessive for the first time with a man, and though my outburst may have scarred our landscape, it had not annihilated it. I hadn't been able to modulate it properly, but at least I had found my voice.

Shortly after this incident, we found a cheaper apartment. It was only two blocks away from the old place, a little closer to the Mercado de San Antonio, the open-air market where you could buy groceries during the week and secondhand books on the weekends.

The house was only half a flat, with one bedroom and a small living room. The tiny bathroom, with a showerhead stuck on one corner of the ceiling and a slanted floor with a drain, had a plastic curtain that could be drawn around the toilet and diminutive sink to create a makeshift shower. There was also a minute kitchen and enough space outside it for a round table with two chairs. The rental was furnished with cheap, modern pieces. Its saving graces were the sunroom that ran along the back wall, opening to a big patio, and the shed at the end of it: two independent spaces to write in. What more could we ask for?

Leo took over the shed and I took the sunroom. We each had a desk, a chair, and a typewriter. We were set.

The first months in the apartment, when my severance pay gave me the luxury of not working, were the happiest. Every morning after breakfast, Leo went to the shed to write for three or four hours. I settled in the sunroom and did the same, working on a novel where I distilled my experiences with Pol and Marea. We ate lunch together, often discussing our work in progress. In the afternoon, we read, went to the movies, and met friends. It was my dream life, but it couldn't last. We were running out of money.

I didn't want to be tied up from morning to evening with work, like I had been the year before. I couldn't bear not having time to write. I found a freelance job with a hostess agency, which served the many conventions and fairs that took place in Barcelona. The agency gave me a uniform, an elegant rust-colored two-piece suit with a knee-length A-line skirt, a short torero jacket, an off-white silk blouse with a bow at the neck, and a pillbox hat. When I put that suit on, I looked like a high-end model. It was a complete transformation from the jeans and T-shirts of my writing days and the tight tops and miniskirts of my dancing nights.

Being a hostess entailed a few basic duties: looking pretty, smiling, and repeating the same information dozens of times a day to distracted convention visitors. Sometimes we had other tasks, like picking up a celebrity in a stretch limo with a uniformed chauffeur and taking them to a TV station for an interview. We watched the program from the green room and took them back home when it was finished. At one point I got a four-month gig that paid enough to support my writing life.

ATM machines had been introduced at La Caixa, the most popular bank in Barcelona, with hundreds of offices across the city. There was one close to our house that catered to seniors. The agency sent me there every afternoon from four to eight, when the bank was closed but your bank checkbook opened the doors to access the ATM. My role was to teach the customers how to use it. To encourage people to come and do their transactions without tellers, La Caixa installed a free coffee machine in the ample lobby and surrounded it with a few dozen plastic chairs.

Every afternoon I stationed myself at a table near the two ATMs. Whenever a senior came to use one, I walked them through the process. They were dumbfounded.

"Poor girl," said a woman once.

"What do you mean?" I asked.

"Well, they have her locked in that machine for hours! Poor girl," she commiserated.

"Oh, no; there's nobody locked in the machine; it's all automatic."

"Don't lie to me! I'm not dumb!"

"I'm not lying. How would she breathe? It's a machine, I promise." She left, muttering insults.

"Just because she's young and cute she thinks I am a gullible old fart. I'm going to teach her manners, I will."

I gave up trying to convince her that we didn't lock young women in a machine and make them count bills for hours under the weak rays of a flashlight.

After a couple of months everybody knew how to use the ATM, but the lobby was packed every afternoon with old folks sitting on the chairs lined against the wall and drinking one cup of free coffee after another. How did they get any sleep?

Sometimes fights broke out when an old curmudgeon who talked too loudly insulted everybody. The floor was littered with empty packs of sugar and used plastic spoons and sticky with coffee stains. If the coffee machine was out of order, I had a rebellion on my hands.

By the middle of the third month, the executives of La Caixa added a small fee per cup of coffee. The pack of old timers who came to shoot the breeze every afternoon thinned out dramatically. Without anybody to teach the ATM functions to and no shenanigans to entertain me, the hours ticked by excruciatingly slowly. I always brought a book, but doing anything besides helping customers was forbidden, and I was scared of getting caught in one of the impromptu inspections. I snuck in a few pages under the table while waiting for it to be time to go home.

With that job close to ending, the severance money spent, and the prospect of inconsistent income again, things got stressful on the home front. Leo's grant was gone, and he hadn't found any work. Not that he'd searched strenuously.

We still loved each other deeply, but I was antsy. Our relationship thrived on intellectual and literary pursuits, with a heaping side of tenderness, friendship, movies, and dance, but a part of me felt constricted, like a foot in a shoe one size too small. Sex had taken a back seat. It didn't drive the car, but neither did it crash it. Leo seemed content with the predictability of our lovemaking. I chafed under the lack of excitement and pleasure. The wide gap between the confident woman who flaunted her sensuality at Tabú and the tame partner I had devolved into at home drove me mad.

I had no role models for long-term lust. When Mama found my birth control pills, she asked me how I could make love with casual partners when it was such a meaningful part of a couple's relationship. At the time, I hadn't yet experienced a complete surrender to my body's wisdom. I thought her comment was hogwash to make me feel guilty, but it may have meant that my parents enjoyed a fulfilling sex life, the kind that erases borders and breeds deep connection. I know Papa at least tried because my oldest brother, who was also a lawyer and worked in Papa's office, mentioned once that he had found books about sexuality hidden behind others on his shelves. You would never have guessed it from the way my parents treated each other. They kept their attraction sealed. Their exchanges were harmonious but restrained and austere.

Shamed for finding self-pleasure at five and treated as a body that could be used and forgotten at six, I didn't know how to be whole. I was either all flesh—meant to be plundered and cast aside—or incorporeal—unable to bring my body in all its glory to the stable relationship where I had found my haven.

And now, after two years of cozy monogamy, I was ravenous. I missed the rush of conquering a man. I yearned for the melting of the gut, the hyper-awareness of the senses. My thirst could only be satiated with the occasional new drink. I didn't crave depth. I craved power.

I partially satisfied my urges whenever I danced with Enrique, our chemistry reminding me that I could still bring any man to attention, but Enrique was out of bounds.

Sergio, however, had potential.

We met Sergio and his long-time girlfriend at a friend's house. During the long boozy afternoon, his girlfriend told me they had problems. Sergio wanted to break up, but she had convinced him to keep trying.

We met again at Tabú a few days later. That night I noticed Sergio looking at me with admiration. He was a pleasant guy, handsome, a little older than we were, in his late twenties or early thirties. We danced a few tunes.

His girlfriend left early, perhaps bothered by the attention he showered on me. Leo and Enrique stayed, but I didn't even see them. I couldn't contain the beast inside any longer. I was on the hunt.

I flirted with Sergio, smiling too much, dancing too close. After a while, we sat at the bar and started kissing. Leo came up to me.

"Isadora, let's go home." His voice was pained.

"No. I'll go home later."

Leo wasn't the type to get into fistfights or create a scene. He was affectionate, thoughtful, and artistic. Having grown up surrounded by women, his feminine side was well developed, his *macho* side non-existent. He left.

How could I hurt so much the person I most loved? I can only guess I was trying to explode our relationship by bringing out into the open what had been festering for months. A lively part of me was asphyxiating.

Sergio and I booked a room in a downtrodden motel near Tabú. He was even more famished for sex than I was. Over the last few years, he had hardly made love to his girlfriend. They got along, but there wasn't any spark.

After the initial high of the seduction, I lost my impetus. My night of lust quickly became a night of camaraderie. Showing Sergio that he could have the stamina to make love multiple times a night (a lesson I had learned from the Madrid playboy), I became his teacher, helping him move along on his journey to reclaim sex and enjoyment, something I needed myself.

As light filtered through the curtains, my thoughts turned to Leo. I had sobered up, and my betrayal was starkly clear. I couldn't hide behind the cloud of booze or the frantic urgency to conquer. I had to face his agony.

I walked back home, hungover and dreading what was waiting. It was nine a.m., Sunday. The streets were almost empty. I marched fast, as if arriving a few minutes earlier would diminish my transgression. I paused before turning the key in the lock. I had no idea what I would find inside. Would Leo be gone? My heartbeats boomed like an ominous drum. Despite our issues, I couldn't stand the idea of losing him. I opened the door.

The house was silent, the curtains drawn, the bedroom door ajar. Relieved to see the familiar shape of Leo's body under the sheets, I left my purse on the dining room table and tiptoed to the bedroom. I sat on the bed.

Leo opened his eyes, and his face crumpled. He sat up, his back against the wall.

"How could you do this to me?" His voice shook, but he kept his composure. "When you kissed Sergio, I felt as if a knife were gutting me."

I had never seen eyes so sad. They wrung out of me the last traces of excitement, leaving only the blunt reality of their anguish.

"I'm sorry. I don't know what got into me. I was so drunk . . ."

"That's no excuse. I don't go around kissing girls when I get drunk. I only want to kiss you."

"I know; I'm sorry. I couldn't stop myself."

"And where were you all night? Did you have sex with him?"

I could have said I had been drinking and dancing in some after-hours club, as we often did. Perhaps that would have erased the grief in his eyes. But lying wouldn't take us anywhere.

"Yes."

Leo covered his face with his hands, as if he couldn't stand the sight of me. I didn't dare say anything. After a few seconds, he lowered his hands. The outer corners of his eyes, which always slanted downward, had travelled down another quarter inch.

"I'll look for an apartment today." His voice cracked.

A moment of weakness was about to destroy two years of love and companionship. I had to stop the train wreck.

"Please don't. It won't happen again. I promise!"

"Why did you do it? Did you like him that much that you couldn't restrain yourself? And why did you kiss him in front of me? I don't understand."

"He was nice, but it wasn't about that." Words cascaded out of my mouth urgently, anxiously. "I craved seducing a man, proving to myself that I could do it. I don't know why. It wasn't even that great."

"I don't get it. Are you going to run off with a man every time you feel the urge to be this great seductress?"

"No! No! I won't, I promise. Please, forgive me. I can't stand seeing you this way."

I touched his hand hesitantly. Leo looked down.

"I love you, Leo; I love you more than I've ever loved anybody. Please, don't leave me. I promise you that I'll never betray you again."

A tear fell on the back of my hand—his tear. My chest tightened. A ball got stuck in the middle of my throat, exerting a pressure so hard I feared it would break through my skin. I hugged Leo and kissed his face.

"Don't cry, please; I love you. I'm sorry I hurt you; please, forgive me."

Leo searched my mouth and he kissed me. We fell into bed and made love with a frenzied desperation.

We tried to keep living together as if nothing had happened, but it was impossible. Leo started going out alone several nights a week. Sometimes he wouldn't come back until morning. He said he was drinking with friends, but I wasn't sure. We fought more often.

Our finances were also in shambles. We struggled to pay the rent. I found a part-time job as a receptionist in a urologist's office and let go of my inconsistent hostess gig. I worked three long days a week. It wasn't my dream job, but I didn't have a dream job. I wanted something that gave me enough money to survive and left me time to write.

Leo stayed jobless. Finding work wasn't easy, especially for an immigrant. Unemployment had climbed steadily since 1975 and it now exceeded twenty percent. Thousands of Spanish immigrants had returned from other European countries now that an oil supply crisis had threatened their economies, joining the masses of unemployed in Spain. The initial support of the unions for industrial recon-version had evaporated, and massive protests took the place of the demonstrations against Franco and for democracy from years earlier. Everything seemed to be crumbling, both at home and in the street.

Leo said it would be good to spend some time apart. He wanted to visit his family in Colombia, but he couldn't afford the ticket. He proposed to use the trip as a way to make money: he would buy women's brand-name clothing that his mother could sell in Bogotá, where those brands were more expensive. I wanted to support him, so I offered to ask my oldest brother for a loan.

I got Leo the money, helped him buy the clothes, and he left. He stayed in Bogotá for a month, but the financial venture wasn't successful. He came back as poor as when he'd left.

What he did bring, though, was a secret. A few days after his return, he got a letter from a woman named Claudia. Another arrived a couple of days later. Leo said she was a friend, but I was wary. Why would a woman write so often to him all of a sudden?

My suspicions were confirmed when the phone rang one morning at five. I picked it up.

"Hello?"

"Can I talk to Leo?" It was a woman.

"He's asleep."

"Can you wake him up?"

"No, I can't, unless it's an emergency. Are you a relative?"

"No, I'm Claudia. Who are you?"

"I'm his girlfriend."

"His girlfriend? He didn't tell me he had a girlfriend."

"Well, he has. We've been living together for over two years."

"Son of a bitch!" She hung up.

I went back to bed, furious. I had kept my promise to remain faithful and try to work things out, but he had gone to Colombia with my brother's money and used it to get himself another girlfriend.

"Who was it?" mumbled Leo.

"It was Claudia, *your* Claudia," I seethed. "You told me she was a friend and she's calling at five a.m. and hanging up on me when she finds out you have a girlfriend? She's not a friend. She's your lover. Don't lie to me!"

He tried to deny it, but I grilled him until he owned up to it. He had met a well-known TV anchor the first week in Bogotá, they had fallen head over heels for each other and they spent the whole month together. All while he kept writing me love letters.

I was devastated. This had not been a one-night stand; it had been a full-blown relationship.

Leo assured me that he still loved me, that he had just been infatuated with Claudia, but he kept corresponding with her. A letter arrived every week like clockwork. He claimed they were just friends and there was no need to stop writing to her. I didn't believe him. I found her letters in the back of a drawer in his writing shed, and I read them. They confirmed that, after the initial disappointment when she realized he had concealed my existence, Claudia still expected him to return and be with her. She described how marvelous their life together would be. What Leo wrote to her in response I couldn't know, but clearly he wasn't denying they would live happily ever after.

He also kept photos of Claudia in the drawer. She was a gorgeous, polished brunette with big hair and sharp suits, nothing like our bohemian, laid-back style. What a confidence boost that must have been, landing such a beautiful, successful woman. After all, in Barcelona he had no job, no money, and a girlfriend who had cheated on him in the cruelest way possible and who didn't desire him.

We hobbled along for two or three more months, trying to regain a semblance of trust. There were tears, jealous fits, and recriminations about his lack of financial solvency. But there was also deep love. We had been so solidly welded to each other that we didn't know how to break apart.

In the end, we separated amicably. He found a cheap room in a shared apartment not too far from where we lived. I helped him move. We didn't have many possessions to divide except for our books. It was hard for each of us to part with half our library but harder still to part with each other.

The first few weeks after we separated, we met often. Occasionally, we made love. We missed each other, but I enjoyed the freedom to go out and have fun without guilt.

I kept my gig at the doctor's office, and focused on writing, working, dancing, and looking for love.

Love I didn't find, but I did find lovers.

A Mirthless Dance

FOR THE FIRST TIME SINCE I'D LEFT my parents' home, I was living alone. I was twenty-six years old. With only part-time work, my finances were precarious. That winter I often went to bed wearing two pairs of socks, two sweaters, and sweatpants because I couldn't afford to replace the gas cylinder for my only space heater. I ate a lot of lentils and very little meat. It didn't trouble me. Living with scarce resources went well with the image of the bohemian writer I believed myself to be.

Writing, however, was the first casualty of my separation. Without Leo to instill in me his disciplined approach to the craft, it became a haphazard activity, ruled by excuses and procrastination. If I was hungover, my mind was too foggy. In the dead of winter, I could hardly type, my fingers stiff from the cold. On Sundays, it didn't seem appropriate.

I drafted a few stories here and there but couldn't gather steam or commit to a serious schedule. I wanted the success, but I didn't have the perseverance and determination to do the work. Much of the time, I was entangled in one love drama or another that took away my focus. I still found my value through a man's eyes. I had no direction. Each lover took me down his path.

My liaisons ranged from forgettable to dangerous. I had a short-lived affair with an Afro-Peruvian guy I met at Tabú who traveled a lot and slept at my apartment during his short stays in Barcelona. I had never been with such a muscular, manly specimen. I tended to like lean, long-limbed men, softer in character and appearance, but he was a true macho man inside and out. Perhaps his booming laugh, self-assured step, and chauvinist attitudes appealed to me because he was the polar opposite of Leo. The contrast helped dig my tender ex-boyfriend out of the burrow he had fashioned in my heart.

This man's raw approach to sex demolished my barriers. When he called from the airport and told me he was on his way, I could hardly contain my excitement. Waiting until he had something to eat was torture. I wanted him right there, right now. He teased me, making me wait a little longer before picking me up and making me vanish, satiated. I eventually realized he was a drug dealer and threw him out of the house.

During that period, Enrique and I became very close. He visited me several times a week, or I would visit him in the tiny apartment where he lived alone. He had a girlfriend, a hardworking single mom, young, petite, and shy, with a dignity and strength of character I admired. Enrique was fond of her, but he was also fiercely independent and kept the relationship contained for a long time, living like a bachelor whenever they weren't together.

When he came to my apartment in the evening, we spent hours sitting on the living room sofa, talking about books and life. I told him about my adventures with my lovers. He told me stories about his childhood and his parents that few people got to hear. Enrique kept a façade of toughness and belligerence, but with me the mask fell off. We enjoyed each other's company, temperament, and intelligence. We were peers.

One Thursday night, I came home with two bottles of champagne that my boss had given me as a Christmas present. Enrique came by a while later and we drank and talked.

Around one a.m., I suggested we go to Tabú to continue the party, as I often did. We had almost finished the two bottles. I was wasted.

"Ah, no, Isadora, you're not going to do this to me again," said Enrique.

"What do you mean?"

"You get me all excited with your sexy stories, we go to Tabú, and after a while you leave alone or with another man. Today we are staying here, and you're dancing only with me."

I tried to convince him to go out because this sounded like a prelude to sex, and I didn't want to mess up our friendship, but he was adamant.

"If you go to Tabú now, I won't come to visit you any longer. I've had it with you leading me on."

I had never led him on; at least, I didn't think I had, except perhaps while dancing, because we had chemistry on the dance floor that couldn't be denied, but it wasn't my intent to seduce him. Our talks about lovers and sex—interspersed with conversations about so many other things—were for me the liberating chance of being candid with somebody I fully trusted. He had a different read.

I agreed to stay in the house, reluctantly. We talked for a bit longer, but when a bolero came on the tape I was playing, he invited me to dance.

I got up feeling wobbly and steadied myself by placing my arms around his neck. He grabbed me and pulled me close to his body. After a couple of turns, he commanded, "Take your pants off."

"What? Why? I don't want to take my pants off."

"Take your pants off. I want to dance with you with your pants off."

He had never talked to me this way, rough, demanding, and unyielding, like an abusive husband.

"That's silly. I won't take my pants off unless you take your pants off."

"I'm not taking them off, but you are."

I tried to joke about it, but he was dead serious. Perhaps if I'd been sober, I would have told him to go to hell, but I had a hard time standing up, let alone arguing. I took my pants off.

We kept dancing. My naked legs against his jeans made me feel vulnerable and humiliated. He passed his hands over my butt. I couldn't bear it. It was a relief when he kissed me. At least that was something we did together.

We went to bed and had sex—quick, perfunctory. We lit a cigarette right after, not exchanging a single word. When we'd finished it, he got up, dressed, and left me.

I fell into a drunken stupor. In the morning I remembered only the humiliation of having been forced to dance with my pants off while he remained clothed and how he'd become ice cold as soon as he lit that post-coital cigarette.

That weekend was the first time in months that two or three days went by without one of his visits. Did this mean our friendship was over? I panicked. I loved Enrique as the close brother I never had, as my pal. I knew his behavior that night was a part of him, not all of him, and that he was better than his actions then. I dismissed it because he had always offered me true companionship. Enrique saw me, he heard me, he shared himself with me, and he admired me, and vice versa. He had made a mistake—and so had I—but we all make mistakes.

By Sunday, his absence rattled me like a chronic toothache. I went to his apartment, unannounced, and rang the bell.

He greeted me coldly.

After some nervous banter, I went straight for it.

"I don't want what happened the other night to spoil our friendship."

"Why should it?" said Enrique, but his posture was stiff. I wasn't discouraged. This was too important.

"I don't want it to happen anymore. And please, don't tell your girlfriend. What would she think of me?"

"She would find you sad."

That hurt. He had demanded sex, but I was the one who inspired pity. I swallowed my pride and continued.

"I would like for us to continue having the same relationship. I want to come here to visit and for you to come visit me at home. I want to keep going out with you and having fun."

He agreed, but he still acted aloof.

It took a few weeks, but we patched things up and continued our friendship as if nothing had happened. His visits to my house became less frequent when he moved in with his girlfriend, and I got involved with other men, but we remained close for decades, even when living continents apart. When he became well known as a writer, radio producer, and event organizer for Latin music clubs, he took on the nickname *El Molestoso*, the troublemaker, which he lifted from the title of an Eddie Palmieri song. It accurately represented his prickly character and his love for a good confrontation. Stirring up debates was a sport that he excelled in, but the arguments with the opposing parties did not preclude his friendships. His authenticity and sense of humor made him popular.

In the last days of his life, when he was battling cancer, he let the mask fall away again and told me how he wanted to let go of that troublesome persona that stuck to him like an inseparable shadow.

"What I want, Isadora, is a simple life. I want to leave the city, live in the countryside with my girlfriend, get a dog, and not feel obliged to come up with contentious opinions and attitudes. Everybody expects it from me, but I'm tired of providing the entertainment."

We never talked again about what happened that night at my place, but, for me, it sowed the seeds of an important lesson: truly committed relationships can weather almost any disappointment. After all, if I hadn't learned to love, mistakes and all, how could I have ever made peace with the person who most disappointed me? How could I have accepted myself?

1973, San Julián
Betrayals

ABUELO HAD A GRAND PIANO in the living room of Santa Margarita, right by his studio. As a child, I had heard him play a few times, and I knew he loved classical music. He told anecdotes about his travels around Europe in pursuit of great concerts and about the famous Russian piano player he had met. All his daughters learned to play the piano. At one point, Abuelo dreamed of having his own musical ensemble at home, with each girl playing a different instrument, so he diversified their classes. Mama studied violin, but she didn't take to it.

Although classical music had been a big presence in Mama's life growing up, we never listened to it at home. In San Julián, we didn't own a record player or a TV. In Barcelona, the turntable was in the dining room, in an alcove by a bay window, where we had two armchairs, a table, and a cabinet with the player on top and a few dozen records in the cupboard. Mama never sat there idling and listening to records, but when a TV program about classical music pitted contestants playing the piano against each other, she watched it and hummed most of the melodies.

Aside from that, music, like most everything else, was a private experience in our house. Whoever wanted to listen to it went into the dining room and spent time alone with the records. We had all the Beatles albums, American and British rock-and-roll bands that my brothers collected, Spanish pop and rock, protest singers, and crooners like Adamo. I don't recall buying any records—literature was my obsession and books my vice—but I went to the dining room periodically to listen to music and dream about whatever boy I had a crush on.

I must have been fourteen or fifteen when I decided I wanted to educate myself about classical music. I asked Mama if Abuelo would be willing to teach me. She immediately got behind the idea, thrilled that I wanted to do something with her father, whom she felt very close to in her quiet, reserved way.

Aside from important holidays, I hadn't seen Abuelo often since I stopped going to Santa Margarita daily at seven or eight years old. These lessons were an opportunity not just to refine my musical education but also to fill the family void. I imagined Abuelo would tell me about his life while we listened to music. I savored in advance the closeness we would enjoy.

Abuelo was happy to share his passion and took pains to prepare a thoughtful program. "We won't start with Rachmaninoff," he said the first afternoon I joined him in Santa Margarita. "That's too advanced and it would scare you off. We will begin with something easy, like Chopin."

We went to the living room, and Carmeta, the cook, brought us tea in green Duralex cups. Abuelo put a record on the turntable and sat down in an armchair facing me. He joined his hands under his chin and listened intently, sometimes closing his eyes to better concentrate. He didn't say a word. When the piece ended, he got up to change the record. As he came back to his chair, he announced the next composer and the piece's title and sat back again in silence. When I tried to engage him in conversation, he wasn't receptive. I was there to learn classical music, and he was there to teach me. Chitchat would keep us from appreciating the mastery of the melodies.

Every session went the same way. Abuelo played three pieces and we drank tea in silence. At the end of the third piece, he asked me if I had liked it, got up to say goodbye and give me a kiss, and handed me a piece of paper with the names of the compositions we had just heard.

After four or five times, I got bored. I told Abuelo I couldn't come back. He seemed disappointed, but he didn't ask questions. I could see now where Mama's reserve came from.

A couple of years later, one of my cousins told me Abuelo had a *querida* for years. A lover? Abuelo? How was that possible? He'd visited Abuela's grave in the little Romanic church across from Santa every day since she had passed away a few years before. He even stayed two extra months in Santa Margarita to be closer to her. And he was a fervent Catholic who for years attended mass daily, sometimes more than one mass a day! My cousin laughed. He said all mid-century bourgeois men had a lover on the side.

I have no idea if this was true or my cousin invented the story to shock me, but he sounded so certain that I believed him. After that, I couldn't bear looking at Abuelo. When I visited him during Christmas or any other holiday, I avoided talking to him.

What an idiot I was. Even if the rumors were true, it didn't make sense to dismiss the whole man for a faux pas. But I was a naïve teenager, and a fracture in the myth of perfect love was not forgivable.

Addicted to Love

MY FINANCES IMPROVED SLIGHTLY when my friend Angela, whom I had met a few years back at La Torre, asked if she could rent the shed at the back of the patio. I also got a second job freelancing as a reader for Seix Barral, a prestigious publishing house. They gave me unpublished novels and I wrote a report either recommending its publication or not. I met biweekly with the editorial director, Pere Gimferrer, a renowned poet, to discuss my impressions. I was reading and reviewing a book or two every week. Finally, a job that used my literary skills!

I toned down my partying. I was busy with work, writing—even if not consistently—and meeting frequently with Enrique and his girlfriend and occasionally with Leo. I still harbored the hope that one day my issues with him would miraculously resolve and we'd get back together, especially now that he had found work designing beach towels (who knew he could do something like that?).

New Year's Eve, we made plans to celebrate at Tabú. Leo showed up past midnight with a girl I'd never seen before. They sat at the bar and started making out.

I turned to Enrique in disbelief. "He's kissing that girl!"

"So what? You guys have been separated for a long time, Isadora. What do you care who Leo kisses?"

But I did care. Seeing him with another woman gutted me. The irony that this happened in the same spot where I had first sabotaged our relationship by kissing Sergio didn't escape me.

I left Tabú in a daze and walked home alone. The first great love of my adult life was over. Would I ever find another man who would love me so tenderly?

Over the next few years, I learned that finding men who would fall for me wouldn't be difficult. I seemed to awake passions—passions that didn't always merit reciprocating, but now that I had experienced what it meant to be loved, I couldn't put the genie back in the bottle. I craved attachment.

That's the main reason I got involved with Fran, even though instead of being my dream man, he was a nightmare.

It was Saturday around one in the morning and I was sitting alone at a bar in the Borne neighborhood, drinking a gin and tonic before going to Tabú, when a guy approached and asked if I had a lighter. I lit his cigarette and he asked if he could sit with me. The bar was full, with only the other chair at my table free, so I said sure.

We talked about music. Fran was well versed in rock, pop, and folk, and I liked people who were passionate and knowledgeable about a particular subject.

During the course of the night, I described to him something unusual that had just happened. The Monday before, I had come home from work and found a single red rose with a card in front of my apartment's door. The envelope had my name on it, but the card wasn't signed. It contained only one typed sentence:

Te esperaré el domingo. (I will wait for you on Sunday.)

Every day that week, when I came home from work, I found another red rose and a card in front of my door, with more verses added. By Friday night it said:

Te esperaré el domingo (I will wait for you on Sunday)

para verte llegar (to see you come)

con tu vestido rojo (with your red dress)

y suave caminar. (and gentle walk.)

Te espero el domingo a las 7 p.m. en el Café Europa

(I will wait for you on Sunday at 7 p.m. at Café Europa)

I didn't own a red dress. I had a tight red knitted top that I wore with a form-fitting, knee-length gray skirt, red tights, and black ankle boots. This secret admirer must have me confused with somebody else.

Fran listened to my story attentively, and at the end of it he said, "Those verses are from a song by Jaume Sisa."

"Are you sure?"

Sisa was a Catalan singer-songwriter. His first record had been the soundtrack of the summer of 1975 in San Julián. I had followed his career on and off, but I didn't recall this song.

"I'm almost positive," said Fran. "If you want, we can go to my place to double-check. I live close to Plaza Cataluña, and I have the album." Seeing my doubtful expression, he added, "Don't worry, I'm not going to tie you up and rape you."

After a moment's hesitation, I said, "Why not? It's on my way home, anyway."

We walked to his home, a second-floor apartment decorated with music posters and pottery. He found Sisa's album and showed it to me, pointing to a particular lyric. There it was: "*Te esperaré el domingo . . .*"

"Would you like to listen to it? I can make tea," suggested Fran.

"Yeah, I'd love to listen to it."

He set the record on the turntable and disappeared into the kitchen while I made myself comfortable on the sofa, reading the lyrics and listening to Sisa's mellifluous voice. The night and the drinks had caught up with me.

Fran came back with a lime blossom tea and some honey. Quica's face floated above the vapors of the hot mug. How many afternoons had I spent drinking lime blossom tea with her in the ironing room, my feet warmed by the lit coals in the brazier hidden under the table . . . Quica, our nickname for Francisca—the same name as Fran, a nickname for Francisco. A good omen?

I examined Fran critically. He was about my height, with short black hair, dark brown eyes, a straight nose, thin lips, and lined, waxy skin that made him look older. Plain-featured without being ugly. But he seemed kind.

We spent the night together. The next morning, we woke up late and hungover.

"I know this restaurant that has the best *caldo gallego*," said Fran. "It raises the dead!"

I had never tried this hearty soup, but I knew it was similar to the *cocido madrileño* or the Catalan *carn d'olla*, a tasty broth with greens, beans, and different cuts of meat. It sounded heavenly.

While we walked toward the restaurant, Fran reached out for my hand. This was a refreshing change—one-night stands typically ended with the guy never calling—but it felt weird to walk hand in hand with a guy whom I had just met and only tangentially liked. I hoped we wouldn't run into anybody I knew.

During lunch, he told me more about himself. He was from a small town in Galicia and had come to Barcelona in search of a better life. He worked as a salesclerk in the men's clothing department at El Corte Inglés, the department store in Plaza Cataluña where Marco had stolen a guitar a few years earlier. Although he didn't love his job, it was a five-minute walk from his home, and he made a decent salary.

I noticed that he chewed with his mouth open and spoke with his mouth full—two things I hated—but he was playing footsies with me under the table. I disregarded his manners.

I told him a bit about me: how I wanted to be a writer and worked as a freelance literary critic for a publishing house and as a receptionist in a doctor's office three days a week. He nodded in all the appropriate places and laughed if I said anything remotely funny.

After lunch, I wanted to go home and get ready for my blind date at seven. The identity of my mystery suitor was too intriguing to let it pass. He offered to go with me and sit at another table to make sure everything was okay, but I declined. The meeting was in a centrally located café, so it wouldn't be dangerous. We exchanged phone numbers and said goodbye.

It was five o'clock. I took a shower, washed my hair, styled it, and dressed in my red top, gray skirt, red tights, and boots. I walked to the cafeteria. I pushed the heavy glass door and marched resolutely from the entrance to the back, scanning the tables and expecting to find a friend laughing his head off.

There were only old ladies having coffee and a guy with long black hair whom I could see only from behind. He didn't ring a bell. When I walked back toward the door, disappointed, I realized that the man sitting alone was none other than Jaume Sisa himself.

I stopped in my tracks. Surely it couldn't be him, the famous Sisa, who had sent me flowers! He raised his hand in hello.

I went to his table, stunned, but trying to hide it, and sat down with fake aplomb.

"I'm glad you came," he said

"Did you send me the red roses and the cards?"

"Yes, I did."

"How did you know who I was or where to send them?"

"It's a long story. Do you want something to drink?"

I ordered a coffee.

Sisa reminded me we had talked a few months ago at Zeleste, a club in the Borne neighborhood. I had been attending a jazz concert with some friends. Sisa was at the counter when I came by dressed exactly like today and ordered a beer. After getting my drink and paying, I'd told him: "You don't remember me, but we know each other. I was the hostess who picked you up at your house with a limousine and a chauffeur and took you to a TV interview. You didn't even say hello or thank you."

Indifference was the usual response from celebrities when we picked them up. With our elegant uniforms, we probably looked like empty-headed, replaceable Barbies.

"Let me correct that," said Sisa. "Hello, how are you, and what's your name?"

"Too late! I'm in a hurry."

I went back to my friends. We left soon after, and I forgot the whole incident.

Sisa didn't. After frequenting the club for a couple of weeks hoping to run into me, he figured out which TV station hired hostesses to pick up the guests. He called the agency and, after a few months of cajoling, extracted my name and address from the secretary, but not my phone number. He devised the plan to approach me using his own song and the roses.

It was a charming story. I relaxed and accepted his dinner invitation. Afterward, I took a taxi home. I had to finish a book report the next day, and I wanted an early night.

I found two messages from Fran on the answering machine. He wanted to know if I was safe. He begged me to call him, no matter the hour, so he would have peace of mind. His concern for my safety was flattering. I called him, and he picked up right away. When I reported that my secret admirer was Sisa, he was impressed. We set a dinner date for Friday.

In the next few days, I received two white roses from Sisa, each with an invitation for dinner. He had explained during our first encounter that red roses meant passion, but he was willing to move to friendship first, as I had requested; hence the white rose. He hoped one day we'd go back to red.

I went to the first dinner, and we had a nice time, but his next invitation, also via flower and card, annoyed me. Why couldn't he call me like a normal person? When he communicated with me via flower and card a few hours before a date, he didn't give me the option to say no. Those days, we didn't have cell phones. I had little recourse but to show up or leave him hanging. I enjoyed his company, but I didn't like him the way he liked me. I decided to end the dates instead of leading him on and disappointing him later.

That evening I went out with Fran, and at nine o'clock, the time of my date with Sisa, I called the restaurant where I was supposed to meet him and asked the waiter who picked up to tell him I wasn't coming. He didn't contact me again.

Why did I choose Fran over an accomplished and romantic guy like Sisa? I wasn't attracted to Sisa, but neither did I feel attracted to

Fran. Maybe I didn't consider myself worthy of a successful man, while a plain guy seemed more in my league.

In any case, my relationship with Fran continued much like our first date. He was attentive and obsessively interested; I was hesitant but letting myself be pursued.

After three months of dating, Fran asked me to live with him. He talked up all the advantages—half the rent, closer to transportation, no need to keep carrying clothes and toiletries up and down, plus he loved me. I wasn't convinced, but he kept hammering me.

"If you loved me, you would commit," he said every day.

I wasn't sure that I loved him, but he surely loved me. After a year of trivial liaisons and regrettable fiascos, that seemed almost enough.

"You are everything to me. What am I for you?" he insisted.

He wore me down. I gave up my half a flat in Ronda San Antonio, the first one where I had lived alone, and moved to his apartment a few streets away. I didn't tell my parents that I was moving in with a guy yet again. Just that I had found a cheaper place closer to work.

Even after bowing to Fran's pressure my feelings were ambivalent, but I was addicted to being loved.

I recall only small flashes of the four months Fran and I lived together. The surprise of seeing him every day in a suit and tie for his job—I had never dated a guy who wore a suit and tie on a regular basis. How I tried to make it work, assuming the role of dedicated wife, doing the laundry, ironing his clothes, keeping the house in order. My attempts to spice up our sex life—for his birthday I had to go to work before he came for lunch, so I left food on the stove and the table set for him, with a packaged gift on his plate and a card that read: "A gift for your eyes only." Inside the package, I placed a set of sexy lingerie that I would wear for him that evening.

Red flags popped up: he didn't like my friends, especially Enrique (the feeling was mutual); he didn't want me to go out on my own; his curiosity about my past love and sex life was insatiable. He would listen with rapt attention, commiserate when I related a sob story, and accuse my former lovers of being weak, depraved, or both.

Fran didn't have any friends, didn't like to read, and didn't enjoy dancing, even though he loved music. He wanted only to work and be at home with me. Our big outings were lunches at the Galician restaurant. His small-minded world stifled me, but his obsessive attention seemed a palatable trade-off.

I tried opening up some space for myself. Since family was sacred for him, a couple of months after we started living together, I said I needed to spend time with my parents in San Julián some weekends. The first time I planned to go, he wanted to tag along, but I claimed it was too early. Mama would never let him stay in the house overnight because she was Catholic. The truth is that Mama had no idea I was living with him or even that he existed.

I left on a Friday night with my brother Diego and his wife. On Sunday in the early afternoon, when I went to Bar Nuria for a coffee, the waitress told me a guy had been asking for me. I sat on one of the little tables outside, my heart racing. A few minutes later Fran parked his car on the side street.

He walked toward me, beaming, and sat by my side.

"What are you doing here?"

"I missed you." He grabbed my hand.

I shook my hand free. "I have only been gone for a day and a half!"

"Aren't you happy I'm here?" he asked with an injured expression.

"I see you every day. I came to spend time with my friends and family."

"What friends?" He raised his voice. A couple of people stared at us. "Do you have a boyfriend here? Is that why you didn't want me to come?"

"Don't shout."

"Don't change the subject! You do have a boyfriend; that's why you came, right?" He talked even louder.

"I have never had a boyfriend in San Julián." I drank my coffee and got up.

"Where are you going?" He grabbed my wrist.

"Let me go!"

I walked rapidly, trying to get as far away as possible from Bar Nuria before any of my friends or siblings showed up. He came after me and changed tactics.

"Don't be mad, please. I missed you, I can't live without you."

He tried to grab my elbow, but I pulled it away.

We were making a scene: me walking fast with my head faced rigidly forward, Fran trotting behind me, imploring to be heard.

I stopped, faced him, and said, "Okay, I will listen to what you have to say, but not here. Let's go back to Barcelona."

I marched toward his car and he drove me to my parents' house to pick up my stuff. He waited outside while I grabbed my weekend clothes and toiletries and threw them in my bag. I went to the backyard.

Papa was asleep in a chair and Mama was reading the paper and dozing.

"I'm going back to Barcelona with a friend," I said.

"So early?"

"Yes, I have work to do."

"Okay, see you soon." She went back to her paper, and I hurried outside.

I didn't even look at Fran while he drove back. My blood boiled. Midway, he said he was hungry because he had come straight from work without having lunch, so we pulled off the highway in a little town. We found a restaurant and sat on the patio.

Fran drilled me again about the weekend boyfriend. I insisted there wasn't one.

"You're lying to me, you whore! You've had so many lovers that one steady boyfriend is not enough for you!" His voice was shrill.

Nobody had ever called me a whore.

"How can you say something like that? That's stupid!"

"Don't call me stupid!"

He banged his fist on the table. The glasses rattled.

"Fran, please don't do that," I whispered.

"Then stop lying to me, you bitch!" he yelled, banging again on the table.

My face got hot. I wanted to get up and leave the restaurant, but we were in the middle of nowhere and I didn't have a car.

A young waitress approached our table.

"Everything okay?" she asked, her eyes darting from Fran, to me, to Fran.

"Yes, everything is fine. Can we have more water?" Fran's voice steadied. He had that fake smile I hated so much. The knot in my throat didn't let a word come out.

The waitress left and Fran turned toward me.

"See what you made me do?"

Tears rolled down my face. He picked up a napkin and dried them. "Don't cry." Voice dripping sugar.

"I'm going to the bathroom," I said.

"Yes, go freshen up, honey."

When I came out of the bathroom, he had finished his meal and was paying at the counter. We drove the rest of the way to Barcelona, me in silence, him dropping uplifting comments about the music, the weather, anything, caressing my thigh.

The next few days he was on his best behavior, but pretty soon the scene at the restaurant became a scratched record. Every night he ranted at me. He asked me if I had done this or that with a lover, threw in my face painful stories I had shared with him in confidence, called me a whore. When I cried or got mad, he hugged me and pleaded for forgiveness.

It was the classic abusive scenario, but for me it was brand new, so the oscillation between the monster and the gentleman kept me dizzy.

The water was getting tepid, and I couldn't hold any longer to its embrace. I slid down the bathtub one more time to cover my face and stayed submerged for a few seconds, trying to squeeze the last bit of heaven out of it. I let my head fall backward as I was coming up for air so my hair would lie smooth like dolphin skin over my shoulders.

I got up and reached for the large pink towel hanging on the wall. I dried my body with it as the water gurgled down the drain. I stepped on the pink rug and wrapped a hand towel over my hair like a turban, feeling sophisticated.

The mirror over the sink was small, but it had three doors. When you opened the two on the sides you saw yourself from many angles. I positioned them just so to play, like I always did.

First, I tried wrapping the large towel over one shoulder and leaving the other bare, but as soon as I moved, the towel slipped, uncovering my young breast. That wouldn't do.

Then, I tried wrapping it tightly under my arms, and tying it behind my neck, imagining myself in an off-shoulder dress, like the stars of black-and-white American movies. I put my left hand on my waist and raised my right hand, index and middle finger clasping an imaginary gold cigarette holder. I brought it to my mouth, inhaled, and exhaled the smoke into my face in the mirror. "You put your lips together . . . and blow," I whispered with the sultriest voice I could summon at thirteen.

The off-shoulder dress was coming loose, and my turban was also falling apart. I let the big towel slide to tighten my turban.

All of a sudden, I felt watched, even though the bathroom was windowless and the door was locked. Instinctively, I crouched and looked through the keyhole.

There was a big fat eye on the other side.

I sprang up, wrapped myself in the towel, and turned the key. I opened the door with trepidation, not sure what I would find. I saw my brother Diego speed-walking into his bedroom. He looked at me over his shoulder, a mix of fear and defiance on his face.

I was enraged, but I didn't know what to do. I swallowed my anger, put my pajamas on, dried my hair, and went to bed.

I woke up a couple of hours later shouting, "Go away, go away!"

My older sister, who was still awake, reading and smoking a cigarette, told me to go back to sleep. She didn't ask what was happening or what I was dreaming, and I didn't offer an explanation. I woke up a few more nights, a knot twisting my stomach.

Perhaps being watched wouldn't have affected me if I had yelled at my brother or if we'd had a close relationship to fall back on. It wasn't that different from being ogled at five while playing doctor, and not too surprising in a place where naked women were harder to find than a pink elephant. But beyond these moments when I was a body, I felt invisible. It was the erasure that hurt, the empty space where my presence should have been. It was walking up Avenida del Tibidabo, turning to open the gate and finding Guille right behind me. He had walked all the way without making a peep instead of catching up and talking to me. It was running into Diego at some club a couple of years later and not even acknowledging each other.

I knew my brothers would help in a crisis. Mama had tattooed family loyalty on our brains with indelible ink. Day to day at home, however, we were strangers, each with a life as unknown as if we lived in different countries.

Fran complained he was getting anonymous phone calls. Men would call while I was at work, and when he picked up the phone they would tell him details about my past lovers that I hadn't shared with him. He used those details to prove he was right when he accused me of being a whore. My promiscuity had often brought me little joy and much guilt, so my protests were muddled with remorse. He said it must be Enrique or another of my friends making the calls, but that didn't make sense to me. I couldn't figure out what was going on.

After a couple of months, I'd had enough of Fran's rants, but every time I wanted to leave him, he threatened to kill himself, going so far as to put a razor to his wrist. I didn't want his death on my conscience, but I couldn't stay caged. I plotted my escape.

One Friday I suggested we go for a beer with a friend of mine after work. I had confided in him that I was planning to leave my boyfriend, and I needed his help.

Although Fran hated my friends, he put up with this one because he was a soft-spoken intellectual who would have given Satan the benefit of the doubt. We met at a bar around the corner. Fran was leery, but after a while and lots of small talk, his shoulders relaxed.

I got up to go to the bathroom, but instead I left the bar while my friend kept Fran distracted. I hailed a taxi and rushed to Diego's home. He and his wife were waiting for me so we could go together to San Julián for the weekend.

A few minutes after I got there, the phone rang. My brother picked it up and he said it was for me.

It was Fran. Once he realized I wasn't coming back from the bathroom, my friend had revealed that I had left him for good and I was with my brother. Fran must have found the number in the telephone book.

I told him not to call me again, and I hung up.

"What's going on?" asked Diego.

I didn't want to drag my brother into my mess, but I didn't have a choice. I confessed I was living with a guy, he had become abusive, and I was trying to leave him. When the phone rang again, Diego picked it up.

"If you bother my sister again, I will beat you to a pulp." His voice was so firm I knew Fran was cowering on the other end of the line. Diego hung up. "That's it; let's get out of here," he said calmly. In a crisis, I could count on my siblings to lend a hand.

When we arrived in San Julián, I told my parents there had been a plumbing disaster in my apartment and I had to vacate it immediately. I don't know if they believed me, but they didn't ask any questions. That Sunday I moved back to Avenida del Tibidabo with them.

A week later, Diego took me to pick up my stuff from Fran's apartment while Fran sat scowling on a sofa. We didn't exchange a word.

Soon Fran started calling in the middle of the night. My parents and siblings slept on the second floor and didn't hear the ring, but I had gone back to my old bedroom in the basement, and I could hear the phone in the ironing room.

It was always the same story: one of my friends had threatened to kill him, they didn't let him sleep, and he was going crazy.

He cried and begged me to do something to help him. I tried to calm him down and puzzle out who could be the anonymous caller. A few nights later the same thing would happen again.

The calls were a thread still tying us, and I couldn't wait to cut it.

Call the Police

Diego,

If I'm not home by Monday, call the police. I may be dead, and the killer is Fran.

María Isidra

I folded the note, slipped it inside an envelope, and sealed it. On the front of the envelope, I wrote "DIEGO."

I left the note on the round table in the foyer and walked to the front door. It was dark on the avenue except for the faint yellow circles beneath the scattered lamplights. The clock struck three times, but its deep voice didn't bring me the usual comfort. There wasn't a soul in sight. The cable car didn't start until six. I wrapped myself tighter in my coat.

Half an hour ago Fran had woken me up, yet again, to complain about an anonymous death threat. He sobbed and whined for five minutes until I told him to pick me up so we could go together to the police. I had to snuff out this torture.

Car lights approached. I rushed down the stone steps to the gate. I didn't want Fran ringing the doorbell and waking my older sister, who was the only one in the house with me. The rest of the family had gone to San Julián for the weekend.

Fran got out of the car. He had a crowbar in his hand.

"What's that for?" I asked from inside the gate.

"It's in case somebody is waiting for me here. You never know with your crazy friends." His voice was high-pitched. He looked around nervously.

"There's nobody here. I'm not getting in the car unless you put the bar in the trunk."

"Okay, okay." He smirked while he opened the trunk and placed the bar inside. I opened the gate.

"Aren't you going to say hi to me?" He opened his arms as if he were about to hug me. I couldn't bear the idea of him touching me.

"Hi." I walked to the passenger door and opened it. I sat inside the car, my back stiff.

He got into the driver's seat and slammed the door shut.

"What shall we do now?" he asked.

"We're going to the police station. I told you when you called me. I'm tired of you waking me up at all hours of the night to complain about my friends. This has to stop once and for all."

"Let's go to the station at Vía Layetana," said Fran. "It's the only one open at this time of night."

The station was located close to his apartment, but I decided not to focus on that detail. I already had too much on my mind.

We drove in silence. There was hardly any traffic, but we caught all the red lights. My hand was on the door handle, ready to open it at the least sign of danger. I lit a cigarette and inhaled deeply. My heart was pounding but I tried to look calm. Fran started with his singsong.

"I'm going crazy, your friends don't let me sleep, they threaten to kill me, each night a different one, it must be your lovers, who knows which one of them . . ."

I stayed quiet. My mind was a jumble. Why would my friends threaten Fran? Getting together with him had been a mistake, but that shouldn't give anybody a green light to harass him. Who could it be? Why did they do it? While I was still living with Fran, I had asked Enrique if he was making the calls because I knew he didn't like Fran.

"How can you think I'd do something like that, Isadora?" he said. "I don't know why you waste your time with this guy, but that's your choice. I would never butt in, let alone make anonymous calls. If I wanted to threaten him, I would tell him to his face."

I felt ashamed that I had suspected him. Months of harassment had increased my stress to an intolerable level, and I was flopping like a fish just caught, trying to find a way out of the net. I would have done anything to end this nightmare.

Below my jittery mind an undercurrent of fear gripped my gut. What if Fran planned to harm me or kill me? At least he would be caught because I had warned my brother.

Fran parked the car right in front of the police station. We stepped inside.

"We want to make a complaint about death threats," I said to the policeman at the counter.

"Death threats to you?" he asked.

"No, to him."

Fran was behind me, shuffling from foot to foot, uptight and silent.

"Okay. Sit over there and we'll call you soon." He pointed to a room behind him.

We sat on a bench. There was only one other person in the room, a man sitting on a chair. He kept falling asleep and jerking back awake when his head fell forward.

The door in front of us opened and a policeman came out. He scanned the room and said, "Fran! What are you doing here?"

Fran jumped to his feet, smiling.

"Alberto! I'm so glad to see you!"

The policeman came up to us and shook Fran's hand.

My stomach turned. Had Fran prearranged this meeting? Were they ambushing me? Should I sprint out of the station?

"How do you know each other?" I asked, trying to steady my voice.

"We do security at El Corte Inglés, where Fran works," said the policeman. "Come in, come in." He pointed to the open door.

It was too late to run.

We entered his office. Alberto sat down behind a desk, and we sat on two chairs in front of him. Fran, now that he was in friendly territory, recovered his nerve.

"This is my girlfriend, María Isidra." Fran had always called me María Isidra, as he associated Isadora with my wild nights.

"Ex-girlfriend," I said. "We separated over three months ago."

Alberto caressed his short, chestnut-colored beard.

"Ex-girlfriend," said Fran. "Well, her friends are calling me every night and they are threatening to kill me!"

"Which friends? Can you recognize their voices?" asked Alberto.

"No. I don't know who they are. But I'm scared." Fran got agitated, and he raised his voice. "I don't even dare go to work some days. You need to catch them and send them to jail!"

"What do you know about this?" Alberto addressed me directly.

"The only thing I know is that it needs to stop, because they threaten Fran and he calls me in the middle of the night to tell me. I can't take it anymore."

"Have there been any threats in person?" asked Alberto.

"No. They are cowards," said Fran, "but they are following me. I've seen suspicious men at the corner of my street when I go out.

I'm sure it's those assholes she used to date." Fran was leaning on the table, his face flustered, his voice trembling with anger.

"When did these threats start?" asked Alberto.

"While I was still living with him."

Alberto posed a few more questions. Then he asked Fran to leave the room.

"I don't want to leave," said Fran. "She doesn't know anything. I'm the only one who receives threats."

"I have to question her in private. I'll question you later," said Alberto.

He got up, walked with Fran to the door, opened it, and said, "It will be short, I promise."

He closed the door, waited a few seconds, and opened it again. Fran was on the other side, bent down, with his ear at the door's lock, like a little kid spying on his parents.

"Please sit on that bench by the wall," said Alberto firmly, pointing to the opposite wall. "This is a private conversation."

Fran walked to the bench. Alberto closed the door and sat back behind his desk. He put his elbows on the table, interlaced his fingers, rested his chin on his hands, and looked me straight in the eye.

"You know this is all horseshit, right?" he said.

"What do you mean?"

"There are no threats. He's spinning this tale so he can have access to you."

"But, but, but . . . That's impossible! He's desperate. He cries when he calls me; he even sobs!"

"I've seen this before, believe me. He spins a story of fake threats to make you feel guilty. As long as you believe your friends are harming him, you will try to help him out."

"But these people have told him things about me that I never told him."

"He may have talked to somebody who knows you and has an ax to grind. He extracted stories about your past to make the threats believable."

I sat back on my chair, my mind shuffling the faces of all the people who may have betrayed me. One came to mind, a girl whom I had once been close to but had become estranged from as I had delved further into dancing, drinking, and flirting, which she found appalling.

"What do I do now?"

"Let me handle it," said Alberto. "I will tell Fran that he should call the police directly when he receives a threat, instead of calling you. That way he can't accomplish his goal, which is contact with you, and there won't be any reason to continue his farce." He handed me his card. "If he keeps bothering you, don't hesitate to call me." I put the card in my purse. Alberto went to the door and called Fran in.

He came almost running, scared and tense. Alberto set his mind at ease. He told him that the best way to handle the situation was by notifying the police immediately when he received a call, so they could trace it and find the perpetrators. He should not call me, because that didn't help. In fact, calling me in the middle of the night was harassment, so he had to stop it.

I sat in silence, trying to digest what Alberto had told me. After my initial denial, it dawned on me he had to be right. Anger toward Fran mixed with relief that mistrusting my friends had been misguided.

Fran took me back home. When he parked in front of my house, he asked, "When will I see you again? Can't we be friends?"

I hid my disgust. I didn't want him to know I knew.

"We can be friends, but not right away, Fran. I need some time to get over everything that's happened. Please don't call me again for a few months."

I closed the car door and went inside the house. It was five a.m. I picked up the note for my brother from the foyer's table and went to bed. I slept soundly for the first time in months.

A couple of weeks later, calls started again in the middle of the night. This time, when I picked up, the caller hung up. I knew it was Fran, but I didn't have proof.

After a few days, I called Alberto. We made an appointment at an outdoor café.

Alberto came dressed in plain clothes. For a moment I wondered about his intentions, but his demeanor was respectful. I explained the situation.

"Yes, that's Fran," he said. "He's never called us to complain about any death threats, and he couldn't call you any longer, so he found a different way to harass you. Don't you worry. I'm going to end it. He'll never bother you again."

"What can you do? I don't have proof," I said.

"I know exactly what to do. I'll give him a scare he'll never forget. I'll pick him up at El Corte Inglés, in my police uniform, and take him to the station for questioning. I assure you he will lose his appetite for bothering you once he learns it could cost him his job."

I don't know what moved Alberto to help me out. And I don't know if his tactics were legal, but a couple of days later, he called me and explained that he and another policeman had visited Fran at El Corte Inglés and, while his coworkers and manager looked on, they had taken him to the station for questioning. They didn't handcuff him, but Fran was livid.

Once at the station Alberto had warned him that if he ever called me again, he would end up in jail. Of course, Fran denied making the anonymous calls, but they stopped.

Alberto helped soften the negative associations with police in my mind from the days of pro-amnesty and pro-democracy demonstrations, when they represented only repression and violence. Although their uniform had changed in 1979 from gray to brown to mark the separation from Francoism, the distrust they inspired had not decreased. They simply went from being *los grises* (the grays) to being *los maderos* (the timbers), but for me this incident opened a truce.

Spain was transforming fast. Ten years before, a *tricornio* had threatened me and Ramón with jail for kissing and fondling in his car at nighttime, when nobody was around. Now the move from dictatorship to democracy and progressive laws like the decriminalization of homosexuality and adultery, the legalization of divorce and abortion, and the removal of the word "Catholic" from the Constitution had ended Spain's isolation and backwardness. We had even entered the European Union. Being "different," the successful marketing campaign from the '60s that had introduced the country to the world as the land of sun, flamenco, bullfights, and paella—blotting out all regional diversity—had fallen out of favor. Being as modern and liberal as the next European neighbor ruled.

But some things and some people never change. A few years later, I ran into Fran on a street close to my house. I turned the corner quickly so he wouldn't approach me. That evening I received an anonymous phone call in the middle of the night. He must have found my number in the directory. Time had not erased his obsession.

When the phone rang again the next night at two a.m., I picked it up and yelled, "I know this is you, Fran, and if you don't stop calling me, I'll go back to that policeman and get you arrested!" I had no idea where Alberto was or how to contact him, but I had to get Fran off my back.

It was the last time I ever heard from him.

Bikini and Lingerie

I LIVED AT MY PARENTS' HOME for a few months while working at the doctor's office, now only two days a week, and freelancing for the publishing house. To save for a deposit on a rental, I took a third job watching kids during lunch and recess at a preschool the three other days. After a while, I dropped the doctor and the preschool, and I started freelancing for more publishing houses, adding translations and book launches to my responsibilities.

I missed being in the thick of the city, but I was grateful to my parents for taking me in while I got back on my feet. The stability allowed me to write again. I added to a collection of short stories that would take a decade to complete. Writing was my refuge, the place where my voice rose free.

By then, five of my brothers had married or left the house. My older sister and my three younger siblings remained at home. We didn't have a cook or maid anymore. A cleaning lady came a few hours a week to scour the kitchen and the bathrooms, but Mama was working a lot and getting worn out.

The house also showed its age and the lack of upkeep. Shutters broke and never got fixed, crumbling paint left white dust in the corners of the rooms, and humidity stains defaced the wallpaper. Our peaceful environment disappeared when our next-door neighbors moved out and rented their property to a nightclub. Music pounded until two, and then there was an hour of loud talking from people lingering on the sidewalk.

Papa's walks around the table in the foyer, hands behind his back, eyes trained on the floor, brow wrinkled, were now a daily, endless habit. His mood veered toward anxiety, while Mama's usual calm was interspersed with sourness.

On Sundays, my brothers came over with their wives and the first grandchildren, and Mama cooked a big meal. Lunch was as boisterous as ever, the animated talk bringing the relief it had always offered to our taciturn family. Sunday was also the only day of the week when conversation filled the living room—conversation between Mama and my sisters-in-law. It was a mystery how she could be so talkative with them and so silent with us. After lunch, the women played cards while the men took a nap, watched sports on TV, or went to a soccer match. I didn't like bridge or sports, so I usually went back to my room.

My experience with Fran had left me drained and distrustful, but now that he had disappeared from my life, I longed to dance again. I went to Tabú a couple of times, but I didn't run into anybody I knew. A call to Enrique solved the mystery. Another nightclub played salsa now, and all my friends had moved there. The club's name was Bikini.

The first few times I went to Bikini, I hated everything about it. At Tabú, salsa was a religion. That dump of a club had nothing to offer except passion for its beats. Bikini, on the other hand, had none of the grit or the intimacy born from sharing an all-consuming ardor for the rhythms that moved your feet and your spirit. The club had two rooms, only one of them dedicated to salsa, and a patio where they projected classic American movies. It was located on Diagonal, the opulent avenue that divided Barcelona's classes, with pedigreed families usually living above it. The crowd was as safe as the location. Barcelona's youth had finally discovered tropical music.

No matter how much I missed Tabú, it wasn't fun to go there always by myself, and the patrons were getting shadier, so I gradually became a regular at Bikini. I went alone and sat at the counter nursing my gin and tonic, ramping up the right kind of buzz to dance with abandon. I was soon on a first-name basis with the bartender, a bald guy in his fifties, as serious as an undertaker.

The club's saving grace was the music. The resident DJ was also a fan of the hard-hitting sounds of La Fania and the sensual cadences of Los Van Van. Once I warmed up, I danced nonstop with friends and strangers.

Every night, the last song the DJ played was "Todo tiene su final" (Everything has an end). Héctor Lavoe's bright voice seduced us while Willie Colón's trombone blew our restraint off the floor. We hung on to the last notes with all our might, as if we could make the song last forever if we wished it intensely enough, even though we had known for the five minutes and four seconds of its duration that our bliss was about to end. As difficult as it was to let go when your hips still demanded movement and your shoulders craved another shake, the lyrics nudged us to the door and made the farewell palatable. The end was inevitable, but so was a new beginning, already hovering like a promise while the ashtrays got emptied and the counters wiped clean.

I roamed the night two or three times a week to unlock that daring girl, Isadora, who swept aside her insecurities with a few drinks. I kept her strictly separated from my daytime persona. In the daytime, I embodied a formal young woman who worked hard at every job she had and was never late for an appointment. At night, I took my wild side on a ride.

During those months, brief romances brought me a step up from careless hookups. Casual sex had been a hopeful path to stumbling into love, the side effect of an urge to be seen and feel less insignificant or a pull to let myself be used—a habit learned when I was six years old. I had become a master in the art of dissociation. When things went wrong, I observed what happened in bed from afar, seeking refuge in a twisted feeling of superiority: I was more aware of what was going on than the clueless man who panted and pounded like a deviant gymnast without the slightest idea that under him was not a delighted woman but a soulless rag doll.

Now I tried to end the drunken one-night stands and go for relationships that had some heft. One had the end date in sight, as my friend was planning to get married once his fiancée moved to Barcelona three months later. Our liaison was his last hurrah. The other was a passionate affair that I ended when I found out the guy was married. Yet another was with a guy who looked like a boxer whom I ran into often at the bus stop. He turned out to be a well-known Colombian writer with whom I shared books, sex, and cognac for a few months.

I broke the one-night-stand ban when I met Abili at Bikini.

Abili was a husky man with a roaring laugh and enough energy to fill up a room. He had that rugged, attractive look you would find in a western gunslinger: semi-longish brown hair, five o'clock shadow, twinkling brown eyes.

After dancing a few tunes, we sat in the outdoor patio and talked for a while. I found out he was a journalist now focused on producing salsa concerts. A settlement from a TV station that had unjustly fired him provided the funds for his business venture. He had brought to

Barcelona some of the salsa greats, like Rubén Blades, for the first time. He intended to make salsa as ubiquitous as rock or pop.

He also told me he was in a long-term open relationship. Lovers were allowed as long as they were kept to one night. He wanted to be with me, but he warned me that he wouldn't call me afterward, as per his agreement with his girlfriend. I was used to open relationships. We were still in that pendulum swing from the repression of the Franco era to the "everything goes" of the post-Franco years. Although I wished I could see Abili again, because I liked him, I decided to spend the night with him. There are few things as sexy as confidence, and Abili's was overflowing.

"If you make salsa very popular, you'll have a lot of competition," I pointed out during our chat.

"Good! I want competition. I don't want to be the *only* one producing salsa concerts and running salsa clubs. I want to be the *best*."

The city hadn't yet caught up with his enthusiasm and he was hemorrhaging money, but that didn't deflate him. Like a true pioneer, he trusted his ability and was ready to bet his last cent on it.

Over breakfast the next morning, he told me a bit more about his personal life. He'd been in his current relationship for a few years and had fathered a daughter whom he was crazy about, but he chafed at monogamy. He had extracted from his girlfriend the commitment of an open relationship as a condition to staying with her and parenting their child together.

After breakfast I kissed him goodbye and went home feeling melancholic.

A couple of weeks later, he called and invited me to dinner.

"Isn't this against the arrangement with your girlfriend?"

"Our arrangement is off. If there is one thing I can't stand, it's betrayal. My girlfriend now says she wants to date a man she likes while she's still with me. I told her to go to hell."

"What do you mean?"

"I've moved out. I'm living at a friend's house. I'm done with her."

"But what about your daughter?"

"I'll still raise my daughter, but I can't be with her mother any longer. So, do you want to meet again?"

"Yes!"

Five months into dating, Abili asked me to move in with him. I hesitated. My decision to move in with Fran too quickly had ended in disaster. Plus, living with a man who despised marriage and disliked monogamy felt risky. Even though I applauded the liberalization of the laws and social customs, I secretly longed to one day be married in Santa Margarita, where I was born, to finally feel like a part of my family.

I stalled, saying I didn't want to live at his friend's house and that I had no interest in sleeping around. Abili said he didn't either. He just wanted to leave the door open in case we needed that relief in the future.

When he found an apartment, I didn't have any more excuses. It was either live with him or break up with him, and I wasn't ready to let him go. I stuffed down my fear and packed.

This time I told my parents I was moving in with a man. I wanted my relationship with Abili to last, and bringing it out into the open was my way of giving it a vote of confidence. Mama and Papa didn't say much, but when I introduced Abili to them a few months later, they made an effort to be warmer than they had been with Leo.

We lived in a small first-floor apartment in the Gracia neighborhood. I hadn't frequented this area much, but I quickly fell in love with it. Gracia had been an independent town until Barcelona engulfed it at the turn of the nineteenth century, and it looked like it. The streets were narrow, and every few blocks they opened up into small squares, including one with a handsome clock tower in the middle and the old City Hall building on one side. All the squares had bars with outdoor seating. The tables were always full of people eating, drinking, and talking. Families rented the same apartment for generations, businesses lasted decades, and everybody knew each other. It was a happy, comforting bubble with a laid-back atmosphere and deep Catalan roots that reminded me of San Julián.

Our apartment had two bedrooms, a living room/dining room, a bathroom, and a narrow pantry next to the kitchen. We slept in one of the bedrooms, Abili used the second as his office, and he transformed the pantry into a room for his daughter. I had a writing desk and my books in the sunroom that ran along the back of the house.

In the summer, Abili organized the First Salsa Congress of Barcelona. He brought icons like Ray Barreto, Tata Güines, and Luis Perico Ortiz for a two-night fest. Even though it wasn't a financial success, the festival became a musical milestone for the city. I helped Abili, doing everything from fetching cognac for Tata Güines, who alleged he couldn't play drums without it, to overseeing ticket sales.

He also organized a concert with legendary salsa and Latin Jazz pianist and bandleader Eddie Palmieri. The band stayed in Barcelona several days, even though they played only one night. I accompanied Abili on outings with Eddie and his wife. If the world-famous musician was shocked to be driven around in Abili's rickety old car, he didn't say so. He enjoyed every minute of the sightseeing, and we had a grand time. Those four days, although I didn't know it yet, would change the course of my life.

Palmieri's concert was also a financial bust—there weren't yet enough salsa fans to fill a big venue—but the performance was explosive. Abili beamed from backstage. The settlement money was dwindling rapidly, but he kept going, as excited as ever. I admired his courage and commitment.

A few months later he landed a gig running a salsa night every Thursday at a club a few blocks from our apartment. He also managed the band, all Catalan musicians who had been bit by the salsa bug. Every Thursday the crowd grew larger. Little by little, his dream of transforming Barcelona's music culture was coming true.

As a salsa fanatic myself, these activities were as enticing to me as they were to him. I never missed a concert or a Thursday night at the club. On weekends, we often went to Bikini to dance. Abili knew Enrique and Leo—everybody deep into salsa knew each other—and he got along with both of them, especially Enrique. We often met him and his girlfriend.

The downside of all this fun was the drinking. Although I continued to keep it contained to two or three evenings a week, it escalated further on those nights. It had come to the point where I couldn't go out dancing without getting drunk. The minute I had that first gin and tonic in my hand I was pining for the second one, and the third. I longed for the liberation that came from booze, the sudden transformation of formal María Isidra into outgoing, vivacious, sensual Isadora.

Blackouts became more common. Once, Abili had to throw me over his shoulder to take me up the steps of the apartment building. This was the first time he told me I needed to take it down a notch.

I didn't heed his warning. Everybody in the club scene drank. A lot of people also did coke, which had become the drug of choice for partiers. I wasn't much into drugs. Alcohol satisfied my needs, and I found it perfectly harmless. It didn't keep me from doing a good job at my various occupations because I only drank when I went out at night, and it hadn't become a daily habit. What I didn't realize is that everybody drank, yes, but not everybody got wasted every single time they went out dancing, like I did.

Although this issue wasn't a deal breaker for Abili, we had more difficult problems. I had gotten into this relationship knowing he didn't believe in monogamy, but I didn't expect him to fool around early on. I was naïve. As soon as I moved into the apartment, it became apparent that Abili hadn't ended his relationship with his ex-girlfriend. They saw each other several times a week when he picked up or dropped off their daughter. At the beginning, she was still dating the guy who had caused the breakup, so it was okay. Once that relationship was over, she and Abili started having sex. He told me right away whenever it happened. I would have preferred not to know, but honesty was sacred to him, even though it tore me up.

I don't know how long I would have been able to put up with this situation, but it resolved itself. The coup de grace came via my new job. I didn't make enough money with the publishing houses, so I interviewed with a travel agency for a gig as a tour leader. The job entailed shepherding groups of tourists around the world. I would be going to Egypt many times a year, the primary destination for this agency, and occasionally to other countries. A local guide would explain the sights; I'd be in charge of logistics, keeping the tourists in line, and resolving any issues that arose. I took the job. In between tours, I kept freelancing for publishing houses.

My first trip to Egypt lasted two weeks. Abili came to pick me up at the airport. He gave me a hug that almost crushed my ribs.

"I missed you so much! Did you miss me?"

I was surprised to be met with such ardor. I had been so busy and so enthralled with Egypt's beauty that I'd barely had time to think of him, but I didn't say so.

When we arrived home, he ripped off my clothes and we made love. "*Ets la meva femella*," he said over and over, in Catalan ("You're my woman," or, more accurately, "You're my female"). It was a primal cry and a sign of ownership, like a man planting a flag on a conquered peak, but it was also a sign that he considered himself owned. He was my man as much as I was his woman.

Afterward, we sat in the sunroom and he showed me two LPs.

"Look what I found," he said. "I missed you so much I had to buy them, one for each of my loves."

He had bought a Celia Cruz LP that included the song "Isadora Duncan" and another salsa record with a song that had his daughter's name in it. The pride and tenderness in his eyes when he showed me Celia's LP moved me.

That's when the sexual escapades with his ex-girlfriend ended. It wasn't my presence that pushed him to commit. It was my absence. Abili thrived on the specific, on flesh, matter, and action. Once I wasn't there, the gap revealed that he truly wanted me as his companion.

I wasn't the only one to notice his impassioned surrender. A friend we knew from Bikini told me once, "The way he looks at you . . . I wish a man would look at me that way." I smiled at Abili fondly. We were settled.

His daughter, though, was anything but settled.

Abili brought the child home for a few hours once or twice a week. Often, he was busy and would close himself up in his office while I sat in the sunroom with the two-year-old and entertained her. At the beginning we got along, but after a while, her attitude changed. Suddenly she didn't want to talk to me. Perhaps she saw her mother's distress once Abili distanced himself from her; I'm not sure. When she stayed overnight, she woke up at one or two and cried until

Abili picked her up and brought her to our bed. Once in bed, she would kick me until I moved to her bed in the pantry.

Soon she had a tantrum as soon as Abili tried to come into our apartment with her. After a while, he stopped bringing her home. Instead, he took her out for various activities by himself.

Through all these challenges, Abili's drive and virility continued to seduce me. I also found his utter lack of modesty fascinating and appalling at the same time. This was the first man I'd met who took a shit and wiped his bum with the bathroom door open so we could continue our conversation. He had no filters.

I had grown up in a family where nudity was so taboo I'd never seen my own sister naked, even though we shared a bedroom for almost two decades. It must have been different among my brothers, since the six of them shared a bathroom and the toilet was right by the shower and the sinks. But in the girls' bathroom the toilet was behind a door, so bodily functions were as hidden as the thoughts crossing our minds. Abili's ease with carnal matters was as foreign to me as the hieroglyphics of Egypt.

I'd had a glimpse of a different way to live in your body when I was eleven and spent a month in France. A friend of my aunt Hélène, a lively brunette with long silky hair and tanned skin, came to visit. They chatted for a while and then she asked Hélène if she would wax her underarms. Hélène was an esthetician, just like Tía María Josefa had been, but she currently wasn't working.

"Of course!" she said.

She heated up the wax. When it was ready, her friend took her top off. It didn't seem to bother her that Hélène's stepbrother was there, even though he was a teenager.

She wore a lacy black bra, as exotic to me as the Grey Poupon mustard that graced the dinner table every evening. At home, the enormous piles of underwear neatly folded in the ironing room were all cotton and white for the men and white or beige for the women. A light blue nylon slip with a thin embroidered band on the neckline and hem was the furthest Mama strayed from sensible undergarments.

I had never seen a woman in her underwear. My sister and I had perfected the nightly Houdini act of disappearing under our night-gowns with our clothes on and reappearing with them off, chastely covered from neck to ankles in our nighties. We'd developed skills that would have made a contortionist pale with envy.

I gawked at this woman—nonchalant and sophisticated, her arms up, her nipples visible through the delicate lace—and was bewildered.

My usual troubles with sex showed up a few months into my rela-tionship with Abili. As had happened with Leo, soon after we became a stable couple, a barricade went up between me and my desire. I couldn't drown my unconscious resistance to being intimate. Giving myself so fully to another person seemed too risky. Even when I sensed a fluttering anticipation in my loins, I contained it.

One afternoon Abili came after me playfully. I ran through the small apartment saying "Leave me alone!" with him at my heels, until he blocked me, my back against the living room wall. I laughed nervously, my lust unfolding in my belly like a tight coil springing loose, while I said "No" and pushed him away—though not strongly enough to deter him. The excitement of the chase had made me want him, but I couldn't admit it.

Pol had been the only steady boyfriend with whom I'd let my

desire run free. Resistance might have eventually shown up if our relationship had been a long-term one, but it had never solidified. It was also colored with transgression and subconscious competition: I had taken the place of Marea, my best friend, a woman I deeply admired. It seemed that without an undercurrent of defiance or misbehavior, I couldn't help but retreat to my subconscious fears.

Abili, however, wasn't satisfied with intellectual discussions or tender hand-holding like Leo had been. He was all guts. Unless I was asleep by the time he came home, I knew what to expect. He wanted sex. He didn't force me, but he was insistent. I usually gave in.

He entered me with the same intensity he did everything else. Without much foreplay and closed off to desire, I often ended up sore. At almost thirty years old, I was still paying the price of being raised in a time when sexual education was nonexistent and sexual shame pervasive. For someone who'd been quite promiscuous, I was remarkably ignorant. I wasn't used to asking a man for what I wanted. In truth, I didn't even know what to ask for. I had never heard of the G-spot. I wasn't aware of the connection between clitoral stimulation and wetness. It never occurred to me to use a lubricant. I didn't even know you could buy them. I thought the throbbing down there was my fault. There must be something wrong with me when an act as natural as having sex hurt.

I couldn't own my sexual drive, but I embraced the hedonistic explosion that had overtaken the country through dancing, drinking, and sexy lingerie. I was coming into the power of my own body, if not to claim orgasms, at least to provoke them. My drawers filled with colorful sets of lacy bras and panties, black garters, and transparent black stockings with a black seam marking the curve of my calves.

We were approaching the end of the '80s, and there was still an air of optimism in the streets. The socialist party had won the election of

1986, again with an absolute majority. The same year, Barcelona had been elected as the site for the 1992 Olympic Games. The economy had rebounded, although in a way that benefited mostly people at the top.

In June of 1987, however, my city suffered a setback. The terrorist group ETA planted a bomb in a supermarket that killed twenty-one people and injured forty-five. I participated in a massive demonstration against terrorism, the largest to overtake the streets since 1977. The government's response was just as swift. They captured the terrorists responsible for the attack and threw them in jail.

The upcoming milestone of the Olympics injected a dose of energy in my battered city. In the next six years, Barcelona would undergo a radical transformation at the same time I renewed myself.

A Place of My Own

BY THE END OF THE SUMMER OF 1988, Abili received a call from a journalist named Chiori Santiago. She introduced herself as Eddie Palmieri's daughter-in-law. She was spending some time in Barcelona and wanted to interview Abili to learn why a Catalan man had become so involved in salsa music. We invited her to dinner and immediately hit it off.

Chiori was a vivacious Japanese American five years my senior. She had short black hair, expressive brown eyes, a beauty mark above her mouth like Mama, and an infectious laugh. She spoke enough Spanish to carry on a conversation, and I was fluent in English. She lived in Berkeley, California, but was on a one-year trip through Europe with her eleven-year-old son, Tito. They had been to Holland, Germany, and a few other countries before arriving in Barcelona.

I admired her gumption. I didn't know any mother who had taken her child out of school for a year to travel the world, let alone without enough savings to sustain them during the adventure. Chiori believed that exposure to different cultures would teach her son far more than any school. Along the way, she wrote articles and submitted them to American magazines and took hourly jobs when she could find them. If she stayed somewhere for a few weeks, she tried to find a school that would enroll Tito, even if he didn't speak the language.

Abili took them under his wing. He found them a room for rent at a friend's house, a school that admitted Tito, and a part-time job for Chiori. The three of us became close. Chiori came to lunch or dinner several times a week, joined my gym, went with us to Bikini, and met all our friends.

One night, at Bikini, she disappeared for a while. When she showed up again, I asked where she had been.

"I was sitting on a sofa back there, kissing a guy," she said. "He reminded me so much of Eddie . . . I miss him." She meant Eddie Jr., who had the same first name as his father and managed his musical career. He had stayed in New York, working.

"But wouldn't Eddie get mad if he knew you were kissing somebody else?"

"I don't think so. I didn't have sex! I would never cheat on Eddie. I wanted to trick myself into believing I was kissing him instead of this guy."

Chiori's lack of guilt surprised me—Catholic prudishness had been hammered into me and whenever I strayed, I felt remorse—but I knew she didn't have an ounce of malice. She was playful, creative, and full of life. I loved her artistic side and the beautiful paper cranes and cards she made that revealed her Japanese ancestry. I loved her fierceness and her loyalty. She was a role model for me because I still lived life at half speed, with a split personality—the María Isidra my family, my bosses, and my childhood friends knew and expected and the sexy, daring Isadora. I was still shut inside my insecurities, blunting their edge through alcohol and dance. I still didn't know where I was going, which kept me lost in the winding road of my life.

I had disconnected from the larger world, living only for the present, content to have work, a boyfriend, salsa, and friends, even if my dream of becoming a writer had stalled and my job couldn't be considered a career. My allegiance to politics, other than voting in elections, had become tenuous. My lifestyle itself, I felt, embodied the change democracy and liberalism had brought about, and that should be enough. Like most of my friends, I lived with a man with no plans for marriage, I had stopped going to church, I had placed art and pleasure at the center of my existence, and I made money by freelancing instead of coveting steady employment. I was the only one among my siblings residing in Barcelona who didn't attend every Sunday family lunch. I had built my own family.

The year before, I had introduced a Christmas ritual for our close friends, many of them immigrants. Abili and I threw a party where we exchanged eccentric five-dollar gifts, choosing the recipient randomly. This Christmas of 1988, Chiori and Gloria Cecilia, who was visiting from Paris, joined the festivities, as did Enrique and his girlfriend and a few other people. Enrique cracked us up with his gift, a pair of black stockings with a little sheath in the middle for a penis. I bought an extra-kitsch bust of Nefertiti at a flea market. Gloria Cecilia contributed a mini-chess board with magnetic pieces, a gift that Enrique derided as too practical.

Chiori's gift was the best. She had put together a small notebook made with sheets of toilet paper she had collected all over Europe. Each sheet had a different color and texture. On the corners she had written where they came from and when she picked them up. She added a cover and bound them with colorful threads. It was unique and beautiful. Who else would have thought of something like that? I was proud to call her my friend.

Right after Christmas, she told us she was going back home to the States.

"But you said you were staying six months and it's only been four," I complained, already dreading her absence.

"Eddie called me yesterday and said he missed me. He wants to start the New Year with me. I thought that was so sweet!"

She found a plane ticket for herself and Tito, and they left right before New Year's Eve. The evening before her departure, we had them over for dinner. She gave me a handmade card with a poem she had written for me in it. I still have it.

I had lost not only a true friend but also a sister who would never betray me, compete with me, or wish me ill. A sister who had become closer to me in four months than my real blood sisters had ever been. Little did I know when I hugged her goodbye that we would keep in touch through letters and that five years later she would open her home for me when I moved to Berkeley.

After Chiori's departure, my relationship with Abili tottered along for a few more months. Our differences were piling on more weight than our commonalities. A pull impossible to deny, no matter how much I tried to drown it, yanked at me: I wanted a baby. Abili, however, already was a father, and he didn't want any more children.

The lack of balance in our sexual needs and his hot temper widened the gap. I had witnessed a few incidents where he almost got into blows with his associates over minor disagreements. The day he turned on me marked the beginning of our separation.

I returned from a trip to Egypt and Abili picked me up at the airport, as giddy as usual. I had turned twenty-nine during the trip, so he brought a box with a birthday gift. It was a set of crimson lingerie, all peekaboo lace. People were rushing on both sides of us, eager to get out of the airport, and he was holding up the bra.

"Let's go home, Abili. You'll show it to me there."

All the way home he gushed about how glad he was to see me. I stayed quiet because I had a secret, and I didn't dare blurt it out in the car. When we got to the apartment, he wanted to make love right away, as usual. I tried to stop him, to say I had something to tell him, but he said it could wait.

Afterward, we sat at the table in the sunroom, and I came out with it.

"I had sex with another man."

"What? Who?" His voice raised, his face got red, and his features moved in different directions as if he couldn't control his muscles.

"The Egyptian guide."

"Why didn't you tell me before we had sex?" he yelled. "I've always told you right away!"

"I tried to tell you, but you wouldn't let me talk."

"You didn't try hard enough!"

"Don't shout, please. The neighbors . . ."

"Fuck the neighbors!" He yelled even louder.

"I thought you wanted an open relationship . . ."

"I haven't had sex with anybody else for a year!" He banged the table with his fist.

Over the next few days, he demanded to know everything, every single detail. He extracted bits and pieces from me. How the local guide looked regal with his white *galabeya* flapping around his legs as he walked, his thick cane with a lion's head marking each step, like a stud disciple of Jesus. How he held his head high, his closely cropped hair shading the perfect globe, his mocha skin smooth as a child's, his eyes penetrating every part of me. How he wooed me every single hour of every single day, asked me to sit with him at lunch and dinner at a table for two on the cruise on the Nile instead of with the tourists as I always did. How he told me to dip my finger in his coffee as a substitute for sugar. How he said he couldn't get me out of his mind, couldn't sleep, couldn't eat. How he wanted to know if I was married, partnered, or single. How he wanted to hear everything about the man I had lived with for a year and a half. How I told him about the open relationship and that my boyfriend had fucked his ex for months, but I had never been unfaithful. How he pounced on it like a jackal. How he weakened my defenses, talking about my right to have a lover. How he couldn't breathe, couldn't drink, couldn't think when I was in front of him. The dark circles under his eyes, the dark circles under my eyes, my skin shuddering as he brushed my fingers, my throat dry wanting to drink the saliva of him, touch his body under the floating *galabeya*. How he said, "I will wait for you tonight; my door won't be locked." How I crossed the narrow hallway from my cabin to his, our doors in front of each other. How those two steps opened a gap wider than the Mediterranean Sea between me and my boyfriend, and I couldn't help but cross it anyway. How I turned the handle and found him lying on his narrow cot, his white *galabeya* still on. How I lay next to him, touched the rod of his sex under the thin cotton fabric and my desire exploded like napalm, burning the last shreds of my indecision. How after sex—quick, hungry, missionary—I went back to my cabin. How for the next three days he sat with the other local guides at lunch instead of sitting with me. How he didn't talk to me except with contempt oozing from his voice. How I retreated into the pain of having been duped. How I felt guilt. How he courted me again the last day onboard so he could use me one last time. How I went back to his cabin at night, how after closing the door I saw his eager face, his hand stretched to welcome me. How I told him from the door he was an asshole. How his mouth opened, his eyes widened in disbelief, his face darkened and closed up in anger. How I demanded that he never speak to me again until the end of the trip unless it was for business. How I left the cabin. How he reverted to politeness but I didn't talk to him except with contempt oozing from my voice.

Abili raged and bellowed. I tried to defend myself.

"You had sex with your ex for months. I've only had sex once, and after one-and-a-half years together. Why do you get so upset?"

"It was supposed to be meaningless, and you liked this guy!"

"I wouldn't have had sex if I didn't like him."

"But he treated you like shit!"

"What do you care how he treated me?"

"I care. You are my woman. Nobody is going to disrespect you!"

It went on and on.

After a couple of months, Abili calmed down. We limped forward, but the stress whittled away our already thinning attachment. Abili suggested talking to a sociologist about my difficulties with sex, but after a few visits, I refused to go back, as I couldn't see any improvement. Abili was disappointed. It became clear we weren't going to make it, even though we still cared for each other.

We broke up. I moved temporarily to my college friend Ingrid's home in a little town fifteen miles from Barcelona. Abili and I still met at Bikini and other salsa clubs, either by design or because we ran into each other. Now that we weren't a couple any longer, an easy affection replaced the resentments that had accumulated. Our separation was harder for others than for us.

"How can you smile and dance as if nothing had happened?" said Enrique's girlfriend. "I'm crushed that you're not together any longer and you don't care a bit! I don't understand."

"Why wouldn't we be friends? We like each other," said Abili.

"We are better friends than partners," I added.

Mama was also disheartened when I told her we had separated.

"I hoped you would settle down," she said. "He seemed a good match for you." She had never told me that before. "What will you do now? Are you coming back home?"

"No, I'm looking for a place. I'll be okay."

A couple of months later, I got a lead on a rental. It was in a two-story building with a restaurant on the ground floor and three apartments. Mine had everything I needed and more: three bedrooms (two small and one decent-sized), a kitchen and a bathroom, a living room/dining room, and a balcony over the restaurant's patio; lots of natural light; and an unbeatable location on a quiet street, only a couple of blocks from the beginning of Avenida del Tibidabo. The train station was five minutes away. The next street over had plenty of restaurants, cafés, and stores, and the rent was affordable. It offered the comfort of a familiar neighborhood without the inconvenience of being far from everything, as we had been when we lived a mile up the avenue.

It was the first time since I had left my parents' home eight years before to live with Leo that I had chosen my own place instead of moving in with a man. I felt exhilarated.

A few weeks later on a work trip to India, I befriended another tour leader. We discovered we lived ten minutes from each other in Barcelona and made plans to meet when we returned. I visited her often, so even though I lived alone, I never felt lonely.

A stable and happy period of my life in Barcelona began. My two jobs—as a tour leader and as a freelance reader, editor, and translator for several publishing houses—provided enough income to sustain me and excitement to entertain me. I embraced my neighborhood, becoming a regular at a modest restaurant around the corner and at the open-air market. The waiters and the grocers greeted me by name. I furnished my apartment simply but cozily, setting up my studio in the largest room. It had lots of light, bookshelves covering a wall floor to ceiling, and a desk with an electric typewriter. It felt like heaven.

Every failed relationship had been a step to learning a small, but necessary, lesson. Now that I had experienced the freedom of being financially and emotionally independent and I owned my own place in the world, nobody was ever going to take it away from me.

Rollercoaster

AS I REVELED IN MY INDEPENDENCE, Spain's people reveled in the freedom to speak up. On December 14, 1988, a general strike protesting an employment law that encouraged short-term, low-pay jobs for youth and made firing cheaper and easier paralyzed the country for twenty-four hours, even interrupting TV broadcasts. It forced the government to repeal the law.

We had been raised voiceless and powerless, but now we expressed ourselves loudly. We had grown up in a country that was old-fashioned and repressive, but now we were the poster children of Europe's liberalism. Almodóvar's irreverent film *Women on the Verge of a Nervous Breakdown*, which had just come out, was nominated for an Oscar. We had arrived.

Meanwhile, I was struggling to fully come into myself. I kept my promise to remain independent in my own home, but the urge to be loved still controlled my every choice. A few months after getting my new apartment, I started dating another guy from Colombia who was introduced to me by a friend.

Luis was shorter than me and had a rotund belly, two things I had always found a turn-off, but my friend talked about him with such enthusiasm that I was curious. I found out quickly what was so great about him. He threw himself into life with boundless intensity and spontaneity. Whenever he liked something, he enjoyed it without measure. You never knew what he would come up with next. He'd just as quickly take off on a trip without a known destination as show up at home with a humongous bunch of flowers before leaving right away.

The first time we made love, as soon as we were naked and in bed, he sat back on his knees and contemplated my pussy for a good two minutes with a beatific expression on his face. I felt uncomfortable lying on my back, naked, my legs spread-eagle, with that Buddha of a man sitting on his heels, his round belly on his thighs, his hands on my knees, his attention laser focused on my crotch.

"What are you doing?" I sat up and grabbed his arms, trying to bring him to me.

"No, wait, wait," he said softly. "It's so beautiful."

I lay back again, speechless. I had never heard a pussy described as beautiful before, and I didn't think about it as such. Weird, ugly, a little ridiculous, and shamefully smelly were the words I associated with it. And here was this man admiring it, as serious as a priest consecrating the host.

With that, he won me over.

When he came a while later, he shouted his pleasure with gusto. His screams were loud enough to be heard throughout the apartment. His roommate, an American woman, was at home, but he didn't care. (I found out later she had been his occasional lover, which explained why she left the house, slamming the door on the way out, right after Luis came.)

I fell hard for Luis. The first few months were a whirlwind. We took impromptu weekend trips, we cooked and ate like the world was ending, we made love, we talked, we laughed.

He was a doctor. In Colombia he had worked in remote rural towns doing everything, from family medicine to emergency surgeries, but he was most interested in the management of chronic pain.

He found a part-time job for this specialty in a public hospital in Barcelona. Once we paid a visit to one of his patients, a lady in her sixties who had stage IV kidney cancer. She lived on a farm with her husband, about eighty miles from the city, and had been too weak to go to the hospital for a while. They were delighted to see us. She brought out homemade cheese and cold meats, bread, and wine, and we sat around the table for an hour. Even though she was too ill to eat, she beamed, grateful that her beloved doctor had taken the time to drive all the way to the farm to pay her a visit.

"You've got a good man, here," she told me.

"No, you're a good patient, that's all," said Luis, patting her hand. His tenderness moved me.

Before we left, they gave us bags to fill up with cherries from their orchard.

"Eat, eat!" the husband encouraged us while we picked them. "They never taste better than when plucked ripe from the tree."

I had never had cherries so sweet. Luis ate so many he got the runs.

We drove back to Barcelona, happy and full, inside and out, but the happiness didn't last. The following weekend Luis's mood turned. He lay in bed all day on Saturday, somber and quiet. From time to time, he got up to make a phone call but he wouldn't tell me whom he was calling. I asked him if it would be better if I went home. He said no but still acted as if I weren't there. I tried hugging him, caressing him, talking to him, not talking to him. Nothing worked. He refused to tell me what was going on.

By late afternoon I'd had enough. I said if he didn't tell me right away what was happening and whom he was calling every hour I'd leave and never come back. He confessed he was calling his ex-girlfriend, a woman he had dated for about a year who broke up with him shortly before we met. It was her birthday, and he missed her.

I was crushed. Until just the day before, Luis had been exuberantly in love with me. Suddenly I wasn't enough. I went home determined not to see him again.

The next day Luis was at my door begging me to take him back. He said it had been a moment of weakness. I didn't need much convincing. Luis was accomplished, caring, exciting. I craved the intensity of his presence, the intimacy we had built.

This started the pattern of highs and lows that marked our relationship. With Luis, there never was a happy medium. Things went from heaven to hell on a regular basis. We made love like dogs in heat, lived in a bubble of harmony, and got each other with a blink and a monosyllable. He captivated me: his mischievous laugh, which started raucous and ended high pitched, his Peter Pan small teeth, the way he covered his black curls in a red bandanna tied behind his head when he drove, the quiet tenderness in his eyes, his passion for the people he cared for. But as soon as I lowered my defenses and gave myself fully to him, he fell into another one of his dark moods. It was as if he couldn't allow himself to be happy. And when he was hurting, he made a point to drag me with him into wretchedness.

Perhaps he had chosen his profession—mitigating others' chronic physical pain—as a way to compensate for the current of emotional pain that drowned his own soul. Luis suffered. The same intensity he lent to the pleasures of life amplified his descent into agony.

I never understood what caused his distress. Part of it was the conflicted relationship he had with his father. He felt his dad had never loved him. He also hated him for having had love affairs that made his mom miserable. Perhaps growing up with the uncertainty of his father's love caused his compulsion to make love uncertain.

Or maybe he suffered from undiagnosed bipolar disorder. Whatever it was, he kept me balancing on a wire, going every few weeks from ecstasy to despair. He would as soon curl with me like a cat or marvel at the song of our bodies as disparage me for staying fair skinned in the summer instead of tanning beautifully like his ex.

As my confidence shattered, I tried to regain it the only way I knew how: dancing salsa. Luis was tone-deaf and he didn't like dancing. For me, it was a refuge. Whenever we had an argument, I jumped in a taxi and went to Bikini to get high on swinging hips, alcohol, and flirting.

We were two broken dolls: he splintered between a powerful zest for life and a bottomless anguish; I divided into formal María Isidra, who longed for stability and a child, and crazy Isadora, who felt most alive when breaking the rules and enacting a drama.

One night, after a heated argument, he dropped me off in front of Bikini, yelling.

"Go, go! Go seduce men, as you like to do! That's what you want, right?" He opened the door and tried to push me out of the car.

"Okay, I'm going, asshole!" I walked to the club door. I heard the shriek of his tires as he sped off. A smell of burnt rubber hit my nostrils. For all I cared, he could go kill himself.

I went home at five in the morning. Luis had a key and was staying at my house as he did many weekends. I liked the comfort of my own territory. When I turned the key, the door didn't open. He had used the safety lock to keep me out.

I rang the bell, but he didn't come. I banged on the door. Silence on the other side. I was wasted and exhausted. I didn't have any money left to go to a hotel or use a public telephone. I didn't own a credit card. Cell phones didn't yet exist. My only recourse was to keep banging on the door. I knew the thumps might awaken my neighbors, whose front door was six steps from mine, but I didn't want to sleep in the hallway. Every few minutes I stopped to cry and feel sorry for myself.

After one of those pauses, the door suddenly opened when I pushed it hard. I had disengaged the safety lock from the wood panel. I went inside, ready to make a scene. Luis was fast asleep. I pushed him a couple of times, but he didn't wake up. I gave up and fell asleep myself, too spent to keep trying to rouse him.

When I woke mid-morning, he was still sleeping. I shook him awake. As soon as he opened his eyes, I recriminated him.

"Are you crazy? Why did you lock me out of my own house?"

He looked dazed.

"I was mad," he whispered. "Then I fell asleep. I didn't hear you ring the bell."

"How come you didn't hear me? I was banging on the door for almost half an hour!"

"I took a bunch of sleeping pills." He pointed to the medicine box on the bedside table. His movements were sluggish.

My heart skipped a beat.

"How many?"

"I don't know, seven or eight."

I looked inside the box. There were twelve empty bubbles in the blister pack.

"We need to go to the hospital," I said. "They'll have to pump your stomach." I had already forgotten about our argument. Luis had a way of bringing things to a screeching halt. You had to forgive his offenses because there was always something more urgent to attend to.

"I'm okay; I just need to sleep some more," he mumbled.

"Okay? You can hardly keep your eyes open and you're as white as the sheet. We need to go now!" I tried to get him seated, but without him cooperating, I couldn't move him an inch.

"I'm a doctor. If I were about to die, I would know. I just need to rest." He lay back again and closed his eyes.

I didn't know what to do. I grabbed his hand.

"Why would you do such a thing? Were you trying to kill yourself?"

"I'm sorry." His voice sounded muffled, as if it came from under a pillow. "I wanted to sleep and forget about my problems."

"Don't ever do something like that again. Please." My voice trembled. I loved this man, and I had almost lost him.

I let him sleep, checking on him every few minutes. While he slept, I cooked a chicken soup, as if I could cure Luis of his anguish and erase my fears with the comforting taste of the broth.

The next few months we were happier than ever. Luis found another part-time job in a new private clinic that performed abortions. They had recently been legalized only when the pregnancy fell on any of three categories: dangerous for the baby, dangerous for the mother's health, or the result of a rape. He interviewed prospective patients to determine if they met any of the criteria. The clinic used "danger for the mother's health" in the widest sense possible, including emotional distress, so that whoever had enough money to pay for the expensive procedure was accepted.

It made Luis uncomfortable to dole out permission to abort to wealthy women whom he would see come back two or three times, as if abortion were a birth control method, but his position at the public hospital paid little, and the private clinic offered an exorbitant salary. He lasted only a few months, but that short time allowed him to pay off his car loan. He also bought me a couple of gifts, one of them a gold ring with a small diamond. The ring didn't come with a request to marry him, but it was his way of showing he was serious about our relationship. I was elated.

We made plans to visit Colombia for a month. We would stay at his family's home in Medellín for a week and go on a road trip to the Caribbean coast, deviating from our course along the way to visit the rural mountain town where he had been a doctor. The last week of the trip, Luis would go back to his parents' home while I went to Bogotá by myself to visit Leo, who had moved back a while ago. Since Leo had a girlfriend, Luis felt comfortable with this arrangement.

Luis's return to Colombia, the first since he had migrated to Spain, was bittersweet. He adored his mother (who thanked me for bringing him back) but he was stiff with his father. He also seemed bothered to have me around his old buddies, as if I were an intruder.

A few days into our visit, he was back to his caustic ways. After he made fun of me while we were in a bar with some of his friends, I got so mad I ran outside and hailed a taxi, giving the driver Luis's home address. Before he took off, Luis ran to the car.

"Go, go!" I urged the driver.

He started the car. I had sat in the back and locked my door, but the window in the front passenger seat was open. Luis threw himself headfirst through the window.

"Hey! What the hell are you doing?" The driver hit the brakes. Half of Luis's body was inside the car and the other half was dangling out the window.

"You need to get out of the car, lady," said the driver nervously, "I don't want any problems." Maybe he thought this crazy man was a drug lord who would shoot us both. The "dirty war" among *narcos*, the guerrillas, and the army was raging in Colombia.

I got out of the taxi, fuming.

"Where were you planning to go?" said Luis. He let out a sardonic laugh, but I saw he was concerned. His eyes darted from my face to his feet. He grabbed me by the arm. I tried to jerk it away, but he had an iron grip.

"You're too sensitive. It wasn't that big a deal. Let's go home so you can calm down."

We got into another taxi and went home. Luis stayed quiet and calm. I was boiling inside, torn between an instinct to run and the fear of not knowing where to go. I had no friends in this city, and it was getting late. I didn't want to wander the streets at night by myself. In Medellín you had to watch your step. Kidnappings at red lights were common at nighttime, so we had a self-imposed ten o'clock curfew.

Still, when we got home, I went straight to our bedroom to pack my suitcase. I thought I'd go to the airport and take the first flight to Bogotá. Perhaps Leo could lodge me longer than planned.

Luis hovered around me.

"You can't go anywhere at night by yourself; it's too dangerous," he said.

"I don't care." I kept packing.

"Why don't you stay? If you still want to leave tomorrow, I'll take you to the airport myself."

I gave in. In the morning, I took my suitcase downstairs. Luis's mom was in the kitchen.

"I'm coming to say goodbye, and thank you for having me," I said.

"Do you really need to go?" she asked softly. "I know Luis can be difficult, but I also know he loves you. Can't you give him one more chance?"

Luis walked into the kitchen. His mom hugged him and left the room, but not without saying first, "See you tonight?"

"I have a great day planned out," said Luis.

I didn't say anything.

"I know I was an ass yesterday; let me make it up to you. We need to talk."

It was hard for me to resist Luis when he deployed his charm, but more than anything, I didn't want to upset his mother. She had been so warm toward me. . . she even gifted me a lovely gold and lapis lazuli set of earrings and bracelet.

I didn't leave.

After we returned to Barcelona, I tried to break up with Luis several times, but he always won me back. His compulsion to suffer and make me suffer dominated our time ever more often. I knew he hurt me because he didn't know any other way to be in the world, not because he wanted to harm me, but I was overwhelmed and exhausted. I'd been with him for a year and a half. I still cared about him, but I also had to care for myself.

I planned a dramatic exit because it was the only way Luis would get the message. He was very private and trusted few people. I called one of our mutual friends and asked her if I could drop off at her house the few things I had from Luis in my apartment. I told her I was leaving Barcelona for an indefinite amount of time. She agreed to take in the items and warn Luis. I knew he would never forgive me for involving another person in our separation, but that's precisely what I wanted.

I left a bag with Luis's stuff, including the diamond ring and a farewell note, at our friend's place. I went directly from there to the airport. I had reserved a flight to Paris, where I would stay for a month. My friend Gloria Cecilia, who lived in a tiny room on the upper floor of an apartment building—a *chambre de bonne,* or maid's room—had offered me her place while she visited her family in Colombia.

That month in Paris was a balm for my body and my spirit. I realized my chest had been constricted for months because suddenly I was able to breathe deeply again. I had brought editorial work, but I mostly wrote, walked the city, and slowly recovered from my frazzled nerves and shattered heart.

It was hard to acknowledge that I had gotten myself involved in yet another destructive relationship. Although I loved Luis with a passion I had never felt for Fran, and I knew his abuse did not stem from machismo but from his own tortured soul, Luis, like Fran, had mistreated me. He had tried to control me by keeping me close, where his emotional blows hit the target more forcefully.

I couldn't blame him as much as I blamed myself. What was so broken in me that I kept attracting broken men? Why was it that when a sane guy like Leo loved me, I pushed him away, but I got attached to others who didn't know how to love without destroying the object of their affection?

There, in that little *chambre de bonne*, I swore I would seek help when I went back to Barcelona. Something had to change, because if it didn't, I would end up crazy or dead.

Family Discord

AS I UNPACKED MY BAG after arriving home from Paris, the phone rang. I didn't answer in case it was Luis. I didn't answer the phone for the next two months.

Mama complained that she never found me when she called, so I called her once a week and went to Sunday lunch every couple of weeks.

Our relationship was somewhat tense, as usual. As the years went by, Mama had gotten harsher instead of softening up. I wondered if we had disappointed her. The three youngest children and my older sister still at home remained problem-free, but several of us had stopped going to church a long time ago, and some had not married in church. That must have been a blow since Catholicism was so important to her. Others had married people she didn't see eye to eye with, or, once their children were grown, started resisting the weekly date for Sunday lunch—a lunch that was the highlight of Mama's week because family was the center of her life.

I must have been the biggest disappointment. Here I was at thirty-one, unmarried, and having lived with three men—Pol (if only for a month), Leo, and Abili—and showing no signs of settling down. I had never told her about Fran or Luis, but she probably had an inkling of their existence. Nothing escaped her watchful eye.

Money was also a source of stress. Papa didn't have a pension. The money he brought home every Friday went in full to support our large family. There was nothing left over for savings. Work was scarcer. They found themselves in their sixties with shaky finances.

As smart as they were, when it came to money neither of them was savvy. When they couldn't afford the maintenance of their beautiful house on Avenida del Tibidabo any longer, they sold it when the real estate market was at a low point and used all the money to buy a big apartment rather than a smaller place and setting something aside for a rainy day. Their new home was on Paseo Bonanova, a street in the wealthy upper side of Barcelona, a few blocks from my former Catholic school, Sagrado Corazón. Mama was thrifty in terms of personal expenses—exaggeratedly so, transforming her extreme austerity into a virtue that perhaps helped her reconcile with the family's descent in status—but having a big living room and dining room to accommodate our family every Sunday and living in a "good," familiar neighborhood was a must for her. If that meant not having enough savings for old age, so be it.

To make matters worse, after Abuelo passed away a few years before, Mama didn't protect her inheritance. Abuelo had invested in real estate. At his death, the oldest male child inherited Santa Margarita, while the rest of his children, including Mama, inherited apartments he had bought in Barcelona decades earlier.

Mama got two great apartments in a posh area. She could have sold them at a good price and never have money worries again. Under the law, however, she had to offer them first to the renters who had leased them for three decades and, if they wanted them, she had to sell them at the market price from thirty years before. The only other option was to give them or sell them to one of her children. Most people used this loophole, giving their inherited rentals to their children and selling them later at current market rates or even selling them to their children at a discounted price close to the current market rate. But Mama wouldn't even consider it. Kicking those families out of their home wasn't the Christian thing to do. She sold the apartments to them for a ridiculously three-decades-old low amount, even though that jeopardized her and Papa's future. She didn't even tell us about it until it was done. That charitable streak that had caused her ancestor, Dorotea de Chopitea, to give away all her fortune had run straight down the bloodline to her.

Mama loved the passage in the New Testament about the lilies that don't need to worry because God takes care of them, so why wouldn't He take care of men? She believed that everything would turn out okay. Papa, however, was a bundle of nerves. His anxiety increased day by day.

What Mama had lost in financial safety, household help, and compliant children she compensated for by exerting her power with a stronger hand than ever. She had always laid down the law at home, while Papa stayed in the background. We toed the line out of respect and, frankly, fear, because hurting Mama's feelings threatened the very foundation of our family.

When we upset her, she didn't yell, but she blurted out a bitter comment or, even worse, gave us the silent treatment. Whenever I took a contrary attitude I felt like a villain, but I was as strong-willed as she was and we often butted heads, especially when she tried to organize my life as if I were still a kid. Perhaps we always had the most conflict because we were so similar in temperament and strength.

Once, when I was a child, Mama returned from a spiritual retreat where several couples and a priest discussed the Bible and made resolutions to live as good Christians. As she drove us to school on Monday morning, she said, "I try to do my best, but if I've ever done anything that hurt you, please forgive me."

I admired her immensely in that moment—her humility, and

her resolve to make amends. But with time, she became less likely to admit error, and I became more prone to accumulate resentment.

During Sunday visits, Mama still talked more with her daughters-in-law than she had ever talked to her own daughters. At lunch, the conversation was limited, as it had always been, to general topics. I had no idea who my siblings were or what their lives were like, nor did they know about mine. I hadn't even mentioned Luis to any of them. We didn't have real intimacy.

I felt detached, but I kept showing up, if intermittently, to keep the family connection, as superficial as it seemed to me. Mama had instilled in us that there was nothing more important than family. She was the one who remembered every birthday, every anniversary, every important occasion, not just for us, but for the more than one hundred people on both sides of the tribe. The one who still gave special gifts to her grown and married godchildren and later to Papa's godchildren after he passed away. The one who gathered her clan at home on Christmas Eve for decades and who pushed us to attend every family party.

Shortly after I came back from Paris, however, we had a fight during Sunday lunch that almost broke my dutiful affiliation to the family for good.

Most of my siblings and their spouses had come to lunch, as usual. My nieces and nephews had eaten before the adults and were playing in the back of the apartment. As we ate, the conversation veered to foreign movies. I was a fan of foreign cinema and the only one at the table in favor of watching movies with subtitles instead of dubbed. The discussion soon devolved into a heated argument.

"You can't appreciate the plot when you have to read the subtitles at the same time," said my older sister.

"Yes, you can. And the tone of the actors' voices is as key to the plot as what they say," I said.

"That's silly," said one of my brothers. "They can reproduce the tone when dubbing it."

"It's not silly," I said. "Take a Kurosawa movie, and the sound of a samurai's voice. He almost barks instead of speaking. You see the same movie dubbed, and the actor has a calmer tone that robs the character of his essence."

"I'm smart enough to understand a movie's essence even if it's dubbed. You just like to complicate things," said Mama.

We kept sparring for a few more minutes, but I refused to give in. Finally, Mama raised her voice and pronounced her verdict.

"You're a snob. You're not happy unless you set yourself apart. You think you're better than the rest of us." She looked at me with a mix of anger and scorn.

"I'm not a snob," I said. "The truth is that whoever has an opinion different from yours has to be wrong. Yours is the only valid opinion in this house."

"Go fuck yourself!" snapped my younger brother.

I looked at him, startled. We never, ever, cursed in front of our parents. The profanity was even more shocking coming from him, a quiet fellow with a stolid face, now white with anger. He was close to my parents, but still, this was out of character.

"What?" I asked. I must have heard it wrong.

"Go fuck yourself!" he repeated.

My other siblings and in-laws were mute, some looking down at their dishes, others at us, forks in the air. I didn't know what to do or what to say. Papa filled in the silence.

"Your brother is right. You shouldn't have talked to your mother this way. That was disrespectful. You should apologize."

I couldn't believe it. Mama had insulted me simply because I had a different opinion, and when I defied her my brother had trashed me and Papa had finished me off while everybody kept silent. Perhaps my being contrarian and rude had hurt my mother's feelings, but did it count for nothing that she had also hurt my feelings?

I pushed my chair back and got up, holding on to the table so my knees wouldn't buckle. I saw the strangers sitting around the table through a haze. I grabbed my purse and coat from the hall and stumbled out the door, down the stairs, and into the street.

There was a bus stop right in front of the house, but I was too agitated to wait for the bus. I walked home. My chest seemed ready to split open, like a rotten melon that you throw to the ground to see it explode in a hundred pieces. Tears were streaming down my face. My shoes kept moving in front of me, pulled by habit in the right direction. I was talking to myself. "I'm never going back, never, I'm done with this family." The hate in my brother's voice kept replaying in my mind. How could Papa, always so peaceful, condone his behavior?

I arrived home and took a long shower, letting the hot water burn away the pain. I was determined to make good on my promise. Never again I would let them shut me down; never again would I let Mama trample me.

A few weeks went by. I knew my family was getting together every Sunday, as usual. They were used to me showing up only once or twice a month, but whenever I didn't go, I would call a few days before to let Mama know I wouldn't make it. Now I didn't call.

I felt adrift. Every aspect of my life seemed as flimsy as a paper house. I didn't have a career, just a series of jobs. I was trying to find a therapist, but I had tried a couple and I hadn't liked them. I longed for a husband and a baby, but I didn't trust my own judgment when it came to choosing partners. And now, I had given up my family.

Two weeks before Christmas, Mama called. I picked up the phone and she asked me straight away if I was coming for the holidays.

"No," I said, curtly.

"Why do you do this to me? We are a united family. Why are you destroying it? Why are you the only one who doesn't appreciate it?" She went on and on.

"Mama," I interjected, "we are not united. I never talk to my brothers and sisters unless I run into them at your house, and even then, we hardly exchange a few words. We are strangers, sharing opinions around a table like the passengers on a cruise ship. Is that being united?"

"We are reserved, but we would do anything to help if one of us were in trouble. Why do you always have to criticize us?"

It was true that we would all be there for each other in a moment of crisis—once every ten years or so—but that wasn't enough for me. Most of my siblings were as reserved as my parents, comfortable with keeping each other at arm's length. I suffered, confined within my shell, and even worse, my upbringing had driven me to hide in a shell in every important relationship.

"Mama, you speak more with your daughters-in-law than you speak with us. We don't share anything except for trivialities. Plus, I'm not going to go so that you can all gang up against me again."

Mama persisted until I agreed to show up for Christmas.

I did as I promised. Everybody behaved as if I had been there every Sunday. Only one of my sisters-in-law acknowledged what had happened. She told me in private that when she'd gotten home that day, she had scolded my brother for not speaking out in my defense.

"It wasn't my place to say anything," she said, "but you didn't deserve that treatment. The problem is all of you are scared to upset your mother. I don't understand it."

I appreciated her words. I filed them in a recess of my mind, and I kept showing up, as usual, a couple of Sundays each month, feeling as lonely as ever.

Endings and Beginnings

THE CONSTANT TRAVELING FOR MY JOB, with a week or two at home in between, was getting to me. I wanted more stability in my life. I gave a two-month notice at the travel agency so I could complete the three trips I was scheduled for: one to Egypt, one to China, and one to India and Nepal. Visiting again the countries I was most familiar with would be the perfect ending to my three-year stint as a tour leader.

I loved Egypt as much as the first time I'd toured it, especially the cruise on the Nile. The simplicity of the views soothed me. The world became the blue of the river, the gold of the sandy riverbanks, the green of the palm trees, and the white of the sails on the *falucas*, the small boats that glided beside us. The cruise ships were small because bigger ones wouldn't have made it on the shallow waters. There was a relaxed, cozy vibe among the staff and the three or four groups of tourists onboard.

Everything went without a hitch in this last trip. No overbooked hotels, delayed flights, or tourists afflicted with the runs. The group I led was easygoing; the Egyptian guide, whom I met for the first time, knowledgeable and friendly.

Mohammed and I got along right away. We discovered we had been born on the same day and year and called ourselves "twins." We talked about everything, like longtime friends. I told him about Santa Margarita; about how I had grown up in that magical world of freedom, outdoor adventures, corn ears picked from the fields and charred on the grill, donkey cart rides, and secret tunnels. I also told him about my dream of being a writer. He told me about his childhood and his ambition to open his own business. We stayed up late playing backgammon or pool. We spent every second together. I had never hung out so little with my group of tourists.

One night, Mohammed told me he was falling in love with me. A devout Muslim and a married man, he had never had sex with a tourist or a tour leader, as other guides did. As for me, after my bad experience with the other Egyptian guide, I hadn't taken any lovers on my work trips.

I liked him, but we agreed to forgo sex out of respect for his religious and marital vows. We allowed ourselves, however, to hold hands discreetly. The warmth of our hands burned all the way through our bodies. We thirsted for that small contact, as the palm trees thirsted for the river.

When we got on the cruise ship, I discovered that my former one-night lover was also aboard, with another group of tourists. He tried to sit with us after dinner, but we made it clear we didn't want company. It was a belated sweet vengeance to see him seething as Mohammed and I laughed, talked, and played games until the wee hours.

In the end, we couldn't contain our desire. Mohammed asked me to join him in his hotel room in Aswan for our last afternoon together before returning to Cairo. We made love, the warmth we had built over the last two weeks coloring our encounter. It was the first and only time in my life when I knowingly went to bed with a married man. I felt guilty but I was weak.

Mohammed reminded me of Jean, my French lover, the first boy who had really cared for me. They shared the same noble spirit, the same tenderness. As had happened when I was nineteen, knowing that our relationship didn't have a future heightened our present. I didn't seek to destroy his marriage. I wanted only to give him a piece of myself, a fragment of love to treasure, as I treasured his.

After I left, we corresponded for a few months. "What have you done to me?" he asked in one letter. "Every time I see cornfields, I think of you. When I play backgammon, I think of you. I can't even be in Aswan without thinking of you."

We stopped the letters so he could recommit to his marriage. Although I never heard from him again, I brought his photo with me when I moved to the United States, together with Jean's poems and letters, and pictures of my family and best friends.

Our romance modeled what short-term relationships could be: caring and passionate. A relationship between equals, the spark of our bodies brightening the bond, without either seeking to use, abuse, overpower, or control.

That intense but fleeting encounter reminded me of something that happened once during a salsa concert, when I was single and lonely. The band played a bolero, and a guy asked me to dance. I usually didn't dance slow songs with strangers, but I said yes. With the first notes, I hugged this man, letting my body fall into his. He did the same. We pressed together from shoulders to feet, my head buried in his neck, his head draped over mine. There were no kisses, hands on butts, or an erection on my hip, but we shared a bond as profound as I had ever experienced. Without an ounce of fear, for three minutes our bodies were one in a tight embrace, as lovers saying farewell at the airport before a long trip. We surrendered to each other.

When the song ended, I said thank you, looking the stranger straight in the eye.

He pressed my hand and sustained my gaze, hushed, his eyes

wide with wonder. We had met. Then we turned away and never saw each other again.

We crave intimacy, pleasure, and love. Often, we don't have a steady relationship to provide it, but that doesn't mean we cannot find it in a short-term lover or a brief encounter like the one I had with the bolero guy. Sometimes words and time dissolve and two souls are left alone, deeply connected in the intensity of the present moment.

Back in Barcelona, my life slowly fell into place. I found part-time steady employment. It was 1990, two years before the Barcelona Olympic Games, but preparations were already underway. The Olympic Committee hired me to translate articles from English, French, and Catalan into Spanish, which were then emailed to the press throughout Spain and Latin America.

The job offered me a daily routine, it paid well, and I found it interesting. I arrived at the Olympic headquarters every day at two o'clock and stayed until six translating the articles journalists in the press department had written that morning.

The Olympic fever seized my hometown and the country at large. The whole city was under construction. Barcelona had often been described as a city that lived with its back to the sea because even though it had miles of beaches, they were dirty, edged by factories, and not suitable for swimming. Now the Catalan government spent hundreds of millions of dollars demolishing the empty warehouses that lined the waterfront and erecting a whole new neighborhood of apartment buildings where the athletes would live. The Olympic Village would become new housing for sale after the Games were over. They also built a harbor for the sailing races, cleaned up the sand and waters, opened up the beaches for swimming, and built promenades for pedestrians, bikers, and skateboarders. New freeways crisscrossed the city. A modern Olympic Stadium rose amongst historic monuments on the hill of Montjuic, overlooking the sea.

It was an orgy of spending that changed the shape and infrastructure of my city. Parallel to these efforts, Seville was preparing for the Universal Exhibition that would open in 1992, and Madrid would be declared a European Capital of Culture the same year. This international splash topped off the Socialist party's decade-long effort to present Spain as a modern country and Barcelona as one of the most beautiful destinations in Europe. After 1992, the economy would crumble, but for the time being we were on a thrilling rise to the top.

Pasqual Maragall, Barcelona's socialist mayor, infected us with his enthusiasm. His campaign, *"Barcelona, posa't maca"* ("Barcelona, make yourself beautiful"), encouraged people to give their buildings' façades a facelift, to fill their balconies with potted plants and flowers, and to contribute to the remaking of the city as a place of beauty, culture, and modernity.

Every aspect of the Games was planned to project this image. An avant-garde designer, Javier Mariscal, was in charge of creating the Olympic mascot, Cobi, a cubist representation of a Catalan sheepdog. The contemporary theater and performance group La Fura dels Baus was hired to put together a show for the innovative and spectacular Opening Ceremony.

As the city remade its image, I rebuilt myself. I found a Jungian therapist and committed to seeing her weekly. I also got involved with a Japanese center that taught *katsugen*, a regenerative spontaneous movement practice, and *yugi*, a laying-on-of-hands technique similar to *reiki.* I attended twice a week.

This dual focus on body and mind transformed me. The Jungian method of analysis was more effective for me than plain talk therapy. I often found the answers I needed were inside me all along. A little push from the therapist to help me decipher my dreams allowed me to hear my own voice.

Discussing the images that populated my nights, the knots that had tied my stomach for decades loosened up. I revisited growing up in a home where the oldest always won, where emotions stayed locked, and where intimacy didn't exist. I talked about the way silence made me feel erased. I dug up how the innocent pleasure my flesh offered me at five years old had become a source of shame and how it made me believe that being loved depended on staying within the norms, and desire stemmed from revolt. I spoke about not feeling seen by men except as a body that could be spied on or trampled upon. I opened up about the compulsions and rebellions I'd concealed growing up and later splashed over my parents' expectations, perhaps as a way to get back at what I had perceived as their lack of love and acceptance. It would be years before I realized that they simply didn't know how to express affection with words or hugs. Love, for them, was opening the door every time I came back, broken.

Bringing up old aches that had been eating my insides made the pain as fresh as if the injury had happened that morning. I often left the therapist's office bawling. But as these long-suppressed emotions fell from my mouth, the weight I had carried inside began to lighten.

I had been living with no purpose other than finding attachment and acceptance, but now, I knew I needed to find me.

The one thing that had never wavered through all my zigzagging from man to man, job to job, and house to house was my passion for reading. I decided to return to academia, hoping it might launch a new path forward.

I enrolled in a PhD program in Spanish literature at my old alma mater, the University of Barcelona. Unfortunately, the program was subpar, a mere formality to get a title that allowed you to teach at college. Classrooms held dozens of students on stadium seating, as during my undergraduate years, yawning and taking notes during boring lectures that an old professor read from yellowing papers. After five or six months, I dropped out.

What next? I was at a loss.

At the time, I was dating a guy from the United States. Daniel told me that PhD programs in the States were top-notch and encouraged me to apply. I thought I would give it a try. I had no idea how the university system worked there, but I went to the North American Institute, where I had studied English for a few years, and dove into their library archives. Applications, I learned, were only part of the process. I had to pass the TOEFL and the SAT exams before I even applied.

I got down to business. Since my job at the Olympic Committee took only my afternoons, I scheduled four-hour study sessions every morning. My spare room became Operation U.S.A. central. I bought books, tapes, and guides and enrolled to take the exams six months later.

I had never been so focused. For the first time ever, I had a clear goal: to enter a PhD program at an American university. It was not a plan that came from my liaison with a man. It was my own. The fact that I was dating an American had nothing to do with it. Daniel had no intention of returning to the United States. He had a job, lots of friends and an enjoyable life in Barcelona.

We were an odd couple. Daniel was only two years younger than I was but looked and acted like a twenty-year-old. I was organized and tidy. He was messy. I was responsible and conscientious. He was undisciplined and rash. I was convinced people were fundamentally good. He was a cynic who thought the worst of everybody. I wanted literary glory. He wanted money. I was serious. He was humorous.

When he pursued me, I held him off for a while because I couldn't see how we fit together, but he made me so horny I could hardly breathe. He also made me laugh more than anybody else I'd ever been with. His jokes were sunny in public but turned biting in private. Even though I couldn't agree with the content, I had to crack up with the form. I decided to give the relationship a chance.

Everybody loved Daniel, including my family. Mama and Papa at first expressed concern when I told them I was dating a Black man.

"Is he very Black?" asked Mama. I had to suppress a laugh.

"He's less dark than you when you get suntanned," I said, "but his features are Black."

"I don't mind his race," said Papa, "but I worry you will be rejected by other people."

As soon as Daniel set foot in my parents' house, however, he won them over. He was so funny every time we went to a Sunday lunch he ended up with my sisters and a circle of nephews and nieces around him. Papa and my brothers stayed on the other side of the room reading the newspaper or watching TV but didn't miss a beat. It was impossible not to laugh at Daniel's tall tales and jokes.

Aside from his comic genius, youthful appearance, and sex appeal, Daniel was smart, intuitive, and didn't put up with crap.

"You keep talking about wanting to be a writer, but I don't believe you," he said one evening. "Either write or stop saying that writing is your lifelong dream."

"What do you know about my dreams?" I was offended.

"I dare you to go into that room and write a story," he said. "I bet you can't do it."

I got up, went to my studio, and locked the door. I emerged two hours later with a new, finished story.

"There." I threw the papers on his lap.

He read the story and didn't say one word, but he regarded me with new appreciation. Not only was it good, it fictionalized our relationship. His dare had been a catalyst to get me off my butt and do what I claimed I wanted to do.

Daniel also demanded that I confront my romance with alcohol. He was a teetotaler and hated seeing me drunk whenever we went to a club. I dismissed his criticism as exaggeration, as I had always done. What? Couldn't I have a couple of drinks? He was such a party pooper! But he wouldn't stop nagging. "One drink, two drinks are okay. But as soon as you have the first one, you can't stop."

When I complained to my therapist about his puritanism, she said, "You know, it's common for people who have felt deprived of love to numb the pain with alcohol or drugs."

I'd never thought of it that way. I saw booze as a crutch to help me drop my inhibitions. It allowed me to hang out with Marea, Pol, and the rest of our friends and be less crippled by my insecurities. Once I discovered salsa, it buried the sad, hesitant María Isidra and propped up confident Isadora, becoming the wind behind the sail of my sensuality, pushing my body's wisdom forward. But it also fueled bad decisions, self-destructive affairs, and a pervasive guilt when I woke up hungover in the morning.

That night I had a dream that shook me up. It was about a little boy who was a troublemaker. The adults in the house—it may have been my family's home—discovered that they only got him to sleep by giving him a shot of cognac. When I arrived in the house and they told me about the cognac, I was horrified. I visited the little boy to explain that cognac was not good for him. When I tried to take away the glass sitting on the bedside table, he transformed into a devil, rose from the bed, and grabbed the bedside table to hit me with it.

I woke up with my heart racing. I knew, even before the therapist told me, that I was that boy. I had been feeding booze to my hurt little child to quiet my troubles.

After that dream, I didn't need to get drunk any longer. It was an effortless change, as if an internal alarm system had launched automatically. When I went out at night, I would drink a couple of gin and tonics, but that was enough. I didn't force myself to stop ordering them or swear that I wouldn't get wasted. It wasn't necessary because I didn't crave the numbing.

That slide from the second drink to the third, the fourth, and the fifth, along with the sporadic blackouts and the crushing morning headaches that had happened several times a week for a decade, evaporated from one day to the next, guided by the voice of my own subconscious.

1992, Barcelona and Berkeley
New Life in a New Land

I PASSED THE TOEFL WITH HIGH MARKS. I barely scraped by on the SAT, but I hoped that the high ratings in the language area would redeem my ineptitude in math.

It was time to apply to colleges.

I spent hours in the North American Institute library researching universities and applied to a dozen colleges. It was time consuming, but I was methodical. The hardest part was getting letters of recommendation from my college professors. More than a decade had gone by since I'd graduated, and I hadn't kept in touch. With hundreds of students in every course, it was impossible for them to remember me, but I was able to track down a couple and convince them to write succinct letters based on my grades, which had been stellar the last couple of years, more than their memory. I also got letters from the directors of two prestigious publishing houses I had worked for.

Once everything went out in the mail, I put it out of my mind. My life was hectic. My tenure as a part-time translator had morphed into a full-time job at the Olympic Committee press department. I worked feverishly translating all the books on the style for filming every sport from Spanish into English and helping organize materials and processes for the press.

Daniel and I dated on and off. We cared for each other, but I wanted to build a family, and he wasn't ready for such a commitment. We were also far too different to tie our lives together. When I got accepted at several American universities, toward the spring of 1992, we broke up for good although we remained friends. There was no point in staying a couple when I was about to leave the country.

The last few months in Barcelona were frenetic. With the Games just around the corner, I worked twelve- to fourteen-hour days, including Saturdays. Evenings and Sundays, I packed items that would remain in my parents' house in San Julián and sold or donated the rest. There was no time for boyfriends or dancing.

Going to the United States felt exciting but also terrifying. It helped that I would be going to UC Berkeley. As a candidate with good grades and a decade of experience in the publishing world, I got accepted by almost every university I had applied to, but I chose that college because my old friend Chiori lived in Berkeley. When I wrote with the news that I would be in her town in August, she was overjoyed. "I'll finally be able to return the favor," she answered. "You can stay in my home until you find your own."

A few weeks before my departure, a phone call woke me up at three in the morning. I thought it must be Fran, again. I got up, angry, but when I picked up the phone, it was my former boyfriend Luis, the Colombian doctor.

"Hola, María Isidra."

I recognized him right away. He was one of the few people—outside my family and childhood friends—who never called me Isadora, guessing, rightly, that the name embodied a persona he would never be able to control.

"Luis? You woke me up! Why are you calling me at this ungodly hour?"

"I wanted to say hi." He sounded composed.

"At three a.m.? Couldn't you call me tomorrow?" I hadn't heard from him in over a year.

"I'm sorry for bothering you," he said, politely, "I will call you another time."

"Well, you woke me up already, so why don't you tell me what's going on?"

"It's nothing, don't worry; sorry for waking you up."

"It has to be something. Just tell me. I'm not mad anymore."

"It's okay. I'll call you another time; it's not urgent."

"Are you sure?"

"Yes, I'm sure."

"Ok, good night. Call me tomorrow if you want."

He didn't call. I was relieved, but also a little sorry. I didn't harbor resentment for Luis. We had loved each other, even if our relationship was unhealthy.

Two weeks later, a common friend called me with the news that Luis had been found hanging in his house. It was hard to believe. How could Luis, who lived with such intensity, kill himself? I stayed seated after I talked to her, too shocked to even cry. Remembering Luis's midnight phone call filled me with guilt. Could I have saved him if I had spoken to him? I knew it wasn't likely, but I would have given anything to go back in time.

I attended the open-casket service. It crushed me to see Luis lying there, so pale, with a peaceful expression that belied his tragic heart. His passion for life, his tenderness, his light—all gone. I might have ended up like him, if not dead by suicide then by other means, had I not dug deep beyond my pain, my shortcomings, and turned my life around.

Four days after the end of the Olympics, I arrived in San Francisco after a cheap, twenty-four-hour flight with three layovers, my old life packed in two suitcases. I had a generous severance package from the Olympic Committee that would take care of my in-state university fees for a few semesters (the out-of-state fees had been waved). I also had a job as a graduate student instructor, which would make me just enough money to scrape by.

Chiori was the only person I knew in this vast land. She was supposed to pick me up at the airport, but she'd misunderstood the date and was not there when I arrived after midnight. I called her. She answered after a few rings, apologized, gave me her address in Berkeley, and asked me to get a taxi.

On my way from the airport to her home, my hands gripped my purse tightly. I sat close to the door, ready to jump out as soon as the driver acted suspiciously. All the stories Daniel had told me about crime in the United States lurked in my head while, weak with fatigue, I tried to pick out my surroundings from the darkness enveloping the lower deck of the Bay Bridge.

The taxi stopped in front of a small house, a light faintly reveal- ing the wooden porch that would become so beloved over the years to come. The door opened, and there was Chiori, in white silky paja- mas and Japanese clogs that resonated on the hardwood floor, with a warm embrace.

I dragged my two suitcases inside, a brand new black Samsonite, hard-shelled and maddeningly heavy but so sturdy it could survive a nuclear war, and an enormous, soft, gray suitcase, where my clothes slept side by side with my life's milestones: a fifty-year-old photo album that I had nicked from Mama where black-and-white images rescued my childhood and my parents' youth; an envelope with Jean's letters and poems; photos of ex-boyfriends that were still tenderly remembered (Fran the only glaring absence); small gifts and mementos from my best friends; some rolled-up art pieces, including a black ink pen work entitled "Dream of Isidra" that my old boyfriend from La Torre, Marco, had drawn for me, and my astral chart, that a wise man from Nepal had painted on yellow parchment paper.

Four days later I was attending classes. Two weeks after that, I had opened a bank account and moved to a rented room not far from Chiori's place.

I introduced myself to every person I met as Isidra. This was the new me. Not the María Isidra that my family had raised nor the Isadora who had been born from the streets and the salsa drums, but someone containing a bit of both as well as all the other versions of myself that had made me who I now was.

I threw myself into my new life, sick with nostalgia for what I had left behind and stressed out by the frantic American busyness. I missed those Sunday lunches when all my siblings talked on top of each other, even if it was about the surface of life. I missed lying on a chaise in San Julián's backyard, taking a nap after a delectable lunch my mother had cooked. I missed walking down Las Ramblas with my friends. I missed dancing salsa until five in the morning at Bikini. Two months after arriving in Berkeley, I had an ulcer.

One evening, after reading a letter from Mama in which she encouraged me to keep strong and told me things would get better, I borrowed a hammer and nails from my landlady. I opened my soft, gray suitcase and, one by one, took out the mementos that tied me to my past. I hammered the paintings onto the wall, placed the trinkets on my bookshelves, and put the photos and letters in the drawer of my bedside table. Tears streamed freely down my face.

That night, feeling anxious and lonely, my hands went to that familiar refuge down between my legs. I couldn't remember the last time I'd tried to find relief in my own body. Used to the spasm of frustration that ended those attempts, I had long ago given up the quest.

As my palms settled over my panties, a tenuous, self-imposed barrier perhaps raised in an attempt to stay on the side of the good girl, I found myself rebelling against a pattern ingrained over three decades of shame. No more frantic rubbing over cotton until my legs became iron rods, lifted from the bed, and my body tensed up, overcome with anxiety. First one hand, then the other, found their way inside my panties, inside a well, on to a flower blooming deep in the hidden, most private part of me, my flesh pulsating, embracing my fingers, my hand firmly holding the bright red balloon of my desire. I flew with it, up, and down, and up again. I had finally met myself.

In the next few months, I found the courage to dig in and look forward. In the old, battered classrooms of Dwinelle Hall, I recommitted to my passion for literature. I learned that not only could I express a dissenting opinion, I was expected to do so. I strengthened my voice. I made new friends in and out of school. And I kept dancing.

Acknowledgments

I COULD NEVER HAVE BROUGHT THIS BOOK to safe harbor without the help of many professionals and friends who supported me along the way.

Sheila Athens coached me to the end when I got stuck in the middle. My editor, Kathy C. Cooper, offered me not only her stylistic savvy, but some key suggestions; most crucially, she encouraged me to change the chronological narrative to an asynchronous structure that moved back and forth in time. It was one of the most difficult rewrites I've ever done, but it also elevated the story by allowing me to play more deeply with thematic echoes. Kathy also advised me to add descriptive titles, including time and location, and several readers have mentioned how useful they are. A second editor, Joanna Mitchell, provided developmental comments on the almost final manuscript for another polish.

My copy editor, Liz Seif, was as professional and accurate as usual. Thank you!

My friends Susan Morrell, Celia Tejada, and Katie Tamony read an early version and offered hearty encouragement and praise that kept me going through the rough times. My correspondence with Scott Adler and his belief in my work were a big boost. Beta readers Judy Blaze, Rachel Abeysekera Lazansky, Sophia Viruly, and Nicole Heydenburg contributed useful comments. As a bonus, the last three were millennials, which helped me believe this book could also find an audience among their cohort. Marcela Landres offered tough love, much appreciated. Thank you as well to the Facebook group We Love Memoirs for keeping the love of this literary form alive.

Emily O'Keefe, whom I met at Sonoma County Writers Camp, came up with the title *Promenade of Desire*, which I love, after my publisher asked me to change my working title. Thank you, my dear roomie!

Authors are notoriously bad at summarizing what their book or themselves are about. I hired Dan Blank, Mónica Moratinos, Graciela Rodriguez, and Caroline Gilman at different stages during this six-year journey to help me figure out who was my target audience, describe my key topics, and how to brand myself as an author on social media. Their expertise was invaluable. Marni Freedman helped stitch together the description on the back cover. Why is it harder to write two paragraphs than 300 pages? I don't know, but that's why I sought other people's help.

For the last year, I've met every Saturday morning with four writers to support each other during our publication journey. Thank you Elisa Stancil Levine, Catherine Drake, Lindsey Salatka, and Susan Speranza, for making this at times very stressful journey much more enjoyable.

To the writers who wrote blurbs for this book—Joyce Maynard, Aaron Shulman, Julia Scheeres, Jeannine Ouellette, and Andrea Jarrell: I asked you this favor because I admire your work. I sent my request with trepidation, thinking you may say no, or say yes and then not like my book. I feel honored you agreed.

Thank you to my publicity team, Chrystal Patriarche, Grace Fell and Hanna Lindsley from BookSparks, for helping get this book into readers' hands.

I am grateful to my publisher, Brooke Warner from She Writes

Press, my publishing manager Lauren Wise, and the rest of the She Writes Press team. I chose this publishing house because it champions the work of women; being part of the community of SWP sisters has been extremely rewarding.

Finally, the biggest thanks go to my husband, Luis, and my son, Adrian. You both supported me when I decided to quit a plush corporate job to commit to my dream of being a writer. Our finances took a big hit, but you never wavered in your belief that it was a worthy sacrifice. I couldn't have written this book without your love and support.

About the Author

© Nathan DeHart

ISIDRA MENCOS was born and raised in Barcelona. She spent her twenties experimenting with the new freedoms afforded by the end of Franco's dictatorship in Spain while immersing herself in books and dancing. She freelanced for publishing houses, traveled the world as a tour leader, and worked for the Olympic Committee. In 1992 she moved to the US to earn a PhD in Spanish and Latin American contemporary literature at UC Berkeley, where she taught for twelve years. She also worked as a writer and editor for Spanish-speaking media and did a ten-year stint in the corporate world as Editorial Director of the Americas for BabyCenter, the leading global digital resource for parents. In 2016 she quit her job to dedicate herself to writing. Since then, her essays have been published in literary journals like *Diálogo, Chicago Quarterly Review, The Penmen Review, Newfound, The Manifest-Station* and *Front Porch Journal.* Her piece "My Books and I" was listed as Notable in the Best American Essays Anthology. Her work has also appeared in widely read online publications like *The Huffington Post, Wisdom Well, WIRED, Jane Friedman's Blog,* and *Better After Fifty.* Today Isidra lives in Northern California with her husband and son. *Promenade of Desire* is her debut memoir.

SELECTED TITLES FROM SHE WRITES PRESS

She Writes Press is an independent publishing company founded to serve women writers everywhere. Visit us at www.shewritespress.com.

No Rules: A Memoir by Sharon Dukett. $16.95, 978-1-63152-856-9
At sixteen, Sharon leaves home to escape the limited life her Catholic parents have planned for her because she's a girl—and finds herself thrown into the 1970s counterculture, an adult world for which she is unprepared.

Anarchy in High Heels: A Memoir by Denise Larson
$16.95, 978-1-64742-136-6
The unabashed story of an all-female performance group unleashing their unique feminine satire in the early 1970s—a time when being a "funny feminist" was considered an oxymoron.

Blooming in Winter: The Story of a Remarkable Twentieth-Century Woman by Pam Valois. $16.95, 978-1-64742-116-8
When Pam Valois met her in the 1970s, Jacomena (Jackie) Maybeck was a model of zestful, hands-on living and aging, still tarring roofs and splitting logs in her seventies—a model for Pam, at the time a young working mother. Here, Pam explores how Jackie's uncommon approach to life encourages us to reflect on our own lives and what it looks like to live exuberantly to the very end.

In Search of Pure Lust: A Memoir by Lise Weil. $16.95, 978-1-63152-385-4
Through the lens of her personal experiences as a lesbian coming of age in the '70s and '80s, Lise Weil documents an important chapter in lesbian history, her own long and difficult relationship history, and how her eventual dive into Zen practice became a turning point in her quest for love.

Redlined: A Memoir of Race, Change, and Fractured Community in 1960s Chicago by Linda Gartz. $16.95, 978-1-63152-320-5
A riveting story of a community fractured by racial turmoil, an unraveling and conflicted marriage, a daughter's fight for sexual independence, and an up-close, intimate view of the racial and social upheavals of the 1960s.